## ADVANCE PRAISE FOR *NO PLACE LIKE HOME*

"In *No Place Like Home*, Jessica Barrett thoughtfully examines the housing crisis from all angles, putting together a clear playbook for one of the biggest problems we collectively face." —Kyla Scanlon, economist and author of *In This Economy?*

"A soulful antidote to our housing crisis. A rallying cry that preserves and decommodifies the very human idea of 'home.' Barrett describes, in elegant prose, why today's conception of shelter as an investor-focused asset is doomed to fail. Then she points the way past toxic real estate and toward real homes and real communities. Vital and fascinating!" —Michael Harris, author of *All We Want* and *The End of Absence*

"*No Place Like Home* is an essential read for anyone who cares about the future of housing. Through sharp reporting and rich storytelling, Jessica Barrett proves that we can fix the abiding crisis of our time. This book gave me hope." —Charles Montgomery, author of *Happy City* and co-founder of Happy Cities

"*No Place Like Home* is an incredible feat: an intricately woven examination of the fundamental concept of home that forces the reader to reexamine the question of the housing crisis from an entirely new angle—one filled with humanity and, somehow, hope. Barrett manages a complex task as a writer in these pages, balancing the vulnerability of memoir with the rigour of journalistic research; the end result is compelling and urgent, personal and political, worrisome and optimistic." —Christina Myers, author of *The List of Last Chances* and *Halfway Home*

# NO PLACE LIKE HOME

Jessica Barrett

## THE MISSING KEY TO OUR HOUSING CRISIS

VIKING

VIKING
an imprint of Penguin Canada,
a division of Penguin Random House Canada Limited

Canada • USA • UK • Ireland • Australia • New Zealand • India • South Africa • China

First published 2026



Viking, an imprint of Penguin Canada
A division of Penguin Random House Canada
320 Front Street West, Suite 1400
Toronto, Ontario, M5V 3B6, Canada
penguinrandomhouse.ca

The authorized representative in the EU for product safety and compliance is Penguin Random House Ireland, Morrison Chambers, 32 Nassau Street, Dublin D02 YH68, Ireland, https://eu-contact.penguin.ie

LIBRARY AND ARCHIVES CANADA CATALOGUING IN PUBLICATION

Title: No place like home : the missing key to our housing crisis / Jessica Barrett.
Names: Barrett, Jessica, author.
Description: Includes index.
Identifiers: Canadiana (print) 20250249030 | Canadiana (ebook) 20250249049 | ISBN 9780735250253 (hardcover) | ISBN 9780735250260 (EPUB)
Subjects: LCSH: Housing—Canada. | LCSH: Housing—Economic aspects—Canada. | LCSH: Home—Canada—Psychological aspects. | LCSH: Home—Social aspects—Canada. | LCSH: Housing policy—Canada.
Classification: LCC HD7305.A3 B38 2026 | DDC 363.50971—dc23

Book design by Dylan Browne
Typeset by Terra Page
Cover design by Terri Nimmo
Cover image: © MicroStockHub / Getty

Printed in Canada

10 9 8 7 6 5 4 3 2 1

Penguin Random House
VIKING CANADA

For Dave,
who keeps our home fires burning,
and Ellis, our light.

# CONTENTS

# NO PLACE LIKE HOME

## INTRODUCTION

# HOUSE AND HOME

Let me tell you how I lost my home.

It started, as these things often do, not with one dramatic moment. There was no thunder crash or bolt of lightning, no life suddenly engulfed in flames. It was more a process of erosion, small drips imperceptibly carrying away bits of my foundation until one day it just couldn't hold me anymore.

I should specify here that I did not lose my house, or rather, my hous*ing*. I have never spent a night on the street or even come close to it, and by the grace of all things good in the universe I hope I never will. What I lost was my *home*, my place in the world, my sense of belonging, my community.

When I moved to Vancouver at 19 I had no inkling of how the blurry lines and fuzzy definitions of home we carry around in our culture would become a defining factor of my life. Even when I left the city 15 years later, a victim of the housing affordability crisis I'd covered so often as a journalist, I still couldn't fully comprehend all the forces—economic, cultural, social—that had conspired to pry me away from the only place I've ever felt I belonged.

This book started as a series of questions that wouldn't stop rolling around in my brain after I landed in a new city, in a different province, struggling to make sense of what had happened to me. How did our housing crisis get so bad—to the point where successful professionals and double-income households can't afford a suitable place to live? Why, despite all the attention, money and effort poured into the problem, haven't we been able to fix it? And when we talk about the obvious solution, creating more homes for more Canadians, what does that actually mean?

In North America, and many other places, housing and home clearly have quite a bit to do with one another. The way we use the words "house" and "home" interchangeably is proof enough of that. But instinctively we know this is an imperfect equation. If I ask you to picture a home, what does it look like in your mind's eye? Maybe it's a classic postwar bungalow with a pitched roof and a white picket fence on a quiet cul-de-sac, or a sleek modern condo with a showpiece kitchen and waterfall marble countertops. Maybe it's a tidy tiny house on wheels full of hidden storage clad in natural knotty pine. No matter what specific shape it takes, you're probably picturing housing—a built structure that offers shelter and some living space. But if I ask you what home *is*, well, we're in completely different territory. You might start thinking about the city or town where you live, or the country where you were born. Maybe you don't think of a physical place at all. Maybe home is a memory—the smell of your grandmother's cooking or the sound of Saturday morning cartoons from your childhood.

Linguistically, this presents a challenge for a writer trying to tease the two concepts apart.

To say "I'm going home" can indicate anything from heading back to your place after work, to visiting your parents, to getting on a plane and flying across the world. Likewise, "house" is also a confusing term. In its most literal form, a house is a particular structure for living in, generally a free-standing building meant to shelter a small group of people, such as a nuclear family. But, if a friend invites you over to their "house" and you arrive to find they live in an apartment, condo or duplex, you wouldn't feel led astray. We rely on context to differentiate between the physical buildings we live in and all the other ways we use these words—house, housing and home. That will be true throughout this book as well. However, it is sometimes necessary to specifically distinguish between these concepts. When this is the case, I will use distinct language to indicate whether I'm talking about specific forms of housing or a more broad understanding of home.

Decoding home in itself presents another kind of challenge.

Home is an unwieldy concept. If you ask 10 people what home is to them, you're going to get 10 wildly different answers. I know this, because I've asked this question of almost every person I've met while researching this book. I've been looking for patterns, something concrete we can point to and say: *This, this is a home and that is not*. It's a difficult endeavour considering the pattern I've found is that there's not much of a pattern at all. When I met Dorna, an expectant mother living in a former factory in Berlin, she told me that for her home is a feeling of being safe to experiment. Home lets you recharge, lets you stretch into yourself, she said. I'd never thought of home as experimental, but I suppose it is. Home, when it's done well, is a foundation that lets you take risks and experiment with the shape of your life—what you do with it, who you add to it, who you subtract from it. It supports you through all the twists and turns you take along the way to becoming all the versions of yourself you will be.

Ellie, a tattoo artist originally from the Toronto area, told me how she came to find home in Kimberley, British Columbia, a ski town of about 8,100 nestled in between the Purcell and Rocky Mountain ranges. "We became really close with a couple here in town and then he passed away in an avalanche," she told me. "We observed through the fog of tragedy how people supported his widow in ways that are so intuitive for a small town, which I hadn't seen before. You know, the freezer always being full of home-cooked meals, the fire out back of their house and all the people who gathered there night after night to share stories and feel some release, some connection. I think being a part of that, it was pretty unmistakable that we'd stumbled into a community."

Among all of the disparate and diverse definitions of home I heard, one commonality did eventually emerge. It was the notable *absence* of the very thing most of us think of as central to the idea of home. Almost nobody I spoke with gave me their current address or talked about a number of bedrooms or square-footage or preferred architectural styles. Out of the dozens and dozens of people I asked, only one person described their physical house as part of their conception of home.

And yet, almost every aspect of our housing policy and every response to our housing crisis is rooted in the belief that housing is the first and often only ingredient required to create a home; that if you put a roof over someone's head the rest will inevitably fall into place. But home is so much more than walls and roofs. It's more than individual boxes piled high in the sky or stretched out in the suburbs. It's even more than a bespoke mansion in an exclusive gated community. What most of us recognize intuitively is that home is a complex confluence of factors, many of them intangible. There is a reason the phrase "to make a house a home" exists. It is a tacit acknowledgement that there is something else required to turn mere shelter into a dignified place to live. We rarely talk about what that "something else" is, but it's time we started.

For more than a century we've based policy and programs on the notion that housing is the foundation of home. I have found this has constrained our imaginations, restricted our options and ultimately corrupted our cultural values, leading to mass confusion about what home even is and what housing is actually for. In fact, as we've become more and more obsessed with housing—how much it costs, where it should be built, what it should look like and who it should be for—we have become disconnected from a more holistic sense of home, one that nurtures our souls and strengthens our social fabric as well as sheltering our bodies. This is not to suggest that people don't need shelter or that housing is not vitally important. But housing alone is not enough to solve the crisis we are in. If we are serious about providing safe, stable, affordable *homes* for everyone, we need to flip the script. We need to recognize that home is the foundation upon which our housing, and our housing policy, should be built.

Finding examples of how to do this has taken me far away from where I live. I have found insight and inspiration in the social housing projects of Vienna, Austria, the Cold War-era apartment blocks of Berlin, and in the slums of Harare, Zimbabwe. I have read reams of academic papers, interviewed dozens of experts and devoured as many books as I could on the subjects of housing and home. I have discovered that restructuring our housing system to reflect the value of home is integral not just to solving our housing crisis but also to addressing many of the other crises we face, from the loneliness epidemic, to social and economic inequality, to climate change.

This book is a first step toward charting a new path.

In Part 1, we'll focus on the problem before us. We'll dive into the history and mechanics of our market-based housing system to uncover how it created the situation we're in now, and how it continues to stymie solutions. We'll also look at the psychological impact this has on how we've come to value and experience our homes, and how our housing system harms all of us, even those whom it financially benefits. We'll also put the concept of home under the microscope and examine exactly what it is that turns our housing into homes. I will articulate and explain some of the intangible qualities that create a sense of home and show you how they can be built, not out of bricks and mortar but out of relationships, connection and social capital.

In Part 2, we'll look at possibilities. We'll get on a plane and go abroad, where we'll discover that not every culture looks at home and housing like we do in Canada, and North America more broadly. We'll learn how Vienna created arguably the world's best housing system in response to a crisis that puts our modern-day version to shame. You'll meet housing activists in Berlin taking on rising rents and corporate landlords—and winning—by leaning into joy, community and radical inclusivity. And you'll venture with me to the outskirts of Harare, where we'll learn the value of refusing to compromise our dreams and our dignity when seeking out home.

In Part 3, we'll look at progress being made right here, and how we can change our system to create not only more housing, but housing that enriches our lives and nourishes a sense of security and connection in our communities using methods and avenues already in place. We will learn that solving our housing crisis is not only possible, but actually much simpler than many of us might think.

Finally, throughout this book you'll learn a lot about me. This is not a memoir in the traditional sense, but I do pull extensively from my own experience of searching for home because it's been fraught with all the forces we'll explore in these pages. I do not exist outside the system. In fact, ultimately I was inspired to write this book because no matter how hard I've tried, no matter where I've moved, I haven't yet been able to escape the insidious grasp of our housing crisis. Perhaps you can relate.

# PART 1: PROBLEMS

*This isn't about blame—it's about unwinding the patterning that got us here.*

—Rebecca Campbell

1

# HEARTBREAK CITY

Growing up in Edmonton, Alberta, I had no real sense of home despite having a surfeit of housing options at my disposal. I spent my childhood shuttling between my mom's rundown bungalow near the centre of town and my dad's spacious two-storey Tudor in an upscale outlying suburb. To say their divorce was messy is an understatement of epic proportions. My parents separated when I was six or seven and were still engaged in court battles as I was approaching my high school graduation. I was often caught in the crosshairs of their mutually unyielding hatred, which eviscerated any sense of emotional safety I might have had in either house. No matter where I was staying I was on high alert, careful not to reveal secrets I shouldn't have known and shouldering the fallout when I inevitably screwed up that impossible task. From my earliest awareness that I would someday be able to choose where I could live, I knew I had to get out of Edmonton. Leaving was the only way I was ever going to break free from the roles cast for me in the ongoing family drama, and as I got older that became a singular goal.

A diehard theatre and dance kid who loved to perform, I figured a bigger city would be more conducive to a career in the arts. I'd planned to apply to university in Toronto but a visit one summer in high school revealed humidity that turned my hair into an impossible oil slick and air that smelled like a combination of hot garbage and wet dog, at least where I was. I just couldn't see myself living there. (No disrespect to Toronto. One thing I've learned about home is that a place that is ideal for one person may be a total pass for another, so as you read, try not to take offence if someone disses your hometown because it wasn't the right fit for them.)

After high school I enrolled in a college dance program with an option to transfer to university in the Vancouver area. I'd always loved the beach, so at 19 I boarded a Greyhound bus and headed for the West Coast.

Vancouver wasn't meant to be a long-term thing, more a launch pad for the glamorous, semi-nomadic life I envisioned for myself, but the chance to travel after I finished school revealed I'm a pretty terrible nomad. I spent most of a post-university "backpacking" trip to South America blogging from an internet café in Buenos Aires. I never made any progress on my plan to venture toward Patagonia, but all the writing I was doing prompted me to think more seriously about my backup career. When I got back to Vancouver I applied to journalism school and attempted globe-trotting once more upon graduation with my first real-world reporting gig that took me all around Sri Lanka for a month. It was an amazing experience that solidified a nagging realization: I am not cut out for a life on the move; it makes me feel unmoored and anxious. I much prefer to spend more time in fewer places so I can settle in and really figure out where I am.

It took me a while to figure out Vancouver. My first year, living on my own for the first time in a new city, was lonely and depressing. But by my second year, I'd moved into an apartment in Mount Pleasant, just off Main and Broadway, with two friends from school. That's when a sense of home started to form.

Today, the intersection of Main and Broadway is a shining example of gentrification, all gleaming condos and trendy cocktail bars, but back then it was still a bit rough around the edges; a working-class area where sex workers sometimes strolled at night, and a spot with a reputation coloured by the fact that it was not far from the Downtown Eastside—the part of Vancouver known for open drug use and street homelessness. I loved Main Street instantly. It was full of funky vintage stores, hippy cafés, discount sushi restaurants and eclectic diners run by Chinese immigrant families that were budget-friendly and welcoming for student artists like me. The transit was good, the rents were relatively cheap and the surrounding area was extraordinarily beautiful. Side streets were lined with elegant Edwardian houses painted in whimsical colours and 1960s walk-up apartment buildings whose utilitarian exteriors were given life by Vancouver's abundant foliage. The whole neighbourhood exploded in pink every spring with cherry blossoms, magnolias and rhododendrons.

To prioritize beauty in one's life is often thought of as frivolous and shallow, but I didn't realize until I moved away how much Vancouver's physical beauty contributed to my quality of life, especially my mental health. Sometimes I'd round a corner on my way to catch a bus or run an errand and be hit by a vista of snow-dusted mountains so stunning it would literally take my breath away. To this day, I haven't found anything as effective at pulling me out of a navel-gazing slump or instantly dissolving an anxiety loop. I felt grounded in Vancouver, specifically my little corner of it. It was the first place I'd ever lived where I felt like I could just be myself. Like I fit.

The city of course had its challenges. Vancouver can be considered patient zero for the housing crisis we are contending with today. As I progressed through my career as a journalist, starting out writing for community papers and eventually for the big daily broadsheet, *The Vancouver Sun*, I noticed a growing sense of concern over the cost of housing roiling under the city's surface. Vancouver was the first place in the country where million-dollar houses became the norm and where terms like "renoviction"—when you get evicted so your place can be renovated and rented out at a higher rate—and "demoviction"—when it gets torn down for redevelopment—first entered our lexicon. But before these trends trickled into every city in the country, the problem was seen as relatively contained. As a cub reporter, I was dispatched semi-regularly to the Downtown Eastside to report on the city's most visibly disturbing issues. Drug addiction, untreated mental health conditions, systemic racism, trauma and poverty all collided in a heartbreaking display of human suffering that never seemed to improve. The pervasive homelessness and housing scarcity in the area was usually chalked up to those underlying issues, a result of conditions affecting an unlucky but decidedly niche population. Rarely was the phenomenon discussed in the context of policy decisions or broader economic trends with the potential to affect everyone. Nobody in charge even seemed to notice when housing issues started to spill over into the rest of the city. First, there were people sleeping on the streets far outside of the Downtown Eastside; then students began complaining that they couldn't find places to live. Lines for viewings at vacant rentals started stretching around the block, and waitlists at every co-op stretched to years. But Vancouver had always been a pricey place to live compared to other cities, so the official line was that the increasing cost of shelter was just business as usual. Those who didn't like it were free to leave.

---

In my 20s, East Vancouver was the cheaper side of town, owing to its distance from the ocean and proximity to the Downtown Eastside. This made it a refuge for students, artists and immigrants and other not-rich people looking to make a go of it. Almost all of my friends lived on that side of town, and it made for a familiar, village-y feel. I ran into people I knew pretty much everywhere I went, at the bus stop, getting groceries, along the bike paths on my way to work. Several of my close friends lived within blocks of the various apartments I occupied over the years. There was even a stretch of time when I lived across the street from one of my closest friends. We had a sitcom-perfect situation where I could literally stick my head out the window and invite her over to watch *America's Next Top Model* on an ancient, rabbit-eared TV I'd inherited from my aunt. We all moved a lot in those days, shifting our housing based on the permutations of roommates or romantic partners. Moving was always stressful and annoying, but most of us landed in the vicinity of where we wanted to be without too much fuss. That got harder as we got older and craved more stability. Rather than improving, the quality of housing we could access seemed to decline as our incomes grew and we sought to become more established.

The hallway in one friend's apartment building reeked of cat piss; another's building was overtaken with black mould after someone triggered the sprinklers and the dampness was never addressed. I lived in a place where I couldn't control my heat for several months out of the year and where I was sexually harassed by the property manager. We considered ourselves lucky. Renovictions had started sweeping the city, and we figured putting up with unsafe or unsanitary conditions was nothing to complain about when there were people being forced out of their homes. Despite all this, I loved my life in Vancouver. By the time I was 30 I had pretty much made up my mind that I wanted to stay forever. I remember coming back from trips and thinking: *This is my place. I'm so lucky to live here.* I was ready to settle in and put down roots. It was right around this time that it started to become clear I might never be able to.

In 2013, I left the city for a year-long reporting fellowship. When I returned I was shocked at how much the housing landscape had changed. Places like the sunny $700 a month ground-floor studio apartment I gave up when I left were going for close to $1,000 just one year later. Without a job or any leads on one, I decided the best thing to do—the most economical thing to do—was to move in with the person I'd been dating for less than a month. When our relationship began to show strain almost immediately, I panicked. If we split up, one of us would be out on the street, and as an unemployed journalist, I felt like I had no chance of winning the fierce competition for an affordable place of my own. Instead of ending the relationship, I doubled down, bending over backwards to try to make it work. This kind of thing wasn't uncommon.

A little-recognized consequence of our housing crisis is how the scarcity of affordable housing plays out behind closed doors. We talk a lot about the less-than-ideal options people are faced with when it comes to housing stock—aging, pest-filled, inaccessible apartments or super-pricey new builds with tiny footprints—but we barely ever talk about the choices people are often forced to make when it comes to who we share those spaces with. My Vancouver life was full of people constantly trying to figure out not just *where* they could live but *who* they could live with comfortably and sustainably to share the cost. This led to all sorts of messy situations. You had roommates scamming each other with subleases where one party would unwittingly be paying the lion's share of the rent, or people wearing out their welcome on friends' couches every weekend while they rented out their place on Airbnb. Occasionally, you'd hear about some really gross situations: people trading free rent for sexual favours or domestic labour, stuff like that. Mostly though, people just stayed in romantic relationships far past their expiration date for fear of being tossed back into the increasingly brutal housing market.

After nine painfully awkward months living with my boyfriend, I finally broke it off. He moved out of our two-bedroom basement apartment and a friend moved in, having also gone through a breakup. We lived happily together for a couple of years, until I rolled the dice on another relationship, this one with much more disastrous results.

---

By my mid-30s things were going pretty well. I was writing a well-read column that had won a prestigious award, and I had various freelance writing gigs that gave me a steady and I thought reasonable income at the time, about $50,000 a year. Then I landed my dream job: senior editor of *Vancouver*, the city's most well-known lifestyle magazine. My job was to steer the news and features section. It was a huge step up in my career. With my professional star on the rise, I was also preparing to close the gap in a long-distance relationship. This new boyfriend had offered to move to Vancouver for me. In an effort to ease his transition and make him feel more at home, I decided we should find a new place together, start fresh in neutral territory. I felt like I was finally on the cusp of real adulthood, and that I deserved to upgrade my life with little luxuries like in-suite laundry or living above ground. It didn't feel like what I was looking for was extravagant, but the market proved otherwise.

It had been just three years since my last house hunt in Vancouver, and in that time rents had undergone a stratospheric rise. I went from splitting $1,400 for a spacious two-bedroom to budgeting nearly $2,000 for a minuscule one-bedroom. And they *were* minuscule.

For years, I'd watched new condo towers spring up all over town, often displacing beloved bars or music venues or quirky (and affordable) older apartments. The city's distinct neighbourhoods had started to blend together under a monotonous sheen of blue-green condo glass. I'd rarely had cause to go inside these new buildings. No one I knew could afford to live in them, and even with my new job neither could I. But these developments—key to Vancouver's affordable housing strategy according to anyone you asked at city hall—boasted features like pet-friendly leases and appliances from this century, so I decided to check a few out. The floor plans seemed like they'd been designed by an AI—some disembodied being with no concept of what it's like to live in a physical body in a physical space. One place we looked at had a full chef's kitchen, complete with a six-burner gas stove, full-sized oven and "luxury" granite countertops, but it was so small you couldn't even have a kitchen table at which to eat the gourmet dinners you could theoretically concoct. As long-term homes, especially for more than one person, these places were absurd, and so was what you had to do if you wanted a chance to live in one. We were routinely asked to provide sensitive private information on application forms that contravened provincial laws and we were punished if we didn't comply. One landlord rejected us because I refused to give her my bank statements.

In the end, we sublet from a friend for a few months before landing in an attic apartment above a millionaire's garage in one of the richest areas in Vancouver, deep on the west side. Our new neighbourhood had the city's most prestigious postal code but it looked like a horror film set full of eerie, abandoned homes. These days, Vancouver has an Empty Homes Tax meant to dissuade people from letting properties sit vacant while they wait for the value to rise (a practice known as speculation), and I'm willing to bet neighbourhoods like this one served as direct inspiration for the policy. The streets were dotted with boarded-up windows, neglected lawns and stately houses where lights never went on. We lived across from a derelict mansion that looked like something straight out of *Scarface*, save for the squatters I'd sometimes see leaving in the morning, careful not to disturb the months-worth of soggy mail that had overflowed the postbox and piled up on the lawn.

Our landlord spent most of her time in California and seemed blissfully unaware of the state of the place. Once we moved in, I discovered our front door wouldn't stay closed unless the deadbolt was locked, the bedroom heater buzzed so loud it kept me up at night, and the windows had been painted shut. When I pointed out these details, our landlord seemed surprised at my concern, implying the place had been that way forever and no one else had complained. Our rent was $1,700 a month—the cheapest we could find and an absolute steal of a deal by today's standards.

Away from my friends and my community on the other side of town I became isolated and depressed. Gone was the feeling of familiarity and belonging that had made East Van feel like home. I started to feel disconnected, not just from my friends but from *myself*. My dissociation was helped along by the fact that my promising new relationship had quickly devolved into a textbook case of intimate partner violence. My boyfriend had a tendency toward volatility, which turned into daily bouts of berating, belittling, gaslighting and guilt-tripping me once we moved in together. We started having all-night screaming matches that more than once threatened to turn physical and made the new neighbourhood feel like a liability. Unlike in bustling East Van, there was no one around to overhear the shouting, the crying or the slamming of doors. As things escalated, I started to worry for my safety; there was nowhere for me to run and no one to intervene if our fights ever took a more sinister turn.

If you've never been in an abusive relationship it'll be difficult to understand why I did what I did next. Abuse is insidious, slowly wearing you down and reshaping you into someone you don't recognize. Before long, I started getting panic attacks and stopped sleeping. I struggled to keep up energy and appearances at work. I felt like I was somehow becoming transparent, as if I was dissolving right before my own eyes. The solution here was rather obvious—kick the asshole out and get on with my life—but in my weakened state I deferred to his take on how we could fix things. During our frequent fights, my boyfriend would often blame his outbursts on the city: Vancouver was full of dumb hippies; it rained too much in the winter and wasn't hot enough in the summer; and it was too damn expensive. I've since realized those first two points were classic abuser tactics—tearing me down by demeaning the places and people that I loved. But on that last one I had to admit he had a point, so I followed him to a different province.

When I looked at the prospects for my future in Vancouver, with or without my boyfriend, I crumbled. The cost of living the life I wanted in the city was a moving target, and it seemed like no matter what I did, no matter how hard I worked, I would never catch it. If I stayed, I doubted I'd ever be able to have even the most basic comforts. A cat. A garden. These simple things had been relegated to luxuries within a housing market that catered to an increasingly wealthy few.

Without realizing it, I had made a fatal error in trying to form a new household and move forward in my life. I'd given up my affordable apartment and, with it, what was left of my foundation. I was falling and there was no safe place I could see to land. So, I gambled. When my boyfriend announced he was moving to

Calgary I decided to go too. Even if my relationship was going to explode on contact in a new city—which it absolutely did—I figured moving at least gave me a fighting chance at recovery. Calgary was a more affordable city, and because of that, I thought I might be able to find the home there that I needed with the resources I had.

It sort of worked.

2

# THE EMPEROR HAS NO HOME

In the years since I left Vancouver, runaway home prices and rampant displacement have overflowed the boundaries of our biggest cities and caused a cascade of ill effects. So-called secondary markets like Hamilton, Ottawa and Victoria are now fixtures on the lists of North America's most unaffordable places to live. Homes in supposedly sleepy cities like Halifax, Kelowna and Kamloops are now out of reach for many locals. It's as if our entire country has been thrust into a high-stakes game of musical chairs—everyone pushing and shoving for a diminishing shot at a dwindling resource. Even those who've managed to clinch a coveted seat are not entirely spared the consequences as they watch loved ones struggle and their communities fracture under the weight of high and rising housing costs.

We Canadians are a compassionate bunch, or so we like to think. Now that headlines scream of record-high housing prices, homelessness and the human toll of crushing rents and mortgage debt nearly every single day, we seem to have finally coalesced around the problem. Our housing system is broken and *something* needs to change. But we are far from consensus about what.

The housing crisis has been met with calls from many disparate groups, from politicians, to housing developers, to anti-poverty activists, to build, build, build. Feeding this common refrain is a belief that the primary cause of our housing crisis is a simple imbalance between supply and demand: there aren't enough houses for everyone who wants or needs one. In response, the Canada Mortgage and Housing Corporation (CMHC), the Crown corporation responsible for administering housing solutions, has called for the construction of 4.8 million new homes by 2035 in order to "restore" affordability to levels we last saw in 2019. The federal government has also cut immigration, an attempt to slow population growth and allow our housing stock to "catch up."

But multiple expert analyses have shown that merely building more housing has had no effect on improving affordability. In fact, data collected in the country's most unaffordable provinces—British Columbia and Ontario—shows the opposite has occurred. Despite flooding the market with record amounts of new housing supply between 2016 and 2021, average home prices in those provinces continued to increase, even though the number of new homes built kept pace with, and in some cases exceeded, population growth.

So, what exactly is going on? According to Andy Yan, director of Simon Fraser University's City Program, who conducted some of the research referenced above, the idea that we can build our way out of this crisis fails to encompass just how complex it really is. "Housing isn't popsicles, or avocado toasts, or widgets or spanners or cars," Yan told me. "There is a complicated series of political, social and cultural actions, behaviors and policies that produce housing." These factors influence not just how much and what kind of housing we build, they also influence how we perceive housing, and the role it plays in our economy and our culture.

For decades now, we have developed a growing tendency to regard and regulate housing as a commodity. Not only has this been ineffective in addressing the affordability crisis, but it is actually a major cause of it.

There was a time when Canadians, if they thought about the monetary value of their homes at all, saw their potential sale as a kind of "rainy day fund"—meaning your house was something you could sell in a worst-case scenario like prolonged unemployment or the death of a breadwinner in order to provide a financial safety net. But over time, specifically since the 1980s, our cultural conception of housing has shifted significantly. We have come to calculate the value of our homes primarily in terms of how well they perform as financial assets rather than how well they function as places for people to live. What's more, we've come to accept this as the natural order of things. Most of us expect, or at least aspire, to become homeowners one day. Once there, we expect our houses (or apartments, condos, etc.) to be nest eggs, to pay for our retirement, to finance vacation properties and second homes, and to pave the way for our children to do the same. And we tend to look at these benefits as a God-given right. As one expert I spoke to put it, we feel as if we've earned the money our homes can make as we eat, sleep and watch TV, despite the fact that most of the value accrued by housing is the result of luck and timing, and a fair amount of public money and policy, not individual effort or expertise. Yet entitlement to housing wealth is so deeply ingrained in our cultural fabric that many of us are incentivized to oppose policy measures that would lower or even stabilize prices. Roughly two-thirds of Canadians and an even greater percentage of lawmakers are property owners. Thus, taking steps to meaningfully reduce the cost of housing, and hence limit its potential for profit, is an unappealing political endeavour.

At the same time, part of the reason we have become so obsessed with maximizing the financial value of our housing is because it costs us so damn much. Whether we rent or pay a mortgage, our shelter costs are the biggest financial commitment most of us will ever have. As that number gets bigger and requires more sacrifice to sustain, it feels even more critical that we continue to believe we will reap a financial reward "in the end." But the more we fixate on the *price* of housing, the less we seem to value what it is *worth*, not in dollars and cents but as vessels for our lives. "People monitor their home prices just like they monitor their equity portfolio," the economist David Rosenberg told me with concern. "I think we've collectively lost our sense of what a home really is."

There are consequences to this that extend far beyond how individuals conceptualize and relate to their own housing; for example, it severely limits the type of housing available for everyone. The unwavering belief that housing must always generate profit—rather than breaking even or becoming self-sustaining—has led to a dearth of housing choice in the market. Once a fixture of the real estate world, modest economical structures known as starter homes have essentially disappeared from the market as developers have pivoted to build primarily luxury housing aimed at affluent consumers. One result of this pivot is the housing stock in most of our cities increasingly sits on either side of a chasm. There are high-end single-family houses, teeny-tiny condos and little in between. The target market for both these types of housing are often one and the same: established property owners who might be looking for a luxurious upgrade for their primary residence or a turnkey condo to purchase as an investment. Often both. This has allowed widespread inequality to flourish within our housing system with inevitable spillover into our society at large.

More nuanced analyses of our housing crisis show the real problem isn't an overall lack of housing, it's a lack of *affordable* housing, and it's worth taking a moment here to unpack exactly what that means. The widely accepted definition of affordable housing used by most governments and institutions is that rent or mortgage payments should cost no more than 30 percent of a household's before-tax income. My personal opinion is that this definition is insufficient. A two-parent family living in the suburbs with small kids and a household income of $84,000 (the median before-tax household income in Canada as of 2025) experiences the burden of housing costs very differently from a working individual who lives downtown with the same household income. For the family, costs such as childcare, groceries and a private vehicle required to shuttle the kids around and commute from the suburbs may mean they struggle to make ends meet, even if their housing costs fall under the 30 percent affordability threshold. The individual, meanwhile, might pay 40 percent of their income, or more, to live in a central location, but without dependents and with the ability to walk or take transit, they might find the cost of housing to be manageable. The other problem with putting a hard threshold on affordability is that it doesn't take into account *how* people are meeting their housing costs and what sacrifices they may make along the way. A person who pays their rent or mortgage in full every month but does so by cutting out fresh produce, skimping on personal savings and racking up credit card debt cannot be said, in my opinion, to be enjoying truly affordable housing. Therefore, my definition of "affordable," the one I'm using throughout this book, means housing costs that leave enough left over at the end of the month to pay for other necessary expenses *as well as* pursue personal interests, prepare for our financial future and be able to enjoy rest, recreational pursuits and leisure.

A number of indicators show the market has epically failed to produce housing that meets either the technical definition of affordable or my more expanded version. A 2024 CBC analysis of rental vacancies in 1,000 Canadian neighbourhoods found that "less than one per cent of rentals are both vacant and affordable for the majority of Canadian renters," according to the 30 percent threshold. Meanwhile, the credit reporting agency Equifax found an alarming increase in missed mortgage and credit card payments starting in 2023, the year after home prices peaked during the pandemic, spurring a hike in mortgage interest rates. And according to Scotiabank, 45 percent of renters and 29 percent of mortgage holders said in 2025 that an unexpected expense of over $250 would "break the bank."

The solution to these problems, touted by a number of housing experts, is indeed more housing, but only certain *types* of housing, such as purpose-built rentals, co-ops and other non-profit options (which we'll get into later), and low-cost, no-frills "starter homes." That is not what our housing market produces, and most of what it does produce gets snapped up by people who already own at least one home. Only about one-third of home purchases in Canada are made by first-time buyers, with the rest made either by established homeowners looking to "trade up" or by investors seeking to acquire additional properties. In many parts of Canada, between 20 and 30 percent of all housing stock is owned by investors, and among condos—the most ubiquitous form of new housing—investor ownership is considerably higher. As of 2022, about 40 percent of condos in Toronto and close to half of all condos in Vancouver were investor-owned. And that's nothing compared to smaller urban centres in Ontario and British Columbia, which have seen a meteoric rise in investor ownership. According to data collected by Statistics Canada, up to 85 percent of new condos—those built since 2016—in places like London, Ontario, and Kitchener-Waterloo, Ontario, were owned by investors in 2022. In Fort St. John, a city of about 20,000 people in northeastern B.C., 90 percent of new condos were owned by investors in 2020. Some of these owners are wealthy foreigners with no ties to our communities or multinational corporations without a conscience, but the vast majority are mom-and-pop investors, people we all know. It might even be you. This call is coming from inside the house.

I don't bring this up to shame or blame those who have made money in the housing market or those who have been seduced by the narrative that investing in real estate is a surefire way to build wealth. An uncomfortable truth is that more and more people are reliant on the promise of housing wealth to fill the gaps left by eroding social safety nets, wage stagnation and the rising cost of living. People and corporations who have profited from housing aren't necessarily bad actors; they are engaging with our system the way it has been designed. What is needed to solve our housing crisis then is systemic, and ultimately cultural, change; a reorienting of our values toward prioritizing housing as a human right and a powerful tool best used to build stronger, safer, healthier, more prosperous communities. Admittedly, this is no easy feat when so many of us are so deeply invested—psychologically and financially—in the status quo. But I believe more people would advocate for change if they understood the many ways our current approach to housing hurts us all, economically, socially and emotionally.

---

These days, it seems like everyone knows someone, a parent, a colleague, a neighbour, a friend, whose house turned into a goldmine seemingly overnight. While it's true that someone who bought a single family house in Vancouver or Toronto in the early 1990s is likely looking at a substantial windfall today, real estate is not as secure an investment as people tend to think, because markets that have been stable for decades can turn on a dime. "A home is bound to a specific geographic location, vulnerable to local economic and environmental shocks that could wipe out the value of the land or the structure itself right when you need it," writes Jerusalem Demsas, a reporter for *The Atlantic*. Even without a catastrophic event, "making bets on real estate is tricky business," she adds. "During the 1990s, Cleveland's house prices outpaced both the national average and San Francisco's. How confident are you that you can predict the ways in which urban geography will shift over your tenancy?"

Daryl Fairweather, a housing economist with the U.S. real estate firm Redfin, told me that just like any other investment there is considerable risk involved in real estate. "It's kind of similar to the stock market," she said. "Just because your friend bought Tesla and Tesla stock went up doesn't mean that if you do the same thing you're going to have the same results." And unlike stocks, the carrying costs of property ownership eat substantially into what money there is to be made. Things like mortgage interest, insurance, maintenance and property taxes really add up, Fairweather said. This is particularly true of so-called income properties like condos, which can quickly become a liability for investors, even in red-hot markets.

Take Toronto and Vancouver, for example. After consistently trending upwards for years, the value of condos in the Greater Toronto Area and Metro Vancouver took a sharp downturn in 2024 and 2025, reflecting increased interest rates and economic uncertainty imposed by the threat of tariffs from the United States. This left many investors shouldering higher mortgage payments than their tenants were willing or able to pay in rent. The result was a wave of investors listing these properties for sale only to have them stagnate on the market for months or even years. A particular sticking point for prospective buyers seemed to be the small footprints of condo units built primarily to appeal to investors. It turns out that even in a housing crisis, nobody looking to buy a place to actually live in wants to pay hundreds of thousands of dollars for a 550-square-foot shoebox that's been designed without their long-term comfort in mind. On top of that, many small-scale investors vastly underestimate the work involved in being a landlord, Fairweather said. "When my friends ask me if they should get into real estate investment or become landlords, I always warn them that it's a job. Like, you have to actually maintain these properties, there's risk involved, you're not diversifying your money the way that you would if it were in the stock market. If all you're trying to do is build wealth, there are easier ways to do it."

Of course, there are other reasons to want to own a home. Compared to renting in a system rife with renovictions and myriad other loopholes undermining housing security for tenants, owning property is virtually the only path to stability our society offers. It's also a powerful form of cultural currency. Renters still face extreme social stigma stemming from our tendency to equate wealth with moral worth. "In Canada and the United States, owning has been held up as a signifier of who's economically stable and who's not and who is worthy of a vote or who is contributing to society," said Fairweather.

Then there's the fact that our economy is overly dependent on people buying and selling housing. In 2024, real estate, rentals and leasing accounted for roughly 13 percent of our gross domestic product, ahead of both oil and gas and manufacturing. But unlike resource extraction, the money generated doesn't easily come back into our communities. Because our system is engineered to encourage prices to trend up, it relies on "a never-ending stream of new people who are willing and able to pay current homeowners increasingly absurd amounts of money for their homes," writes American housing expert Daniel Kay Hertz, who likens the North American property ladder to a Ponzi scheme. When someone does sell their house for substantially more than they paid for it, almost all that equity is eaten up instantly by the purchase of their next home, which will also have increased in price. The few people in the position to actually pocket a profit often do so by leaving their communities, or even the country. This also has negative repercussions. From South America to southern Europe, many cities have been hit with rampant gentrification and waves of evictions hastened by a recent influx of North Americans who consider foreign housing costs a bargain compared to what they're used to paying, but whose buying power ends up pushing prices far higher than locals can afford.

Back in Canada, governments are so gun-shy about the political fallout of falling home prices that they engage in some serious financial gymnastics to prevent that from happening. We spend billions each year on back-end programs such as tax-sheltered savings accounts, publicly funded mortgage insurance and shelter subsidies for low-income households, all of which are in place to ensure people can continue to qualify for ballooning mortgages and pay ever-increasing private market rents. Meanwhile, there are almost no mechanisms to recapture the public money that keeps the system afloat. For instance, the mere suggestion that we tax profits from the sale of primary homes, as we do with the sale of other assets, is widely considered political suicide.

Maintaining an open-ended system that continually funnels public money into the creation of private housing wealth has serious downstream effects for our entire society. Every dollar that goes into ensuring our population can continue to pay inflated housing prices is one that doesn't go into any number of other areas in sore need of public investment. It means less funding for things like health care or education or recreation or the arts. Less funding for infrastructure, public transit, scientific innovation or research. Less money to mitigate the effects of climate change or to find ways to green our economy. As individuals, putting more money toward rent or mortgage payments means we have less money to spend in our communities and to support local businesses. We have less money left over at the end of the month to save for an emergency or invest in other, more reliable and beneficial, wealth-building avenues.

Experts have even started to eye high housing prices as one reason Canada persistently lags behind peers like the United States and Australia in worker productivity. According to a report from Alberta Central, the trade association for Alberta's credit unions, home mortgages are sucking up so much of our country's available credit that there is little left over for lending to businesses that need money to invest in machinery, equipment and intellectual property—things that create jobs and grow industries. "As most businesses need to borrow money to invest, a lack of available money or high financing costs will hamper the capacity," the report states. As well, multiple studies from the CMHC show the cost burden of housing causes brain drain from our cities. People in their peak working years tend to flee when housing costs get too high, or they flat-out refuse to move to cities with pricey housing markets to fill job vacancies.

Meanwhile, the financial underpinnings of our housing sector have created a house of cards. Canadians shoulder the highest household debt levels of any nation in the G7. Collectively, we owe more money than our entire economy produces. Three-quarters of that debt is due to our mortgages. While our financial system has fairly good safeguards in place to weather normal market fluctuations, experts increasingly warn we are just one global recession away from a total market collapse. While a sharp decline in house prices might seem like welcome news to people who've been priced out of the market, examples from south of our border show it could actually make the problem of housing inequality even worse.

When U.S. home prices bottomed out in the depths of the Great Recession, it was corporations, not people, who swooped in to buy them. In the wake of the subprime mortgage crisis, government bailouts focused on keeping hedge funds, private equity firms and banks afloat in the name of rescuing the U.S. economy. Working-class households who had lost their housing and/or income were offered no such safety net. As a result, it was these corporate entities—including many of the same hedge funds, equity firms and banks that helped create the subprime mortgage crisis in the first place—who had the resources to buy up the houses that suddenly seemed so cheap. And they did. Since the Great Recession, the U.S. housing market has been utterly transformed in many communities as hundreds of thousands of single-family houses once owned by middle- or modest-income people have become the property of institutional landlords.

Backed by global private equity players like Blackstone, these companies have turned single-family homes into an asset class through the creation of real estate investment trusts, or REITs, a financial product that allows organizations and individuals to buy shares in properties as they would in corporate stocks. That means entire neighbourhoods once owner-occupied are now owned and managed by inscrutable subsidiaries uniquely designed to maximize shareholder profits, chiefly by raising rents, adding fees and downloading responsibility for things like landscaping onto tenants without making any meaningful improvements to the dwellings, much less creating more housing. A *New York Times* investigation characterized the situation as "a housing recovery without a homeowner recovery," and revealed that although many residents of these houses had been allowed to remain in place, they were now paying considerably more in rent than their original mortgages demanded.

The phenomenon of banks, private equity firms and other corporate financial entities finding ways to slice and dice our homes into pieces they can buy, sell and trade has been given a name—the financialization of housing—which the United Nations has flagged as a major threat to human rights. "Financialization is linked to expanded credit and debt taken on by individual households made vulnerable to predatory lending practices and the volatility of markets, the result of which is unprecedented housing precarity," a Special Rapporteur on Housing wrote in 2017. Beyond simply driving up housing prices to the point where we can't afford them and setting us up for financial ruin, the financialization of housing wreaks havoc on everything from our psyches to our communities. "Capital investment in housing increasingly disconnects housing from its social function of providing a place to live in security and dignity and hence undermines the realization of housing as a human right," the report states. "Housing and financial markets are oblivious to people and communities, and the role housing plays in their well-being."

These financial forces act on our lives in ways that can be difficult to notice and even harder to talk about.

We are well aware of the scourge of homelessness on our streets and can likely imagine, to a degree, the suffering of those caught in its midst. What we are less aware of is all the ways our profit-driven housing system negatively affects even those of us who seem quite far removed from that fate. We don't talk about the people stuck in abusive relationships because there is nowhere else to go, or the toxic stress of living in fear that your rental home will one day be sold. We don't talk about the anguish of being forcibly relocated, of leaving behind a cherished garden that gave you and others joy, of having to rehome a pet or the impossible heartache of pulling your children away from their school and uprooting their tiny, fragile lives. We don't talk enough about how the trend of millennials and younger generations toward staying single longer and having fewer, if any, children is tied to the fact that many can't anchor into communities that have the connections and support networks necessary to form the families they might like to have.

It's difficult to articulate all the ways our market-based housing system requires us to contort ourselves, to shave down our ambitions and shave off bits of ourselves in order to fit into whatever box happens to be available that we can also afford. It's almost impossible to quantify the cumulative impact this has on us as a society, but if you scratch the high-gloss surfaces and marble countertops of our real estate fantasies, you'll find an awful lot of loss, grief and pain. Most of us may never know the vulnerability and fear of being left without shelter, but many of us are living with an aching sense of being unrooted and adrift—of being in a very real sense, homeless.

---

It is devastating to lose a home, or live with the fear that you might, but there are not a lot of outlets for those feelings. I think this is a big reason why so many of us opt to discuss the value of our homes purely in financial terms, especially when those who dare to publicly venture into more emotional territory often face ridicule.

Around the time I left Vancouver there was a wave of open letters published by anguished people who felt they'd been pushed out. These letters were easy to make fun of. Though their complaints were legitimate, many of the authors came across as sore losers who just didn't have what it took to "make it" in the big city. I saw myself as an entirely different case. I felt like I *had* made it, and becoming successful in a challenging career in a challenging city had formed a huge part of my identity. So, I surprised myself when I decided to write a letter too.

I was reluctant to add my voice to the chorus of disaffected former Vancouverites, but I had a *lot* of feelings about leaving. When an editor I trusted asked if I'd write a piece I said yes, assuming my essay would just be another entry in an already saturated market and fade into internet obscurity within days. I was mortified when the thing went viral. For weeks I was the face of Canada's broken housing system, appearing on talk radio and national TV news. I was also satirized, crucified in the comments and ripped to pieces in the meanest corners of the internet. Meanwhile, my inbox filled with private messages from people just like me looking for advice. Should they also move to a new city? If so, where should they look—and what should they look *for*—in their search for a home? I had clearly touched a nerve. And I had no idea what to tell these people.

In my attempt to avoid being cast as another sore loser (and it's highly debatable whether I succeeded) I'd tried really hard to frame my story in a certain light. I wasn't *forced out* of the city; I had made an *empowered choice* to go somewhere that allowed for the possibility of the life I wanted. I certainly didn't mention the relationship dynamic at play or how much shame I was feeling. In reality, I found the transition to Calgary extremely difficult, and I blamed myself for the situation I was in. Sure, the housing market didn't help things, but if I hadn't been so *stupid* as to give up my apartment, so *selfish* as to want—to need—my own space, so *sentimental* as to desire a garden, or a pet, maybe I'd still be there, in the only spot on the planet where I felt like I belonged. Maybe if I'd been smart enough to give up journalism and get some higher-paying job, or learned how to live with 10 other people in a decaying mansion, I could have made it work. Maybe if I'd been a quicker study about my relationship patterns or just a stronger person generally, I could have avoided the whole messy business.

I've learned that this is a central feature of our housing system.

It thrives on, depends on, us blaming ourselves instead of interrogating it. And we are complicit. We encourage people to believe that if they can't afford the housing where they live and work, then it's due to their own poor life choices. When we beat ourselves up in this way, it's hard to muster the dignity to demand better, and so we put our energy into fixing our perceived personal failings rather than challenging a system that exploits our deepest human needs. This pattern lets our leaders and institutions off the hook of accountability and pits us against one another instead. Rather than working together to demand the change we need to see, we resort to slinging blame. We quietly compete with and compare ourselves to our neighbours without really getting to know them. As a result, we don't develop compassion for their struggles or even realize that we share them.

Blame, shame, social alienation. These are the feelings and forces that emerge from a housing market that is fuelled by our suffering. And it is. When we suffer, we are willing to pay more for our housing—as much as we can muster—to make it stop. If we have money, we will pay that. If we don't, we will leverage everything we have to get loans. If we don't qualify for loans, then many of us will pay with our souls, our mental health, our emotional well-being, our sense of community and belonging. We will pay with an ever-shrinking sense of self, self-expression and self-worth. Any way you slice it, we pay. What we get in return is seldom worth that price.

This even goes for people who've managed to hack the system—the winners, if you will.

I don't know what it takes for someone to evict an entire building or double the rent in the name of business and still sleep well at night, but it can't be good for your soul. Similarly, the logic behind investment maxims like *rent where you want, buy where you can* is inherently self-defeating. If *you* are eyeing other people's homes as commodities to be bought and sold on the whims of the market, it follows that someone else is looking at *your* home the exact same way. Buying a house because you think it will be a *good investment* rather than a *good home* is seriously twisted logic that has us living with kid gloves on. Many owners look at their homes as an investment to "protect" for a future return, forgetting that our quality of life, our experience of home every day—*is* the return, or should be anyway. By this logic even people with money, and lots of it, make absurd and limiting choices when it comes to their enjoyment of their own homes: Don't paint that bathroom flamingo pink, even if the thought of it sets your heart on fire. It might hurt your resale value. Renovating? Bathrooms and kitchens are where you'll make your money back; just be sure to keep them sufficiently greige. Considering turning your living room into a play space or a workshop so it works better for you or your family? Oof. That's a risk. The message is this: Whatever you do, don't get too colourful, too creative or too weird in your home lest you repel some hypothetical future buyer—as if there is another, more appropriate place than your own home to be your most creative, colourful or weirdest self.

I love a good home makeover show as much as the next person, but HGTV and its spate of programs like *Income Property* or *Flip That House* reinforce the narrative that the purpose of housing is to generate financial rewards for landowners rather than provide a high standard of living for the people who will ultimately occupy them. The language used to describe homes is similarly detached and dehumanized. Terms like "investment property," "mortgage helper" rental suites and—my favourite— "unit" linguistically suck the soul out of dwellings that are meant to envelope the broad and complex intimacies of human life. And what about the things these shows leave out? You never hear about what happened to the former occupants of that old abandoned house, or how that million-dollar sale kicked off a wave of speculation and gentrification on the block.

The removal of real human considerations from the pursuit of real estate profits might make for clean and compelling TV, but in reality, it's leading to tragedy. In March 2023, seven people died in a fire in Old Montreal in a poorly maintained apartment building that had mostly been converted to illegal Airbnbs. Former tenants told the press the landlord had long neglected safety provisions in the building, which had been cited for multiple bylaw infractions. An investigation after the fire revealed the building did not have proper emergency exits or working fire alarms. There was exposed wiring, and at least one suite had no windows. In May of that same year, the city of Hamilton was rocked by the murder of a young couple in their 20s, who were shot and killed by their landlord after allegedly complaining about mould in their apartment. In December 2022, a 73-year-old man in Vaughan, Ontario, went on a shooting spree, killing five people—all connected to his condo building's strata council—before being fatally shot by police. Court records showed a years-long battle between the condo board and the shooter, whose declining mental health had been exacerbated, in his view, by noise from the electrical room below his suite. These are extreme examples, but they are the result of an increasingly toxic environment where our relationships with those we live closest to are now characterized almost entirely by estrangement and conflict. Provincial residential tenancy boards report an unprecedented volume of disputes between landlords and tenants alleging abuse of the system on both sides; development hearings at city halls are beset by battles between community members with wildly different ideas of who their neighbourhoods are for and how they should evolve; and, as sociologist Alan O'Connor has pointed out, management of condo buildings has become so impersonal and litigious that our first interaction with neighbours in a multi-unit building is less likely to be a warm welcome than a written notice of a noise complaint.

All this points to a society reaching a boiling point. For a great many of us, our experience of home has become rather fraught as we have become more isolated, polarized and distrustful of one another. We are not living well together, and we are not happy in our homes.

The thing is, we are extremely emotional about our homes, and we should be. At our core, we *are* emotional beings. There is nothing that has a bigger impact on how we feel walking through our lives, how we perform at work, how we show up for our friends and our families, than whether we can feel relaxed, nurtured and well supported *at home*.

Finding our way back to a version of home that extends beyond the roofs over our heads to include the people, relationships, lands and ecosystems that support our very existence isn't just vital to improving our own quality of life; it has wide-ranging societal implications. As we'll discuss later in this book, it is no coincidence that the rise in anxiety, depression, and other mental health conditions, social isolation, addiction, distrust and political polarization in our society has come at a time when fewer and fewer of us feel we have a home, a place or community where we belong. Rethinking the way we produce housing so that it is not only affordable and attainable but also encourages social connection, belonging, purpose and stability is a cornerstone of improving mental and physical health and reducing polarization at a population level. It's also critical if we are to successfully adapt to the effects of a changing climate.

From Paradise, California, to Lahaina, Hawaii, to Lytton, B.C., we've already seen wildfires wipe entire cities and towns off the map. Meanwhile, the risk of increasingly devastating floods and storms has rendered some residential areas of the United States and Canada uninsurable. Our climate crisis and our housing crisis go hand in hand. Unless something drastically changes, the next several decades will see more people forced from their homes due to natural disasters and climate-driven poverty as habitable areas of our planet become fewer and farther between. This means we will have—in the medium-term at least—more people sharing less space; more people looking to make a home where others already live. Failure to prepare adequately for this eventuality is a recipe for disaster.

Fear of losing our homes—either through forced displacement or an influx of perceived "invaders"—is the source of so much conflict. It's the starting point of wars, whether waged between nations or between neighbours. But it doesn't have to be that way. We can find examples of how to make room for one another by looking to systems that already exist, and we can demand that our leaders make it possible to create better homes for more people. We can find ways to live well while living closer together.

Or we can continue the status quo. We can continue fighting amongst ourselves and competing with each other for homes. This will only increase our suffering while making a tiny percentage of already rich people inconceivably richer.

My hope is that we will pursue the path that leads us toward a more harmonious way of living. Because making better homes for ourselves and everyone around us is not only possible, it will positively transform almost every aspect of our society. But in order to get there, we need to start with the basics: What even is a home if not a simple collection of bricks and sticks and mortar? We've all heard the old adage *home is where the heart is*. As cheesy as it sounds, I have found that's largely true. The tricky part is figuring out just what our hearts actually want.

3

# THE ELEMENTS OF HOME

I did eventually land on my feet in Calgary. I easily found a sweet little two-bedroom, postwar bungalow in a trendy inner-city neighbourhood for a manageable $1,300 a month, $400 less than my last place in Vancouver. It had a red front door, a picture-frame window with a matching origami-inspired porch light, and at over 1,000 square feet, was much larger than it looked from the street. I'd intended to live there with my abusive boyfriend, but thankfully he never moved in. I finally worked up the courage to dump him shortly after I arrived. Then, I promptly fell apart. For months, that house was the only thing that held me together, and I rarely left its cradle. I did all the cathartic breakup things—sang sappy ballads, made extravagant meals at unusual times, sobbed and screamed in the middle of the night curled in the fetal position on my IKEA pull-out couch. I had no job, so my mom, bless her, helped pay my rent for the first little while. It was an altogether humbling and humiliating experience.

Eventually, I started to right the ship. I went to therapy, picked up more freelance work and spent a *lot* of time polishing my countertops and organizing and reorganizing the dry goods in the kitchen pantry. After what I went through in Vancouver, having an entire free-standing house to myself felt extravagant. Being able to do what I wanted, when I wanted, in a space that worked for me felt like I'd just shrugged off an itchy sweater I hadn't realized had been giving me hives. As far as houses go, this one was everything I'd hoped for.

In his beautifully esoteric book *The Poetics of Space*, the French philosopher Gaston Bachelard compares humans and their houses to snails in their shells. As containers for our lives, houses, or housing, in whatever form it takes, gives us a shape to grow into. In Bachelard's view, we fill the nooks and crannies of our houses with our beings until they are fused into one identity—one concept of home. It's a beautiful image, but as my experiment asking people to define home revealed, we all have vastly different ideas of what home is, and it doesn't necessarily connect to any structural form. This presents quite the problem when trying to have a practical discussion of how to build or provide a sense of home at scale. Pity the poor policy-makers, elected officials and even real estate developers trying to make home happen for the masses when definitions range from one person's specific childhood neighbourhood to another's country of origin or connection with their spouse. Because individual conceptions of home are so diverse, attempts to build consensus around what constitutes a "good" home in this culture have coalesced around its most tangible expression: housing. This is actually a rather contentious approach.

Scholars who study the varied nature of home are loath to pin the concept to any kind of physical structure, noting that there are many cultures in the world where housing and home have almost nothing to do with one another. "For nomadic peoples, for hunter-gatherer societies which followed food sources and such, home moved," Joseph Moore a sociologist at Douglas College in Metro Vancouver told me. "Their idea of home was materially quite light, but there was a strong sense of home in the relationships to people and also the relationship to the environment." This isn't just a vestige of history. There are an estimated 40 million people on this earth right now—from Mongolian herders, to Kenya's Maasai, to the Romani people found in many parts of Europe and Asia—who are part of existing nomadic cultures. They have likely never equated a pitched roof, or a plot of land, with their conception of home. In Canada, many Indigenous cultures still regard the idea of permanent settlements as a curiosity that runs counter to their traditional ways of living.

For many people in mainstream Western culture, though, the idea that home could exist without some type of permanent dwelling at its core is almost inconceivable. But removing housing from the equation for a minute is a useful exercise. Without the image of the white picket fence or the walk-up apartment—whatever it may be—clouding our vision, we can start to see clearly the true foundations of home: the qualities and connections we need in order to set down roots where we live. Only then can we fully assess how well our current approach to housing does or does not meet those needs.

---

When I was reporting on housing and homelessness in Vancouver, I met a lot of people living on the streets who would rather bunk down in doorways or sleep on park benches than enter the shelter system or live in chaotic and squalid low-income housing. Their reasons for this were manifold. Supportive or subsidized housing often came with strings attached, such as requiring residents to be sober or working toward sobriety. Or you'd be separated from friends or partners or have to leave beloved pets at the door. Emergency shelters in particular could be hellish places where residents had no privacy and risked having their few belongings rifled through or stolen during the night. Sexual assault was rampant.

These are some of the reasons why, even in the depths of Canadian winters, some people will still risk death from the elements rather than try to get into an overcrowded shelter on even the coldest of nights. It's also why housing advocates have pushed for so-called no-barrier or housing-first philosophies when it comes to providing shelter for people on the street; the more you can take people as they come—with their pets, addictions, partners and all—the more you can build relationships and, the idea goes, help them connect to supports that could lift them out of crisis. But even this approach has its limitations. It's actually pretty common for street-entrenched folks to wind up back on the street after being placed in housing. A lot of people find the silence of a still room deafening, or are completely overwhelmed by the logistics of housing—paying rent, maintaining appliances, stocking a fridge. Others just find they can't settle in.

And for some people, the barrier to accessing housing comes down to something many of us would consider rather arbitrary when faced with sleeping on the street: location.

One interview that's stuck with me all these years was with a man named Arthur whom I met in a back alley in Kitsilano early in my career. Kitsilano, or Kits, is an upscale neighbourhood on the west side of Vancouver whose residents are known for their clean-living lifestyles and dedication to yoga. That Kits was the first place in Vancouver to get a Whole Foods and proudly boasts its status as the birthplace of Lululemon should tell you a lot about the vibe. Geographically, it's only a few kilometres from the Downtown Eastside, but psychologically it's about as far away as you can get, and that's exactly what Arthur liked about it.

In his 50s with a salt-and-pepper beard, wearing a yellow raincoat and pushing a shopping cart, Arthur told me he'd lived on the streets of Vancouver for eight years, five of them in Kitsilano. He'd taken to hanging around the intersection of Maple and Broadway, a quiet, residential area lined with single-family homes, upmarket condos and a nearby elementary school. Through his years in the area, Arthur had gotten to know some volunteers from a coalition of Anglican churches nearby. This is why we were talking.

I was writing a story about the volunteers' efforts to identify the local homeless population and ensure they were first in line for a new social housing site slated for the area. This was a rare occurrence on the west side, where residents were known to storm city hall meetings in order to keep services like this out of their very expensive backyards. The church volunteers were doing double duty. On the one hand, they were tracking down people living rough in the area and helping them with the necessary paperwork to get into housing. On the other, they'd undertaken a kind of public relations campaign with their congregations to help them recognize and accept the street population for what they already were: neighbours, many with long histories in the area.

For Arthur, the prospect of staying on the west side was what finally prompted him to try to get off the street. "It's a friendly neighbourhood and I know quite a few people now," he told me at the time, adding that he'd been approached about applying for housing before but never followed up for fear it would have taken him out of Kits and likely to the Downtown Eastside. The chance to stay in his neighbourhood was the difference maker, and he was pursuing housing more seriously than he ever had before. The week before we spoke Arthur had met with some of the church volunteers and government staff to fill out the housing forms.

Meeting Arthur and others like him made me realize that even in average North American cities, home is not necessarily built with bricks and mortar but in how we relate to what's around us, be that the people in our sphere, a given landscape or the rhythms and intricacies of a certain intersection. People like Arthur, and those who work with them, know this better than almost anyone. That's why there's been an important shift in language over the last few years regarding people with no permanent shelter. The reason you may hear people referring to these populations as "unhoused" rather than "homeless" is because there's an important difference between the two. It's possible to be homeless and not unhoused; for instance, if you're living in a shelter or couch surfing without a place of your own. And, as Arthur helped me understand, it's possible to be unhoused, or unsheltered, but not entirely homeless. A major aspect of Arthur's definition of home had been met when he found a community in Kitsilano where he felt he belonged. Preserving that sense of belonging had taken precedence over his need for shelter for five *years*. "I like it because you build up trust with people," Arthur told me when I asked him why it was important for him to stay in Kits. "After a while, when you build up your trust, it feels more like a home than it does a big city."

If home, as Arthur described, is a *feeling* more than a physical thing, that particular definition opens up a can of worms. How exactly can you foster a single feeling for a whole society? Is it even possible? As diverse as our ideas of home can be, are there any universal factors that are likely to make each and every one of us *feel* at home, wherever and however we find it?

I found some answers to these questions in the work of Dutch sociologist Jan Willem Duyvendak, who analyzed a good chunk of his colleagues' investigations into just what home actually is. What he found were the typical academic vagaries and debates around the highly individual and relative nature of home, but he also managed to identify some much-needed common ground. The literature he surveyed agreed on two main points: Home is a fundamental human need; and there are three fundamental elements that are essential to eliciting "home feelings" in nearly everyone, no matter where or what their home tended to be. They are: familiarity, haven and heaven.

**Familiarity**, at first glance, seems like the most straightforward of the three. It's the experience of knowing your home. You gain familiarity by exploring all the nooks and crannies of a new house and learning its quirks: the way the tap needs to be cranked just so to stop the leaky faucet, or the way you close the curtains every afternoon to keep the sun from blinding you while you cook. Familiarity extends outside our dwellings too—the routes we take to work, the neighbours we know by sight if not by name, the businesses we frequent to fulfill our daily needs. Familiarity in our neighbourhoods is something we build over time, but we can lose our sense of familiarity without ever moving. When long-standing neighbourhoods change rapidly through gentrification, development or neglect, our once-familiar surroundings can become strange. There's even a word for this, "solastalgia," which researchers coined to describe the sense of loss or distress people experience when faced with a shifting environment. The researcher Leslie Kern calls this process "un-homing."

Familiarity isn't just important to homebodies. Those who move around a lot also seek it out. Digital nomads are afforded their globe-trotting lifestyles in part due to the availability of familiar amenities—from WiFi connections to Starbucks to co-working spaces—in once-remote corners of the world. Expats and travellers tend to congregate because they find familiarity among strangers sharing a similar experience. When you arrive on vacation and immediately try to get your bearings ("Okay, the subway station is four blocks from the hotel, by the bodega where I can buy some coffee in the morning"), that's your biological need for familiarity kicking in and giving you a little sense of home, even when the goal is to be away from home.

Haven and heaven bear a bit more explanation.

**Haven** refers to a place of refuge and retreat where we are safe to tend to our inner worlds. A haven is invite-only, a sanctuary, a protected place where we can have our most intimate moments and be our most authentic selves alone or with people we trust. It's an escape from the outside world, providing shelter not just from the elements but also the judgments, expectations and aggressions of daily life.

Ideally, at least in the West, our haven is our physical dwelling, our house, or a part of it. Home yoga studios, spa-like bathrooms, "man caves" and "she sheds"—these are some ways the real estate industry markets to our desire for haven-like spaces. But design features can only go so far in instilling the necessary sense of safety that haven requires. A great many of us don't have a sense of haven within our physical dwellings, and indeed our security is often threatened from within. Everything from the simmering frustration with an inconsiderate roommate, to the actions of an abusive partner, to arbitrary restrictions imposed by a landlord or a condo board can undermine the sense of security and autonomy we need to feel at home in our housing. That's why many people seek havens outside their dwellings, such as a child's tree house retreat, a rented workshop space or an escape to the backcountry to sleep under the stars.

The most excellent example of haven I can think of is the case of a mysterious tunnel discovered in a Toronto ravine by a park worker in 2015. At 10 metres long and 2 metres wide, with structural supports, electrical wiring, a rosary and a Remembrance Day poppy pinned to the wall, the tunnel sparked international speculation. Many feared its creator harboured nefarious intentions. For a time, the worry was the tunnel was somehow related to a terrorist plot to upend that summer's Pan Am Games. It turned out it was the work of Elton McDonald, a 22-year-old construction worker who lived in a nearby public housing development with his mother and two sisters on one of Toronto's toughest streets. With violence common in his neighbourhood, the ravine had long been McDonald's haven. Building the tunnel was simply a way to give it some infrastructure. When he was finally identified in the media and peppered with questions around his intentions, McDonald's answers were so unexpectedly uncomplicated it left nearly everyone speechless. The tunnel was a quiet place for him to sit and think, simple as that. "I was getting away from regular things, away from life," he told *Maclean's* magazine. "Nothing in particular. Just life itself."

**Heaven**, on the other hand, refers to our place in the outside world. Broadly, it's the idea of **belonging**, which is how I'll often refer to it going forward. Heaven is feeling like we are part of a community, that we fit into our surroundings and understand the culture and customs common to the places where we live. Heaven feelings can occur at the national, regional or extremely local level; we can find belonging through a proud sense of citizenship in our country, our region or our city block. And we often find it as members of a specific group with ties to a physical area. Immigrant enclaves, religious communities, gay villages or artist colonies are all examples of the way people geographically self-sort along identity lines. This has pros and cons. On the upside, there's nothing quite like the ease of moving around in a community where you know you are welcome, understood and protected; where the language, customs and unspoken social signals need no explanation; where you are spared the stress of being scrutinized as an outsider. For marginalized, racialized and minority groups, finding a sense of heaven isn't just necessary for home feelings but is often a matter of survival—there is safety in numbers.

But, as Duyvendak pointed out, belonging also has a dark side. Taken to its extreme it can lead to xenophobia and discrimination—the idea that if some people belong in a given community, others do not. We've seen this expressed through things like segregation laws and the red-lining of neighbourhoods, or even the more subtle influences of economic gentrification.

Building a diverse society where everyone can belong is, in the West especially, one of the biggest, most necessary challenges of our time, and I believe it is possible. But, as we'll explore in the next chapters, our current market-based housing system makes it difficult for people to feel like there truly is room for everyone to find their own version of heaven.

Duyvendak's research gives us a good foundation for expanding our understanding of home and determining where "home feelings" come from—and, conversely, why they are often lacking. But it clearly doesn't cover the whole gamut. Anyone who's gone on a house hunt or contemplated a move to a new city or even another neighbourhood knows there are some more practical considerations we make when considering where to go or whether that place eventually starts to feel like home. Through my research and my own experience, I've boiled these down to four additional elements: space, place, need and time.

**Space.** I realize people like Arthur, though more common than you'd think, are the exception. For most of us, shelter is an essential component in our conception of home, and it generally comes in the form of housing. This, in turn, delineates a certain amount of space we can reasonably claim as our own.

In the era of "McMansions," monster homes and subterranean "iceberg" basements meant to circumvent zoning rules with hidden square footage, much of the discussion about the space of our homes comes down to the obscene amounts of it they consume. Over the past several decades the average single-family house in

North America has been getting bigger while our household size has shrunk. In 1975 the average Canadian home was a little over 1,000 square feet for a household of 3.5. By 2010, it had almost doubled in size, to nearly 2,000 square feet. Household size, meanwhile, shrank by a whole "person," to 2.5. That, combined with our continent-wide preference for detached single-family houses, has led to the suburban sprawl that is threatening important ecosystems, eating up farmland and taxing municipalities' abilities to pay for things like utilities, emergency services, roads and transit.

In response, the housing pendulum has swung in the other direction. While single-family homes have been growing, condos have been shrinking, from an average of about 1,000 square feet in the 1990s to less than 650 square feet by the 2020s. The logic is simple: Put more people in smaller housing forms. But the details matter when it comes to how well these new builds foster home feelings.

For a conventional developer, there are two main ways to deliver more affordable housing: You can build far away from the city centre where the land is cheaper, or you can build really, really small. If you can do both, you can deliver some of the cheapest housing around. Because of this economic reality, one of the fastest-growing sectors of the housing market is something called "suburban multi-family"—basically, apartment and condo buildings placed on the outskirts of cities. These buildings do offer inexpensive housing options for people who need them, but they often come with other costs, like giving up access to transit, schools, services and employment opportunities—all without the benefit of personal space, which is the primary value the suburbs are supposed to offer.

And even in more urban settings, the trend toward tinier homes begs the question: How small is too small? The emergence of "micro suites" and "junior one-bedrooms," coming in at around

300 square feet or less, has raised concerns about mental health and long-term livability for their occupants.

Some proposals for packing in more housing seem patently absurd, if not entirely inhumane. The University of British Columbia in 2019 caused a stir when it opened a new student residence featuring 71 "nano units" at 140 square feet each—that's smaller than a standard city parking stall. But the controversy over that project pales in comparison to the outcry billionaire Charles Munger caused in 2021 when he released his design for a student dormitory at the University of California, Santa Barbara. It called for 4,500 students to be packed into single-occupancy rooms measuring only 70 square feet, slightly larger than a prison cell. Of particular offence to the architecture community was Munger's insistence on a peculiar design detail in order to ensure his funding: Over 90 percent of the rooms would be windowless, lit by LED panels with no access to fresh air or natural light. Thankfully, the proposal was abandoned after significant protest.

The way our need for space in our housing relates to our feelings of home is complicated. Most of us can probably agree that 5,000 square feet should be enough to enable a family of almost any size to feel at home, while the idea of anyone living in 70 square feet, particularly with no windows, makes us deeply uncomfortable. But the truth is, our needs regarding space change throughout our lives and vary according to our desires. A parking stall–sized apartment may be a perfectly comfortable haven for an extroverted university student on a bustling, walkable campus. Less so for a work-from-home professional who likes to entertain or a couple expecting a child. The amount of space we need in order to feel at home directly corresponds to how much space it takes for us to live comfortably and pursue our individual life goals. If we want to have children or share our homes with other people, then we will probably need more space. If we are content living on our own, we might be happy with less. But the question of just how much space it takes for each one of us to feel at home in our housing has an answer that is frustratingly imprecise: enough.

**Place.** In December 2022, a 33-year-old Ontario woman named Jackie Thomas briefly became internet famous—and not in a good way—for the seemingly ordinary act of moving.

In an as-told-to piece in *Toronto Life* that ran under the headline: "I moved to Alberta and hated everything about it. After three months, I came back to Toronto," Thomas summed up her boomerang journey as a kind of cautionary tale. She'd made frequent work trips to, and had a few friends in, Edmonton, so when the Alberta government launched an aggressive ad campaign promising a lower cost of living and plentiful jobs to lure Ontarians to the province, she gave up her Mississauga apartment and took the leap.

"I snagged a newly built 1,600-square-foot home with two master bedrooms and a large backyard, 30 minutes south of the city, for just $400,000," she told *Toronto Life*. But she soon found herself hopelessly isolated and depressed. A self-described Black Carrie Bradshaw type, Thomas found the deep suburbs of Edmonton to be distressingly quiet. She missed her old life hitting up shisha lounges or the Cactus Club after work with friends.

For this admission, she was resoundingly mocked online. Commenters, positively glowing with schadenfreude, declared her an imbecile who clearly hadn't done the necessary research for such a serious move. Either that, or she hadn't given Edmonton a fair shake. The consensus was that she deserved to pay the consequences, about $12,000 in moving expenses, for her lapse in judgment.

Now, it does seem fairly obvious that buying a house in a distant suburb of a substantially smaller city several thousand kilometres away from the only home you've ever known might set you up for some serious culture shock. But I can absolutely understand why Thomas thought it was a good idea. There is a powerful narrative that's emerged in the midst of our housing affordability crisis: Price trumps place. Thomas unfortunately discovered through her expensive error, however, that place matters greatly to our experience of home—more than many people bargain for.

In this, we find another paradox. Home may be more of a feeling than a place, but place influences our feelings of home. There is no getting away from the fact that we are physical beings in a physical world.

Like home, place is a layered concept and a linguistic shapeshifter. It can refer to our physical dwellings, the streets of our neighbourhood, our broader city, region, nation or continent, any or all of which can have significant bearing on our individual sense of home. Meanwhile, local history, landmarks, infrastructure and architecture can coalesce in a shared identity, even a shared language, that sparks a collective sense of home among people in a certain place. When Drake reps "the Six" in his songs he's telegraphing the connection between his identity and his roots in Toronto. In my much maligned hometown of Edmonton, people wear sweatshirts with the slogan "Still In Edmonton"—a kind of dog whistle to the legions of young, creative, liberal thinkers who find the city an excellent and nourishing home even though it seldom ranks on lists of the world's, or even Canada's, most exciting locales. Then there are the landscapes, ecosystems, climate and weather patterns unique to the places we live that inform everything from our daily routines to the economy to the celebrations and rituals we share with our neighbours. Think of coastal fishing villages or mountain ski towns and the way the natural elements dictate the rhythm of life, attracting and retaining people who tend to share the values they instill. Or the fact that you can draw a direct line between Canada's status as a northern nation and our predilection for hockey—even the most ambivalent fan goes nuts when we make the Olympic Final.

No matter how we encounter a sense of place, it enhances our sense of home. Environmental psychologists call the emotional bond between people and place "place attachment," and research has found that the stronger it is, the stronger our sense of belonging (heaven) and safety (haven). The opposite is also true.

One thing I didn't account for in moving to Calgary from Vancouver is my strong attachment to the climate and landscape of the West Coast. Objectively, where I live now in Calgary is also a spectacular part of the world, just an hour away from the famous Rocky Mountains, but the landscape just doesn't stir my spirit like being on or near the coast. I find the moss-covered trees and misty air of the Pacific Northwest deeply comforting, almost cocooning. For me it's like being held by the earth, a feeling I just don't get in sunny, wide-open Alberta, which lots of people love for its expansiveness. Our individual affinity for one particular landscape over another also has a name—"topophilia," from the Greek words for "place" and "love"—and this aspect of home is truly a bit of a mystery. No one can really say why one person gravitates to the ocean while another longs for the plains. Nevertheless, people who rate highly on place attachment scales tend to be healthier, happier and more involved in their communities. They are more likely to defend it from threats, volunteer to help neighbours and even cheer on local sports teams during a losing streak. They are much more likely to feel at home.

**Need.** Not long after I left Vancouver, my friend Hilary announced via social media that she and her young family would also be leaving the city in favour of a more affordable long-term home. After "auditioning" nearly the entire country, Hilary said that they'd settled on Duncan, a town on central Vancouver Island in the Cowichan Valley that, to be honest, had a reputation as a bit of an armpit.

Of all the places I could imagine Hilary—a vivacious community builder who works with social enterprise companies—it was hard to imagine her in a town I'd heard most often described as a nondescript nowheresville in a part of the island overrun by an oddly conservative confluence of "hicks and hippies." I wanted to know why, after considering virtually the entire country, including centre-of-the-universe Toronto, this particular town had won out. I was even more curious when I heard Hilary had intended to, and nearly did, move her family to Salt Spring Island.

If you know anything about Salt Spring Island, you know it should have been the obvious choice compared to Duncan. Salt Spring is the largest and most developed of the Southern Gulf Islands, just a 90-minute ferry ride from Vancouver. It's a favourite holiday spot for city-dwellers drawn to the bucolic scenery, seemingly untouched beaches and a cool artisanal community of cheese makers, lamb farmers, kombucha brewers and soap makers who conspire to put on a truly epic Saturday farmer's market. Making Salt Spring their forever home had long been a dream for Hilary and her partner Eduardo, who at the time worked for Greenpeace. But when they looked into moving there, they realized they would just be trading one housing crisis for another.

Skyrocketing costs in Metro Vancouver had spillover effects on the island, because many people who lived on the mainland owned rental properties on Salt Spring. When housing costs in the city got too high, they decided to move to the island—into the suites they'd rented out to tenants. The result was a wave of evictions. The local paper filled with heartbreaking stories of long-standing island residents pleading for somewhere, anywhere, to live. Strong resistance to densifying the island meant there was little chance of new housing being built any time soon to alleviate the situation.

Hilary and Eduardo realized they needed to recalibrate their dream. "It was just like: We're not needed in Salt Spring. And Salt Spring doesn't want us," Hilary told me.

When it comes to home, the waters of want and need must be carefully tread. History is full of examples of discriminatory practices to keep unwanted populations out of certain communities by claiming they are "full." Nearly every public hearing I have ever covered on increasing density or changing residential zoning has featured opposition groups claiming the scarcity of resources ("Where will all these new residents park?") or fearing the influence of unfamiliar groups ("Renters will destabilize the neighbourhood! Transit users will bring crime!"). On the flip side, there is something to be said in our current climate, especially when you are in a position of relative privilege and choice, for looking at prospective communities not just from the perspective of how they can meet your needs but in terms of whether they need you.

Most of us, without thinking too hard about it, can rattle off a fairly long list of the things we need in our homes: a certain amount of space, affordability, proximity to jobs or the ability to work remotely. We need creature comforts and conveniences like restaurants, coffee shops and grocery stores that stock the foods we eat. We need to be able to get around, so we need roads and parking or, better yet, good transit, bike and pedestrian infrastructure. If we have children, we need to be close to childcare and schools. There are certain phases of life where we need to be near family or other support systems, such as when we are rearing young children, caring for aging parents or going through a health or other personal crisis.

What many of us fail to consider, however, is that need is a two-way street. Our experience of home can be made infinitely richer when we find home in a place that needs what we have to offer. Looking at home as a reciprocal relationship doesn't just help the communities where we live; it can help us strengthen other elements of home, like place attachment and belonging. It can also lead us to find really great homes in places we otherwise wouldn't think to look.

When Hilary and Eduardo realized Salt Spring Island didn't need any more people like them, and indeed, that their presence might add to the island's housing crunch, they opened their search. When a friend suggested Duncan, Hilary was initially skeptical, but they decided to pay it a visit and "everything just flowed." In Duncan, they found housing that suited their needs—a newly renovated five-bedroom rental house where their two boys could "literally run in circles." But more than that, Duncan seemed to really need them. Hilary began working with local start-up groups and social enterprises, helping to build capacity for small businesses and diversify Duncan's traditionally resource-based economy. She also became highly involved in her children's school, a one-of-a-kind nature school with a curriculum informed by local First Nation traditions. Eduardo worked remotely at first, but soon found his experience as a community advocate was uniquely suited to doing reconciliation work with the Indigenous groups in the Cowichan Valley. A couple of years ago he ran for, and won, a seat as a school trustee. All this has led them to become deeply committed to Duncan and to the community—Hilary's mother even moved from Indiana to join them there a couple of years ago.

During one trip to the coast, I spent an afternoon with Hilary and she showed me her town. Situated off the side of a highway in a string of small communities ringed by big-box stores and strip malls, it's nowhere near the pastoral ideal of Salt Spring Island, and it has many of the same social problems as Vancouver. There's an addiction crisis, and housing affordability concerns have crept up to the central island now too. Transit is extremely limited and the boys' school is a 20-minute drive away. Duncan is far from perfect, but it's definitely home.

Walking through the town's tiny downtown with Hilary I could see how connected she is to her community. Every few steps it seemed like we ran into someone she knew. We stopped to pick up a hat and lend a shirt to the woman who runs a used book store—the first good friend Hilary made in Duncan. We filled up her household cleaners at the local refillery, where she chatted easily with the woman behind the desk. At the Garage, a kind of one-stop shop for coffee, organic veggies and locally made goods, we even ran into Eduardo working on his laptop in a quiet corner outside the coffee stand. "I can't imagine living anywhere else," Hilary told me as we sat down to lemon bars from the bakery. "Like, I would love to live in Amsterdam or Portugal, but then I think about it. I'm just like, this is our place."

Another way to frame being needed is to call it "having purpose." The benefits of purpose, of being part of something larger than yourself, have been well-documented in relation to work. We know that people who feel a sense of purpose in their jobs are more likely to report higher rates of satisfaction, stay longer, go above and beyond for co-workers and report lower rates of burnout than colleagues who look at work as just punching a clock. As author Melody Warnick points out in her book about place attachment, similar benefits can be found when people see themselves as necessary contributors to their communities. Rather than simply viewing their homes in an extractive capacity—what can this place give me?—looking at what you can give back leads to a more connected and infinitely more fulfilling experience of home.

**Time.** Of all the elements of home, time is the most important for the simple fact that home is a feeling that develops and strengthens over months, years, decades, a lifetime. Time intersects with nearly every other element of home. You simply can't become familiar with your surroundings without spending time with them. The deep sense of belonging and community we all crave usually requires years to cultivate. Researchers aren't totally sure where place attachment begins—do people tend to stay in places they like or do they grow to like the places they stay?—but the correlation between time and attachment is clear. The longer people have been in a place the more strongly attached to it they become. Space, haven and need all affect how much time we will spend in a given home. It's hard to stay in a place where you don't have enough space, don't feel safe, or that doesn't suit your basic needs.

On the flip side, the feeling that we are running out of time can devastate our experience of home. Our sense of security or safety is eroded when we fear our haven will be ripped out from under us. We won't put effort into connecting with a community when we know those ties will be severed before they have a chance to grow strong. Like houses, homes are slow to be built and can be demolished in an instant. Nothing more efficiently or brutally demolishes a sense of home than telling someone their time is up.

---

Looking back, what the little bungalow with the red door really was for me was a haven, something I had lacked in my housing for the previous several years. It was easy for me to attach to the house because it looked familiar to me—it reminded me so much of my mom's little bungalow where I grew up. Because I lived there by myself, I had a lot of space to experiment and fill it with things that reflected and reinforced my sense of self. After a while, these elements formed a foundation that enabled me to seek out and develop some of the other elements of home.

You see, we don't need all the elements of home in equal measure all of the time. There are times in our life where one or two might take precedence and the rest feel secondary. And just like that, they might flip. In my 20s and early 30s heaven was my priority. My sense of belonging in my community was more important than my address or the characteristics of my physical dwelling, and this grew as I learned more about Vancouver and explored the West Coast through my work and with my friends. This helped me build a strong sense of place attachment and nurtured my growing connection to the environment and the culture around me. Vancouver also met a lot of my needs. It had good transit and bike routes. There were jobs in my field, and through my work I felt like I gave something back. All those elements were enough to sustain me through fairly regular upheavals in my housing, where I didn't feel particularly safe or secure. By the time I hit my mid-30s my priorities had changed. The lack of haven became a dull ache, and then a searing pain point in my life. It was the thing I needed more than anything, and not having it negated almost every other element.

The first brutal winter after I moved to Calgary, I burrowed into my haven, but as the weather warmed I started to venture outside. I became friendly with some of the people who lived on my street. Even though I had a yard where I planted my own veggies, I volunteered at the neighbourhood community garden to meet people with similar interests. After almost a year in the house the beginnings of a community had formed and I opened up my home a little more.

An acquaintance who had just gone through a breakup knew I had an extra bedroom and asked if I'd consider letting her move in. I thought about it and decided I'd done what I needed to do alone in that house; I'd begun a process of healing and my spirit felt much stronger. When Kari moved in, we formed a community together, hosting dinner parties on the sun deck and fires around the pit in the backyard underneath the canopy of our Manitoba maple tree. We started to get to know the single mother who lived next door who shovelled our sidewalk in the winter and sometimes ran an extension cord to our place in the summer when her power got shut off. It was a far cry from the well-rounded sense of home I'd felt during my heyday in Vancouver, but it was the start of something good.

After years of dodging demovictions in Vancouver it's almost comical that I faced my first one in Calgary. The news came about a year and a half after I moved when I got a phone call from someone I'd never met at a company I'd never heard of asking where my rent was. When I said I'd paid as per usual on the first of the month I learned the house had been sold to a developer. Neither my former nor my new landlord had thought to inform me. You would have thought my years of living in Vancouver would have hardened me to the instability of renting, but I was an anxious mess. There was no timeline on the demolition, but knowing I could be uprooted at any moment felt like living with my head in a guillotine. Things got worse when I opened the front door a few months later to find a surveyor on the lawn who casually informed me the house was part of a land assembly with three neighbouring properties, including the one next door with the single mom and her teenage kids. A few weeks after that, a sign went up on my lawn heralding what it was to become: "21 Luxury Townhomes."

Within a week of the sign going up, my neighbour had packed up her kids, mentioning in passing that they were headed back to the B.C. interior to stay with her parents. Her house remained vacant. At some point somebody jimmied the lock on the front door and left it flapping in the wind and it stayed like this for months, casting an ominous pall over the block, which became especially creepy as winter set in.

I reached my limit when I started getting routine wake-up calls from the cops banging on my door asking for info on the derelict property that was generating complaints. All I could do was give them the number for the landlord who, like the house next door, had gone completely dark.

Clearly, it was time to go.

4

# TRICKLE-DOWN HOME ECONOMICS

If you stop to think about it, really think about it, a lot of the roadblocks that continually keep us from creating and maintaining affordable, good-quality housing that meets a variety of needs stems from a cultural definition of home that is limited to housing. When we think of home as beginning and ending with shelter, we don't consider all the elements—familiarity, haven, heaven, space, place, need and time—that interact to make us truly feel at home, or not, in the buildings where we live. Nor do we recognize how different priorities pertaining to these elements of home play out within our housing system, often causing conflict and impeding or eroding our home feelings.

So-called NIMBYs (not-in-my-backyard change-resisters) who storm city hall in predictable opposition to any development or neighbourhood evolution are acting out of fear of a loss of *familiarity* in their surroundings. Similarly, our attachment to single-family homes comes down to a lack of familiarity with other forms of housing that are more affordable, environmentally sustainable and encourage better social cohesion.

*Space* has become so unevenly distributed in our housing stock that it has become the physical manifestation of the emergent class divide between the housing haves and have-nots. The glut of tiny condos designed primarily to appeal to investors in many markets has created a class of households living in spaces too small to allow for the privacy and sanctuary required of a *haven*.

The development industry, meanwhile, has done its best to downplay the concept of *place* and our attachment to it by making many places seem as if they are interchangeable. On one level, it has succeeded. Every corner of this continent is filled with identical houses on nondescript cul-de-sacs orbiting commercial plazas with big-chain businesses. That doesn't change the fact that our hearts know the difference. In Toronto-transplant Jackie Thomas's case, it wasn't that Edmonton didn't have a Cactus Club—it actually has two—it's that none of them were *hers*. She discovered the hard way an awkward truth many people encounter in their search for more affordable housing: There are certain places that feel like home to us, and others that just never will.

When we are either forced or forcibly encouraged to cut our *time* short and move away from places to which we are attached, the message we hear is: You are not *needed* here. Your contributions, your purpose, your commitment to your community, that's all meaningless. We are left demoralized, dehumanized and deterred from making the same effort in a new location, lest we suffer the same humiliation and heartbreak anew. This, in turn, affects our sense of *belonging*.

It is easier to be mean than to be vulnerable, and so our culture has adopted a decidedly cruel tone when it comes to how we talk about the pain and suffering the neglect of our home feelings can cause. Rather than deal with difficult albeit natural emotions, we resort to stereotypes and name-calling. NIMBY has become a kind of slur used to negate the fears of residents who feel they are being progressively un-homed. We regard these change-resisters not as people grappling with a sense of loss but as out of touch elites who have no concept of their privilege. People who struggle to cram their lives into too-small footprints aren't recognized as being caught on one side of a widening class divide; rather, they are maligned as materialistic packrats who simply need to embrace the "freedom" of a minimalist aesthetic. People who are attached to specific places—those who won't leave their hometown despite an economic downturn or the apartment slated for demolition—are seen as sentimental relics clinging to a bygone world. Renters are still regarded as transient spendthrifts who should have the discipline to cut out avocado toast or whatever in order to get into the market.

This is getting us nowhere. We are locked in an impasse, each of us dug in around whatever trauma our housing system has wrought upon us, unable to consider other points of view.

Here, we've arrived at another of my burning questions: How did we get here? How did we arrive at a system that reduces a fundamental human right to a commodity and then moralizes our access to it? There's the simple answer: money. Cynics among us might argue that people can't help but abandon their morals as soon as there is cash on the table. But that doesn't actually explain it. There are many examples of ways in which we have protected, or at the very least shielded, human needs and desires from the influence of market economics, even when there is a great deal of money to be made.

In the Canadian context, health care is a prime example. In the United States, the for-profit health-care industry is worth hundreds of billions, but on this side of the border we regard universal health care as a sacred part of our collective identity. Our system is surely not without its flaws, but for the most part we hold fierce beliefs that everyone has a right to health care no matter their economic or social status. When our system looks to be in danger, governments fall.

Education is another area where we have cordoned off some parts of the system from private interests, deeming it necessary—required, even—for every child to have access to free primary and secondary education. Then there's daycare, roads and public infrastructure, parks and green spaces: all things we deem worthy of substantial public investment and protection from privatization because they pay dividends in the form of a more productive and free society whose basic needs are largely cared for and whose rights are, at least in principle, respected.

Housing is this weird outlier. For some reason, we've chosen to treat it more like a discretionary consumer good backed by some seriously wonky logic. We don't buy cars expecting them to go up in value as we drive them around town. We don't buy furniture, clothing or household appliances and expect to flip them for a profit when we're done with them. We buy these things with the understanding that their value comes from how well they meet our needs while we need them. Their utility *is* the return on investment. So, what is up with housing?

Well, the ridiculous gains in financial value attributed to your average suburban rancher have pretty much nothing to do with the house at all. They're about the land it stands on.

---

Winston Churchill famously called land the source of all wealth and railed against consolidated land ownership as the "mother of all other forms of monopoly." He would know, Britain having spent several hundred years trying to clinch a monopoly on nearly all the world's productive land. Nothing puts the scope of this in context quite like a visit to the British Museum in London. Walking through the marbled halls and climate-controlled exhibition wings, I couldn't help but marvel at the sheer size and breadth of the collection. Among the more famous offerings on permanent display are the Rosetta Stone, used to decode ancient languages; a moai from Rapa Nui, one of those heavy-browed, strong-nosed busts from what is also known as Easter Island; and a huge array of ancient Egyptian artifacts, including a colossal granite statue of King Ramesses II, complete with some of its 3,000-year-old pigment intact. But for me, visiting was also an uncomfortable experience—the museum being basically a trophy case for the spoils of imperialism.

Recent years have seen Britain and other former colonial powers called to answer for their habit of stealing priceless cultural artifacts during often bloody occupations of sovereign lands. The museum, for instance, is engaged in the process of repatriating or making reparations for some of the stolen items in its keep. But that complicated process may pale in comparison to the task Britain faces in unwinding the impact of its centuries-long land grab from its own citizens. Well before the British sailed the world kicking people out of their ancestral homes and pillaging artifacts, they honed this practice on their own people by displacing peasants on British soil and progressively privatizing fields and forests once available for the common good. This has laid the groundwork for the crippling housing crisis Britain faces today, which, not coincidentally, bears eerie resemblance to our own. If you boil it all down to its roots, the beliefs that underpin Canada's housing system, and consequently our housing crisis, stem from the customs and practices of the damp island that gave rise to so much of our culture and our laws. Specifically, they were set in motion nearly a millennium ago when someone looked out over a bunch of land a lot of different people were already living on and declared, rather arbitrarily, "This is mine now."

Ever since humans figured out how to farm the same fields year after year there have been ownership claims on land, with tribal leaders of agrarian societies eventually becoming the monarchs who controlled land through their noble classes and fought with other monarchs over other lands. Few have done it so effectively, or so brutally, however, as William the Conqueror.

Back in 1066 William made the voyage over the English Channel from Normandy in what is now northern France and quickly set about dispensing with the Anglo-Saxon rulers of the time. In the wake of the Norman Conquests, as they came to be known, William carved up what was then the Kingdom of England into large plots of land he handed over to his cronies to rule. Feudalism, the practice of granting land rights to the noble classes in exchange for loyalty and military service to the Crown, was nothing new in Europe. But William put his own spin on things.

First, he greatly reduced the size of the aristocratic class, installing fewer than 200 Norman barons in an area once controlled by more than 4,000 Anglo-Saxon nobles. Then he instituted a system of male primogeniture, ensuring these large tracts of land could only be passed on to the eldest son rather than spread between all heirs, as was the custom in many other parts of Europe. This had the effect of not only keeping these massive estates intact as they passed from one generation to the next, but they also grew considerably as the descendants of those early aristocrats acquired more and more land, generation over generation.

Fast-forward a few centuries and the concentration of land, and hence wealth, in Britain is one of the key sticking points in its centuries-long class struggles. According to extensive research by writer and activist Guy Shrubsole, an estimated one-third of England and Wales today is still in the hands of the original *landed* elite, while around half of England is owned by less than one percent of the population. Those landed elite continue to benefit monetarily through rents, development opportunities and industrial activities on their properties. One proclivity of William the

Conqueror that has been particularly vexing to land reformers in England throughout the last 1,000 years is the amount of public space privatized purely for the leisure pursuits of the wealthy—things like stag hunting, grousing or horse racing. Overall, the Norman Conquests saw nearly three-quarters of what is now England fall into private hands. This includes Sherwood Forest, of Robin Hood fame, a real place that used to be common land where peasants could hunt and forage for food until William claimed it as a royal hunting forest. (Learning this really made Robin Hood's drive for vigilante justice make a lot more sense.)

So extreme is the impact of land and wealth accumulation on ordinary, non-noble Britons that Gerald Grosvenor, the sixth Duke of Westminster, once quipped to a 21st-century audience of young entrepreneurs that the single best thing they could do to succeed in modern Britain was to "make sure they have an ancestor who was a very close friend of William the Conqueror."

Commoners left to compete with each other for dwindling tracts of public land didn't take kindly to this, of course. There were many peasant revolts over the years, including a big one in 1381, but the nobles' claims on land ultimately remained. The introduction of enclosure acts in the 1600s cast another blow to the peasant classes, privatizing a further 6.8 million acres of common land between 1604 and 1914. Only property owners could vote at the time, rendering the vast majority powerless to stop the sweeping legislation. Making matters worse, the onset of the Industrial Revolution around the same time eviscerated cottage industries like weaving and metalworking as it concentrated the means of production in fast-growing urban centres. Many rural Britons, faced with paying extortionary rents to live, farm and forage on once public lands, and with their livelihoods increasingly made redundant by machines, had no choice but to abandon their traditional villages and flood to the cities in search of work. There, they encountered a housing crisis far worse than the one facing the country today.

---

If the British Museum is an ode to imperialism's winners, the Museum of the Home is an ode to everyone else. On the east side of London, about a 30-minute tube ride from the city's central museum district, the Museum of the Home sits in the working-class area of Hoxton in an unassuming two-storey building of faded brown brick and moss-covered shingles. Compared to the throngs of tourists downtown, the vibe here is much quieter. On the day of my visit, a couple dozen visitors strolled through the exhibits and wandered through a tranquil courtyard with native English plants sprouting in neat rows. A few of the staff prepared for the imminent arrival of a school group.

Director Sonia Solicari met me at the entrance and took me back to her office, leading me through a winding path of creaking stairs as she told me about the building's history. Built in 1714 as the Geffrye Almshouses, it was once an early form of low-income housing that arose during the Industrial Revolution as an attempt to offset some of the human suffering the era ushered in. Privately funded by trades guilds or wealthy industrialists—in this case an ironmonger by the name of Robert Geffrye—almshouses gave shelter to those with few other options. Most residents of this home would have been the widows of factory workers, or perhaps the working poor, Solicari said, such as single women working as governesses whose wages wouldn't cover market rents. Life in the almshouse wasn't glamorous by any means, but it was stable and safe. Each resident had a private bedroom with a small adjoining kitchen and access to shared communal spaces such as the chapel and the courtyard where they could grow their own food. Though few aspired to wind up in the "poorhouse," as almshouses were (and still are) colloquially called, historical records show a strong sense of community between these residents and those of the surrounding community of worker tenements. "They were good places to live," Solicari assured me.

Since it opened in 1914, the Museum of the Home has evolved from a furniture museum to a reflection of our own cultural understanding of home. Exhibits showcase the architectural evolution of housing from Victorian-era parlours to sleek modern lofts, but they also speak to contemporary issues like increasing social isolation or the impact of technology on how we interact with our domestic space. Many of the discussions they spark are universal, but some are more unique to London, harkening back to a time when a great many residents had virtually nothing in the way of home and when the city turned on the labour of a seemingly limitless supply of untethered, often violently uprooted people.

In the basement, Solicari pointed out a handwritten letter hanging in a transparent frame, telling of one young man's disillusionment with the city. In an elegant cursive hand he described streets rife with human waste, overcrowded slums, air heavy with soot, and a rank River Thames that was little more than toxic slurry. Beside that sat several servants' boxes, meagre vessels where domestic workers, many of them children, would have kept their few belongings for easy transport from house to house. "They never had their own home, all they had was their box," Solicari said, noting domestic workers depended on their employers to provide lodging in the servants' quarters of their grand estates. In another corner, an etching of something akin to a women's shelter showed a particularly barbaric scene: anguished bodies laid stiffly in so-called coffin beds, narrow wooden boxes placed together side by side. Above them on the wall were the words: *Are You Ready To Die?* Indeed, for the truly destitute of industrial London, death was often the only escape from grinding poverty.

Seeing evidence of a grim reality, I had renewed appreciation for why so many people of this place and that era opted for an untested life in an almost unfathomable land an ocean away. Faced with the dismal option of eking out an existence among London's inhumanity or extortion by the elite in the countryside, the idea of settling in the New World would have seemed incredibly enticing. Land, which was in such short supply in Britain, which had been so mismanaged and caused so much strife for so many, was plentiful in this far-off world. So plentiful, in fact, they were literally giving it away. The central promise North America made to white Europeans was that it was a place where anyone, regardless of class, could expect to one day own property if they were willing to work for it. And for the first few hundred years at least, this was true.

---

It is a fact that the country known as Canada exists on Indigenous land, much of it forcibly claimed by the Crown and distributed to European settlers through disingenuous, often violent means. In tracing back the origins of Canadian housing policy, it was clear that the Indigenous people who'd lived on and shared North America for millennia were not a consideration. The New World was incorrectly presented to prospective settlers as a vast expanse of unoccupied, uncharted territory, and from this colonialist perspective, there was more land available than anyone knew what to do with. So much that it posed a problem for the people who were initially tasked with distributing it. In Europe, the scarcity of land and the glut of peasants made property expensive and labour cheap, but in North America that dynamic was reversed.

It didn't take long for peasant farmers to realize this, and they enjoyed rights and freedoms unheard of to their transatlantic peers. It was, in the parlance of today, very much a renters' market. In what is now Quebec, habitants farmed land technically owned by seigneurs, an aristocratic class similar to British lords, but they essentially operated as independent landowners, easily breaking ties with seigneurs they found to be overly demanding or neglectful. They could even sublease the land and keep any profits from the produce it reaped.

Meanwhile in English Canada, the British first granted land only to high-ranking members of the military as a reward for their service and fealty to the throne, but the abundance of space put a wrench in that tradition as well. By the 1800s, land use, not ancient social pedigree or dubiously acquired acreage, determined who could rightfully, and legally, claim ownership. In French Canada, habitants were granted legal rights to the lands many had already been farming for generations, while in English Canada, particularly in the wide open west, anyone willing to stick out a few years farming a chunk of the prairies would be given a deed of ownership.

This did not translate into settlers building palatial dream homes, as we might expect today. Interior domestic comfort was a fairly low priority in the newly forming Canadian psyche. One- or two-room dwellings remained common for farming families well into the 20th century, with governments actively encouraging settlers to deprioritize their own houses and focus instead on developing their farms. While many settlers did eventually build more comfortable and spacious dwellings as time and resources allowed, the official policies that influenced how people lived were firmly focused on spreading them out over all this land. It wasn't until the early 20th century—in the aftermath of a great tragedy—that anyone paid much attention to the structures that sat atop it.

---

On December 6, 1917, two steamships attempted to weave their way through Halifax Harbour, at the time a bustling hub of wartime activity. The first, the *Imo*, was a Norwegian vessel on its way out to sea with a load of humanitarian supplies for the people of occupied Belgium. The second, the *Mont-Blanc*, was a French munitions ship packed to the gills with explosives that was headed into the harbour to join a convoy destined for France. For reasons that are not entirely clear despite more than a century of analysis, the *Imo* wound up in the wrong shipping lane, where it plowed straight into the *Mont-Blanc*. The collision tore a hole in the munition ship's hull, spilling several barrels of flammable liquid that were instantly ignited by the sparks flying from the grinding metal ships. In no time, a deck fire broke out on the *Mont-Blanc*, drawing thousands of Haligonians who were going about their busy morning routines to the water's edge—just in time for the explosion.

At the time, the Halifax disaster was the largest human-made explosion ever recorded. The carnage was grisly and intense: nearly 2,000 people killed instantly, 9,000 more injured—many of them blinded by flying shards of glass—and 25,000, half the city's population, left homeless or without adequate shelter.

Among the legacies of the Halifax explosion are the seeds of what would become Canada's first official housing policy.

Up until that devastating moment in 1917, settler residents in a still relatively young Canada had been entirely on their own when it came to finding shelter. There were few building codes or zoning requirements, and no high-interest savings accounts in which to sock away a down payment. Mortgages were rare, and most were obtained through handshake deals with wealthy acquaintances. For the vast majority of Canadians, whatever lodging you found yourself in came down to what you could afford to pay in cash or build with your bare hands.

Despite this, the barrier to entry for housing was quite low. Renters often found room and board in family homes, while those with the means to own land had many options when it came to building. Through the 1910s and '20s, for instance, you could order a flat-pack prefabricated house through the Eaton's catalogue and assemble it like an IKEA bookshelf. Another easy option was to grab some neighbours and a pile of lumber and start building a simple timber house of the sort that was common in Halifax's North End—specifically in the neighbourhood of Richmond, which was essentially flattened by the blast.

The widespread, instantaneous homelessness created by the disaster was a first in Canadian history, and the ensuing humanitarian crisis is what prompted the Canadian government to end its hands-off approach to housing. Within weeks of the disaster the government committed $30 million 1918 dollars, nearly $600 million today, to the rebuilding effort, establishing an independent commission to disperse the funds. The money was to be split between a variety of projects, chief among them building new housing for those whose homes had been lost.

Rebuilding Richmond was a true community effort. Locals pitched in with supplies. Unions and contractors contributed labour and materials at below-market rates. But rather than pass the savings on to vulnerable residents whose homes had been destroyed, the commission opted to charge market rents, with a plan to funnel the money into a pension fund benefiting the survivors. The intentions were good enough—use money collected today to provide a financial safety net for the victims in the future—but the immediate impact of such a move was to price those very same victims out of their new homes.

"Many soon found the high rents unaffordable, and over half the units became vacant," wrote H. Peter Oberlander and Arthur L. Fallick in their book *Housing a Nation: The Evolution of Canadian Housing Policy.* Nonetheless, the project was considered a resounding success as the first official instance of government involvement in housing. Though comprehensive housing policy would still be decades away, the government response to the disaster contained a glimmer of the ideology that would come to be its backbone: Houses needn't be mere places to live; they can also make an awful lot of money—and if we're playing our cards right, they should.

It's taken several generations for this ethos to seep into our collective consciousness in the way it shows up today, with housing treated like stocks and government policies engineered more to protect property values than people's right to housing. From the outset, though, housing policy in this country has always been more, or at least as much, about making money as the human need for shelter. Poring over the excerpts from government speeches, news articles and transcriptions of parliamentary proceedings that Oberlander and Fallick drew upon liberally in their book, I found it remarkable how rarely the word "home" was actually used by the people who created our housing system.

There is one notable exception, however: "Home," when it does appear, is almost always in conjunction with another word—"owner."

---

Given this nation's history as a place of opportunity for the (white and European) landless, the aim to make homeowners out of all Canadians can be seen as an attempt at egalitarianism. Indeed, many Canadians did long to own property. It was the promise this nation was founded on, after all. So making that the "clearly articulated, overriding goal" of our first National Housing Act (NHA), established in 1938, would have been a popular political move. As Steve Pomeroy, one of the country's leading housing policy consultants, put it, "Everyone wanted to be homeowners, so the politics sort of followed their will." That's probably true to an extent, though the entrance of government into the housing sphere also provided ample opportunity for lawmakers to embed in legislation their own moral judgments and personal views about who deserves housing and the "right" way to live.

Those applying for government assistance in the wake of the Halifax explosion, for example, had to swear off alcohol, while women were not allowed to entertain men in their homes. Some historical documents also suggest one reason government officials so readily took the lead on the rebuilding effort was to prevent the community from recreating the ad hoc neighbourhood some well-to-do constituents had considered a slum. Racist, classist and elitist notions of home continued to permeate housing policy throughout the 20th century, often slipped into laws under the guise of health and safety. The evolution of the single-family suburban house as the epitome of home was ostensibly developed in response to fears about the health impacts of pollution and overcrowding in urban centres. Conveniently, it also served as an effective way to exclude poor, racialized and immigrant groups from the emerging North American ideal by essentially outlawing multi-family buildings and multi-generational households more common among those demographics. Some scholars have posited that the design of postwar houses set far back from the street behind expansive lawns became ubiquitous not because of the lifestyle they enabled but because they visually emulated the rural villas of the European elite. Essentially, they signalled wealth. At the same time, those who dared demonstrate a preference for alternative ways of living that were less individualistic were continually and actively penalized by the state. Canada's legacy of barring people from sharing land and establishing collective approaches to home continues to this day. For instance, very few financial institutions provide mortgages to unmarried or unrelated adults who wish to purchase a property together, and up until the last decade or so these didn't exist at all. In many cities, bylaws restricting how many unrelated adults can share a home, no matter how big it is, remain on the books. Co-operative housing, a type of non-market collective ownership, provided hundreds of thousands of affordable homes to Canadians during the 1970s, '80s and '90s, and many are still in operation today. But almost none have been created since, owing, until very recently, to a complete lack of government support. Then there's the thorny issue of zoning. Despite a growing trend in some jurisdictions to end what's known as exclusionary zoning, the vast majority of residential land across North America allows only single-family houses, effectively banning more affordable, more creative options. All of this has had a lasting impact on our cultural conception of home and the housing available to us. Even as so many people are locked out of the sanctified structure of the privately owned single-family house, we cling to a deeply ingrained skepticism of the many viable alternatives.

It might be difficult to recognize the cumulative effects of institutional policies on a personal level, but on a population basis we can clearly see their influence. In housing circles, Canada and the United States are frequently and unfavourably contrasted with Western Europe, where lifelong renting is normalized, and where social or non-profit housing constitutes a much larger part of the urban landscape. Unsurprisingly, in places where owning a home isn't the only path to stable and secure housing, people aren't so obsessed with it. In countries like Austria, the Netherlands, France, Denmark or Sweden people don't tend to look at their homes, even ones they do own, as a vehicle for profit. Nor do governments rely on credit and dangerous levels of household debt in order to catapult people into the market.

The difference between the North American and European approaches to housing is often chalked up to culture. We think about housing one way, and they think about it differently. But it's important to delve into why that is. Culture is not a fixed thing; rather, it is a malleable force shaped by many factors, from the environment to the economy to religious traditions—and culture shifts over time. When it comes to contemporary culture around housing and home, nothing has been more influential than policy decisions made since the First World War.

---

We can consider ourselves lucky in one respect when it comes to the Halifax explosion. It is one of the only modern instances of a North American city being physically altered by war. Europe obviously hasn't been so lucky.

In the wake of the world wars, housing stock and critical infrastructure in cities like Vienna, Berlin, Paris and parts of London were in shambles. Survivors were left to shelter in overcrowded buildings without proper sanitation where disease flourished. Faced with a humanitarian crisis, European governments had no choice but to invest heavily in social housing lest their remaining populations, and the hope of economic recovery, slowly succumbed to waves of cholera and tuberculosis. Now, a century or so later, policies that treat housing as a public good have become ingrained in the cultural fabric of many of those societies.

In Canada, by contrast, legions of soldiers returned from serving overseas, often with war brides in tow. Not content to return to isolated family farms, many chose to settle in cities, increasing pressure on limited housing stock and instigating a change in the makeup of the country. Rather than build them all housing, we built a *housing market* instead.

One can't necessarily fault the leaders of yore for choosing a market-based approach over that of the systems in Western Europe that heavily favoured social housing. In theory, it could have worked. Things get morally opaque, however, when you see how our leaders clung to this ideology despite mounting evidence that it didn't. Louis St. Laurent, prime minister during the Second World War, was vehemently opposed to public housing as a matter of personal principle. Other prominent figures were equally enamoured with the promises of a free market. David Mansur, the first president of what would become the Canada Mortgage and Housing Corporation, saw himself not as a provider of homes but as a "mover of money."

In fact, the founding fathers of Canada's housing policies (and yes, they were all "fathers") almost all viewed the act of actually housing people as a secondary goal. In many of their debates, declarations and speeches, providing places for people to live was often framed as a happy by-product in the pursuit of other aims—everything from creating jobs, to courting the business community, to fulfilling colonial aspirations, to expanding "construction and development capabilities from coast to coast." To this end, our National Housing Act is primarily a financial program guaranteeing qualifying Canadians access to loans with a stated purpose to "contribute to the well-being of the housing sector in the national economy." Curiously, it makes no mention of the well-being of actual Canadians. Even so, its first iteration in 1938 was undeniably a game changer for this country.

The NHA massively reduced the financial barriers to buying a home by making credit widely available. Even so, the dream remained out of reach for many. By the early 1950s, population growth was outpacing housing construction, and a growing number of Canadians were feeling squeezed by the market. The baby boom, immigration, increased longevity due to better health care and a rapidly urbanizing population put pressure on existing housing supply. After an analysis found that only the top third of Canadians could afford to buy a house, the government allowed banks to enter the mortgage market and increased the amount of debt prospective buyers could take on. The minimum down payment for a home dropped from 20 percent to just 10 percent, encouraging households to rely even more heavily on debt in order to get into the market.

Meanwhile, increasing calls for the government to build non-market, low-income and rental housing, or perhaps tie home values to income rather than to the whims of the market, went largely unheeded. Leaders of all political stripes remained resolute in their belief that the market alone could house this nation, which is notable because most of our peer countries did not. Compared to Australia, the United States, even Britain, which had made considerable efforts to improve housing standards after the wars, Canada lagged substantially in its per capita production of affordable, rental and non-market housing throughout much of the 20th century.

Central to our system was a concept known as "filtering," which still drives much of our behaviour and beliefs around housing today. Similar to the idea of "trickle-down economics"—the belief that tax cuts for the wealthy stimulate the economy and eventually benefit the lower classes—filtering holds that if you help people at the top of the property ladder continually move up, the more affordable stock they vacate then filters down to lower-income groups. In theory, everybody wins. But like trickle-down economics, filtering doesn't quite work in reality. Even in the booming economy of the 1950s cities were beset by housing shortages, with affordable areas either gentrified or bulldozed under the guise of "slum clearance" and "urban renewal," leaving even less for those at the bottom of the ladder.

It wasn't until the 1960s that the federal government started to acknowledge that the market it had meticulously created had left so many Canadians out in the metaphorical cold. Buoyed by the economic halo of the postwar years, the 1960s were an era of unprecedented global optimism among wealthy Western nations, with both public sentiment and political leaders focused on the greater good. "The climate of opinion was that governments could largely 'solve' poverty, and that the welfare state should not only offer security against sickness and old age, but give the poor a better slice of the pie," writes housing researcher Greg Suttor. It was during this time that enduring programs such as public health care and Old Age Security emerged in Canada, along with an epoch housing scholars have come to refer to as the "golden age" of social housing.

At first, federal public housing programs were aimed only at low-income groups, but by the 1970s the program had evolved to produce socially diverse, mixed-income developments built and managed by non-profit housing co-operatives. According to Suttor, this "made in Canada" approach not only prevented low-income "ghettos" from forming, like the ones that had become a public relations nightmare in the United States, but it garnered us international recognition as a trailblazer. Production peaked in the mid-1970s, when then–Prime Minister Pierre Trudeau successfully ran for re-election on a platform that included significant investment in social housing, and by the 1980s institutional support of housing "alternatives" had begun to worm its way into our collective psyche. This era saw an average of between 12,000 and 20,000 units of federally funded affordable, non-market housing added to the landscape *each year* for nearly three decades. And we've barely built any since. As of 2023, 87 percent of social and affordable housing still in use in this country was built prior to 1996 under these golden age programs. All told, Canada made leaps in closing the housing gap during this period, putting us in league with our international peers.

Finally, it seemed like the cultural tide was starting to turn. Then, macroeconomics got in the way.

---

As any baby boomer will tell you, the 1970s and '80s were tough decades on the economic front. Gas shortages, the energy crisis, rising inflation and historically high interest rates hit middle-class Canadians hard. Mortgage rates reached double digits, peaking at 21.75 percent in 1981, causing a precipitous decline in home building and buying. Developers, feeling the pinch of a challenging economy and unfavourable lending terms, saw federal support of the non-profit housing sector as unfairly bankrolling their competition. They began aggressively lobbying for more market-friendly policies. Meanwhile, the optimism of the 1960s had started to fade and a new era of austerity rose to take its place.

"Neoliberalism" is a term that gets tossed around a lot these days, but it doesn't always get defined. For those, like me, without a poli-sci degree, it's basically the political philosophy behind the hard shift toward small government, deregulation and privatization that defined the 1970s and '80s. Former U.K. Prime Minister Margaret Thatcher and former U.S. President Ronald Reagan—both trickle-down evangelists—were icons of the movement, with their well-publicized campaigns for low taxes, free markets and a good life defined by individual freedoms unencumbered by the state. Costly public housing programs were high on their hit lists. Thatcher's "Right to Buy" program in the 1980s effectively privatized much of the social housing built in Britain after the war and primed the pump for the housing crisis the country faces today. Reagan, meanwhile, slashed funding for low-income housing and successfully rebranded poverty as a personal failing rather than a systemic issue worthy of collective action. In Canada, a booming oil sector insulated this country somewhat from the economic climate affecting our closest peers, but not from their cultural influence. Soon, Canadians developed an appetite for austerity that was cemented in our psyches by the 1990s, when a deep recession finally hit home and the housing market crashed. Ironically, this appeared to bolster the case for a government retreat from housing.

The early 1990s saw home prices plummet by as much as 40 percent in some Canadian cities. Interest rates soon followed as the central bank tried to entice consumers to borrow and spend in order to stimulate the economy. Those who'd been locked out of the housing market in the preceding decades flooded in, spurring a huge jump in ownership that fundamentally changed the fabric of our society. At last, it seemed, the dream of a white picket fence for every Canadian might actually be achievable. Concern for social welfare began to disappear from public dialogue as the federal government transferred social housing programs to the provinces and then cut their funding to the bone.

It didn't take long for the cascading effects of this policy shift to spill over onto city sidewalks, back alleys and park benches, where it remains painfully visible today.

Before working on this book, I'd never really thought about the origins of visible street homelessness, by which I mean unsheltered people sleeping outside. Perhaps because unhoused people are such a permanent fixture in North American cities, I'd assumed that being left without shelter was a tragic but unavoidable part of the human condition—one that had ever been thus. Like untimely deaths or disease, it seemed as if a certain sector of society had always been struck by this unfortunate fate. Imagine my surprise when I learned that this isn't true. Just as the squalor of industrial London was the result of political decisions and economic shifts, so too is the rise of visible poverty in North America. I always thought it was kind of funny when my parents would visit me in Vancouver and seem so surprised to encounter unhoused people living rough like Arthur. I chalked this up to their sheltered, suburban existence. Not enough time spent in big urban centres. But there might be more at play. It turns out that the presence of panhandlers and squeegee kids, who have been a constant urban fixture throughout my lifetime, are a fairly recent phenomenon. According to a wealth of research, the street homelessness that has become a defining characteristic of modern city life didn't really exist before the '80s. That's the *1980s*.

Terms like "hobo" or "vagrant" started to appear in the North American lexicon in the 1800s, but according to scholars, homelessness back then was a very different beast. It was mostly a temporary occurrence, increasing during times of economic depression and abating once conditions improved. And being "homeless" didn't necessarily mean being unhoused or unsheltered. The mostly white, mostly single, mostly able-bodied men who famously rode the rails in early America and ambled into towns in search of casual work could often avail themselves of shelter in the form of flophouses, single-room occupancy hotels or cheap tenement flats. Conditions might not have been great, but in most cities there was always a skid row one could rely on to put a temporary roof over a road-weary head. In fact, part of the reason these untethered men drew such ire from mainstream society—as well as the adoration of authors like Jack Kerouac—is because they were seen to have *chosen* their condition, to have had the audacity to reject the traditional trappings of family and home in favour of absolute freedom.

But the neoliberal policies of the 1980s and '90s saw the nature of homelessness fundamentally change. The rapid globalization of industries and the offshoring of jobs evaporated income for those working in manufacturing or other blue-collar sectors. At the same time, an influx of young adult baby boomers, just then entering the housing market, as well as waves of new immigrants, increased the pressure on a stagnant number of affordable dwellings. Gentrification became common in cities, spurring the multi-decade rise in property values and rents that have led to the exorbitant prices we see today. Rather than able-bodied single men, the homeless population now spanned the gamut: women, children, whole families, the elderly and disabled, immigrants and a disproportionate number of Indigenous people—populations that had previously been served by low-income housing programs. When those programs were cut, along with the shuttering of institutions serving those with mental health concerns, they "filtered" right through the floor of the system and wound up on the street.

The overwhelming need at shelters and soup kitchens and the noticeable increase of aimless bodies shuffling around city centres prompted public outcry. Only this time around, the concern was framed as being less about social welfare and more about public safety. Politicians beat the drum of law and order, vowing to clean up the streets, and peddled band-aid solutions like more funding for homeless shelters and low-income housing subsidies—cash that would directly supplement private landlords charging market rents. Bureaucratically speaking, these were low-cost, low-effort programs that offered crumbs to the very poorest rather than creating affordable housing for all.

The justification for this was, and remains, a belief at the core of neoliberal thinking: that governments are ill-equipped to meddle in private markets, which should be left to their own devices for optimal results. But this belief ignores the fact that, especially in housing, keeping the private market afloat has required considerable and ongoing government intervention and constant feeding from the public purse. As University of Toronto housing scholar David Hulchanski has pointed out in his work, governments take great pains and dedicate billions to maintaining the *appearance* of a self-sustaining housing system guided only by an invisible hand. The reality couldn't be farther from the truth.

Over the years we have had a laundry list of publicly funded incentive programs aimed at enticing Canadians into the market and ensuring they can stay there. To name just a few, there was the Assisted Home Ownership Program, the Registered Home Ownership Savings Plan, the Canada Mortgage Renewal Plan, the Mortgage Rate Protection Program and the Canadian Home Ownership Stimulation Plan. More recently, we have had the tax-sheltered First Home Savings Account, and the First-Time Home Buyer Incentive, basically an interest-free down payment loan from the government in exchange for an equity stake in your house. Each of these programs directed public money toward ensuring people could continue to pay higher and higher housing costs, rather than investing in housing programs that keep costs down. As if that weren't enough, Canadians are exempt from paying income tax on profits reaped by the sale of a primary home, as they must do when they sell other high-value assets such as stocks or a business. This free pass on paying capital gains tax means almost all the public money that helps people get into the market remains in private hands, requiring more public money to be continually pumped in. The result is a system propped up by falsely inflated buying power, which in turn simply encourages prices to rise.

The cost for this, of course, is astronomical. The capital gains tax exemption on primary home sales cost our economy $5.5 billion in 2024 alone, while attempts to make up for the decades-long shortfall in affordable housing investment come with an even more staggering bill. The National Housing Strategy, a 10-year plan launched in 2017 to address the housing crisis, has a budget of upwards of $115 billion, most of it earmarked for private, for-profit housing initiatives that have had little impact on affordability. In fact, federal government data from point-in-time homeless counts shows the overall number of people experiencing homelessness—those with no permanent address, including people who are couch surfing or in the shelter system—actually *grew* by 20 percent between 2018 and 2020–22 (the 2020 count in some communities had to be delayed due to the COVID-19 pandemic, so the data collection took place over two years). The number of unsheltered individuals—those sleeping on the street or in encampments—jumped by a whopping 88 percent during that time. Canada's Parliamentary Budget Officer, meanwhile, projected in a 2024 report that 2.6 million Canadian households will be in core housing need by 2027, an *increase* of 926,000 households over 2017. By measures both social and fiscal, our blind adherence to a market-based approach has largely been an expensive, inefficient boondoggle when it comes to meeting the human right to housing. However, it has been tremendously effective at shaping our collective psychology.

The underpinnings of a financialized mindset have existed in our housing system all along, though many experts agree we hit a turning point sometime around the 1980s, when a confluence of factors conspired to permanently shift the way we think about housing. That decade's high inflation meant that anyone who already owned a home saw its value rapidly increase, turning it into a tax-free windfall. Consciously or not, this is when homeowners began to see their houses less as places to live and more like tax-sheltered assets to be cashed in one day or borrowed against to finance other large purchases, like, say, a *second* home. Condominium legislation, which started creeping across the country around this time, put a perfect product on the market for those looking to invest. It sounds wild, but up until about the 1970s or '80s, if you wanted to buy an apartment you'd have to buy the whole apartment building. Breaking up units for individual sale was intended to increase affordable entry-level housing in a country chronically starved for it. But as we can see from the condo market today, first-time buyers weren't the only ones drawn toward the idea of cheap, low-maintenance housing. Existing homeowners with access to equity-backed financing started snapping them up as well, and voila!, the concept of an "investment property" was born.

The growing trend of mom-and-pop real estate investors happened to come at a convenient time for governments keen to divest from housing. As politicians cut programs aimed at creating both market and non-market rentals, they found that private investors rose up to fill the void. As much as small-scale investors have contributed to our crisis by outcompeting potential owner-occupants and skewing the market toward producing increasingly unlivable housing, without them the situation might be even worse. Today, a substantial portion, up to 40 percent or more in some cities, of our rental housing consists of investment properties (like condos) or "mortgage helpers" (like basement suites and laneway homes) meant to help owners shoulder mortgages that would otherwise be financially crippling.

As we discussed in chapter 2, income properties don't always live up to their names. I've often wondered if one reason we don't hear much about that side of the story is because the narrative of real estate as an iron-clad investment has become critical to propping up our housing system. It is the promise of passive income and ongoing guaranteed rewards that often convinces private individuals to take on the responsibility, and the risk, of providing the kind of housing that was once made available through government programs. There is, however, definitely a large and prominent segment of our society for which the story of housing wealth has proven undeniably true. If there is a modern-day equivalent to being pals with William the Conqueror and stumbling into an eternity of generational wealth, it has to be having bought a single-family house in Vancouver or Toronto—or, increasingly, any major city—during the 1970s, '80s or '90s. But there's a pivotal difference between the property owned by your average person and the kind of land wealth of the British aristocracy. In general, our houses don't stand on vast acres of productive land. They don't host working farms or quarries or horse stables and racing grounds that bring in consistent income. They don't contain whole villages bound by law to pay rent in perpetuity. They are just houses. Mostly very ordinary ones. The simplest way to realize the value of the land they sit on is to sell them and move somewhere else. Of course, to do that, you need to have somewhere else to go.

5

# MOBILE HOMES

My dad is a total technophile. The kind of retired baby boomer who's got enough time and money on his hands to not only acquire every digital device that strikes his fancy but also to figure out how to use it properly. He's got an Apple Watch strapped to his wrist 24/7 and ski boots with sensors that assess his technique and give him feedback via a Bluetooth headset embedded in his helmet. When he goes for a bike ride, he has the choice of going electric-assist or old-school pedal power, and either way he reviews his mileage on any number of apps. There seems to be no tech function too small, too fiddly or too redundant to pique his interest. Therefore, when some iPhone update made it possible to add subject lines to text messages, my dad was one of about five people whose hearts leapt at the prospect. He wasted no time integrating them into one of his main love languages, which is sharing information.

My dad has been sending me links to news articles he thinks I might find interesting for decades now. In the beginning of my journalism career these were mostly stories about the declining fortunes of media companies and massive rounds of layoffs. Eventually I asked him to stop with those, since I was intimately familiar with the reality of trying to eke out a living in my chosen field. Once I got on this kick with housing, though, he switched gears and started sending articles he thought might be relevant to my research. One text, which arrived early on a summer morning as I was packing up for a camping trip, came with a bit of personal exposition that made a familiar headline hit home in a new way.

Subject line: Empty Bedrooms. Text body: This is us.

The article was about seniors unable, or unwilling, to downsize from their large suburban homes. According to Statistics Canada, nearly 95 percent of people aged 55 to 74 have one or more spare bedrooms in their home. It's not a new phenomenon, certainly, but it is a trend that's receiving new interest in relation to our housing crisis, and something I'd never really thought about in relation to my own family.

In the abstract, it's hard to feel sorry for people like my parents who are well off, partly because they were born into the most prolonged period of economic prosperity humankind has ever known. It's not that the baby boomers didn't work hard or face any adversity in their lives—their generation certainly isn't a monolith, and not everyone fell into a charmed life of easy upward mobility. It's just that, historically speaking, they are likely to be the most financially prosperous of any generation to come before or after them. Mostly this comes down to luck. They were born into a ridiculously good economy that lasted well into their early adult years. For the most part, this generation landed secure, decently paying jobs right out of school, which they were able to pay for without student loans, and worked their way up to even better-paying jobs as a matter of course. Without student debt, they were able to save their paycheques to make down payments on reasonably priced houses that accrued more wealth than anyone could have imagined while they were busy working and raising their kids.

Many experts have posited that these houses are now poised to become part of one of the biggest transfers of wealth the world has ever known as members of this "silver tsunami" start to pass away or otherwise pass that wealth onto their kids. But it might not work out exactly as anticipated. As they get on in years and their housing needs change, people my parents' age are butting up against the same problem young families, students, new immigrants and just about everyone else out there has been contending with for decades. When they need to move, there are few options that are both affordable and appealing.

When I talk to my parents about it, moving to a condo is out of the question. They love their house, of course, but equally important, they have friends in the neighbourhood; they take regular bike rides past the old elementary school; and they start most mornings sitting out on their deck with a cup of coffee, even in the dead of winter, watching the birds flutter in from the woods behind their house. Holding on to these relationships and rituals, plus their raft of empty bedrooms, might seem selfish, especially at a time when so many other people could use that space. But the instinctual drive to hold on to their homes might actually be a matter of survival.

Moving house is widely recognized as one of life's most stressful events, and when elderly people move from a place they've lived for a very long time, that stress can be catastrophic, even lethal. People who work in geriatric fields are familiar with a condition known as relocation stress syndrome, or sometimes transfer trauma, characterized by the rapid declines in mental and physical health many older people experience after moving out of a long-term home, especially if the move is involuntary. Essentially, seniors who may be dealing with certain health issues but are overall doing pretty well tend to tank rather quickly when removed from their homes. (When I think about how stressful it was for me to move in my mid-30s with lots of energy and no health issues, this tracks.) Moves go better when seniors have agency and can decide where they want to go, but people my parents' age often find the choices lacking.

For all the "luxury" and "convenience" they promise, many condos are as impractical and uncomfortable for downsizing seniors as they are for younger demographics. There's no space for guests to stay the night, no place to host a big family meal, not enough outdoor space, and, due to the zoning restrictions discussed in the previous chapter, they're often far away from the familiar single-family neighbourhoods they have long called home. There are some exceptions, but the condos that tick all these boxes are often so in demand and so expensive, the purchase price would eat up any equity seniors have stored in their existing homes. That's a big problem for the more than half of Canadian seniors who say they plan to use home equity to fund their retirement.

Of course, there may come a time when holding on is no longer an option, when living in a big suburban house full of stairs becomes untenable or even unsafe. The options in that scenario don't get much better. At anywhere from $1,000 to $6,000 a month, or more, assisted living facilities can be so expensive that people like my parents, who are hoping to be around for a while yet, worry about running through their entire life savings before their life has run its course. And even before the pandemic exposed the shortcomings of many long-term care facilities, most seniors dreaded winding up in them. Survey after survey consistently shows that seniors want to age in place, meaning in their family homes, and when that's no longer possible, still within their neighbourhoods.

However, the fact that baby boomers in their golden years are bumping up against some of the same housing issues hitting younger generations in their family-forming years could be a golden opportunity.

Though millennials have now surpassed baby boomers to become the largest generation in Canada, there is no question the cohort born in the postwar years from 1946 to 1965 remains a powerful political and economic force. In order for our housing situation to improve at the pace we need it to, more members of older demographics will have to advocate, and vote, for policy shifts away from the system that created their comfortable surroundings and, quite frankly, made many of them rich. Paul Kershaw doesn't think this outcome is as unlikely as it may sound.

A public health researcher at the University of British Columbia, Kershaw started Generation Squeeze, a movement for "generational fairness," off the side of his desk in 2012. Since then, it has become a non-profit "think and change tank" that advocates for a more even playing field among the generations when it comes to government spending and policy. Though Kershaw cautions against blaming any one group for our current housing woes, data shows there is a clear generational component to this crisis that must be taken into account when devising solutions. According to data from Generation Squeeze, it would've taken someone in their 20s or 30s 17 years to save for a 20 percent down payment on a typical home in Canada in 2022, compared to five years for the same age group in 1976. In Vancouver and Toronto, it would have taken 27 years. Younger generations also face barriers to accessing financing that their parents did not, like the mortgage stress test that requires first-time buyers to prove they can withstand a sharp jump in interest rates. By Generation Squeeze's estimates, housing prices across Canada would have to come down by more than *half* their current value in order to be considered "affordable" for people earning average incomes today, which would mean a huge hit to the housing wealth many baby boomers are sitting on. If there's any hope of even inching toward that kind of equilibrium, it comes down to finding common ground between the different generations and their distinct experiences with housing.

"I think the solution can be found at the intergenerational table, at Thanksgiving, or the winter holidays," Kershaw told me. "We'll have multiple generations around that table and they love one another and that intergenerational love can be the root." Just like I don't want to see my parents shuttled off to an old-folks home against their will, where they might very well die of a broken heart, parents don't want to see their adult children struggle to find affordable housing that will allow them to build their own families or whatever kind of household they desire. It's because of this that so many aging parents are helping their children get into the market. One 2024 study found a whopping 48 percent of first-time homebuyers made their down payment with a loan or gift from family, while a further 20 percent used money from an inheritance. But just because some families have the resources to hack the system doesn't mean it's not broken, Kershaw said. Even hefty withdrawals from the "bank of mom and dad" often prove inadequate to fully shield loved ones from the effects of declining social mobility wrought by high housing prices. Nowhere is this more evident than in patterns of residential mobility.

Would-be downsizers aren't the only ones who feel "stuck" in their suburban homes. Among young adults aged 20 to 34, more than 35 percent live with at least one parent, many in their childhood houses. No doubt for some this is an intentional exercise in multi-generational living, but for others it's a default option that can feel like delayed independence. And when those young adults do finally cobble together the resources to make a move, many are forced to go much farther afield than they would have liked.

---

Mobility is a defining feature of our modern age, almost universally celebrated as a net positive largely because it is the beating heart of our industrialized economy. For the past 250 years we've been relying on people to move where work, education and other economic opportunities would take them in order to boost productivity and prosperity. Our housing crisis has disrupted that pattern. As housing prices have gone up over the last 40 years, residential mobility has declined, while those who are moving are doing so, according to some, for the wrong reasons. "Many Americans are stranded in communities with flat or declining prospects, and lack the practical ability to move across the tracks, the state, or the country—to choose where they want to live," writes American historian Yoni Appelbaum. "Those who do move are typically heading not to the places where opportunities are abundant, but to those where housing is cheap."

Indeed, in the United States, housing affordability now trumps any other consideration for new home buyers, ahead of size, quality, or location, which was the top consideration as recently as 2014. Meanwhile in Canada, nearly 40 percent of prospective homebuyers say they'd move cities in order to afford a home, and another 25 percent say they'd consider moving to a new province. While these trends are worrying to economists, there are social and emotional ramifications as well, notes Kershaw. With the age of first-time home buyers creeping ever upwards—43 percent were 35 or older in 2023—many millennials and Generation Z are delaying having children until they can find secure housing, meaning they may not have as many children as they would like, or have none at all. The impetus to drive—or fly—until they can qualify for a mortgage on a home they want often means the distance between adult children and their aging parents increases at a time in life when they might otherwise rely on each other for support. Kershaw is hopeful realizations like this will unite extended families in petitioning for change. "I think when you're gathering around these intergenerational tables people will say, 'I want my kids to be able to have homes somewhere near to where I live and I want my kids to feel like they can afford to have [our] grandchildren,'" he said. "That can be the source for people saying: 'You know what? This system is broken. I realize it's been giving my demographic maybe some benefits financially, some more security in this system, but actually the cost is too grave.'"

The costs for those without generational housing wealth to draw from, and without the prospect of becoming homeowners, are even higher. Not only are renters locked out of one of the primary wealth-building tools—home equity—in this country, but they devote a greater portion of their income to housing costs than homeowners, making it even harder to save for a down payment or save at all. And for lifelong renters, the precarity of the rental market can come with a level of forced mobility that is far greater than many can tolerate.

---

The day I visited Breton and his family was the kind of spring day where the warmer weather finally beats the dregs of winter into a decisive retreat. As we sat in the yard of his rented mobile home on the boundary between urban Metro Vancouver and the rural Fraser Valley, we both peeled off layers to reveal bare arms desperate to be warmed by the sun. An aura of new, almost neon green glowed around the trees and bushes against a backdrop of freshly tilled black dirt and a horizon of evergreen-crested mountains. Breton's two-year-old daughter Emily napped inside, a tangle of soft brown curls and purple leggings on a tan microfibre couch.

His wife Christina was still at her job at a veterinary clinic. It was peaceful on a Saturday morning, though like everywhere in the Lower Mainland, Breton told me the area was beset by the sounds of residential construction throughout the week.

Breton, 35, is not one of those lucky millennials poised to benefit from his parents' housing wealth. They don't have any to share. As the child of lifelong renters, his early life was marked by housing instability, with his mother embroiled in near constant battles with unscrupulous landlords or fighting dubious evictions through British Columbia's Residential Tenancy Branch. As an adult, Breton vowed to break the cycle of housing instability that he'd watched erode his mother's mental health, at times rendering her homeless. His greatest dream was to give Emily a more stable childhood than the one he'd had, ideally a permanent home in a single-family house in the suburbs—a place with a basement to stash boxes of childhood mementos, walls to mark up with her growth spurts and a big tree to climb in the backyard. But unless something miraculous happened, it was looking like Emily might face even less housing stability than her father. "There might be some help from my grandparents," Breton said, but he couldn't count on it. And if any money did come, it would likely be too late to provide the childhood home he wanted for his daughter. "Emily will be in high school by that time."

As a kid, Breton's family followed the doctrine of mobility down to a T, moving to pursue economic opportunity. When Breton was a baby, his dad worked in the shipyards on Vancouver's North Shore, but when that industry started to slow down, the family moved to the province's Interior region to pursue work in forestry. Breton's youth was spent bouncing around rental homes in rural communities, which made the constant moves a little easier—he was already used to having to drive or cover distances to visit family and friends. But the physical disruption left a mark on who he is that has only deepened with time. His childhood memories are tinged with a sense of loss, of constantly being torn away from the things that are meant to reinforce a child's developing sense of self—leaving a tree with initials carved in it; photos and mementos dumped out in the rain or otherwise lost during a move; burying pets in the yard only to have to leave their little bones behind. Of course, most people expect to leave their childhood home at some point, Breton told me. But this? "It was just too often, too frequently. It's like every year at every opportunity, every time you make a permanent mark on the world it disappears."

By the time he was a young adult, climate change was taking its toll on forestry jobs in the Interior, turning occasional blazes into yearly acts of devastation. Breton's parents picked up again and moved back to the coast. He followed and soon found work in construction. Breton's job gave him an insider's view into Vancouver's worsening housing disparity. He already knew he was building homes he'd never have a hope of living in—but eventually he realized he wouldn't want to anyway. Shoddy workmanship, cut corners and rushed timelines transformed perfectly good, relatively affordable houses into high-end mansions his team would be told to pump out as fast as humanly possible only to have many of them ultimately sit empty. When he worked on condo projects, the small footprints seemed ridiculously proportioned, especially for their price, and it made no sense to him. "I thought the whole point of having a dense city was so you could create space out of thin air, quite literally," he said. He was never too sure who these condos were for—some units changed hands multiple times before the crew had even broken ground—but he knew they weren't for working-class people like him.

When he met Christina, the couple started looking for a bit more space, heading east toward the more affordable suburbs and migrating further out with each successive move. Sometimes this was by choice, like when they lived in a basement suite below a family with three kids under 10 whose relentless screaming and stomping became a "mental health issue." But there were other places where they would have liked to stay, like the place in Port Coquitlam, the next city over, where Breton got to know his elderly neighbours by pitching in to help shovel snow or chatting about their careers on the corner. When that place was sold they wound up out here in his mobile home in an area in the midst of an identity crisis. Zoned as agricultural land with housing supposedly for farm workers, the region has become a hotspot for speculation, with developers and property owners taking advantage of loopholes in various pieces of legislation to build mansion-sized houses intended to catch the spillover from the city. It's not where they expected to be, but Breton said he didn't mind it; he could actually see his family living there long-term. There was a tree with a swing, just perfect for Emily to carve her initials in, and a big yard with space for her to run around and maybe even plant a garden. The mobile home itself was nothing fancy—it was showing its age—but Breton had the skills to fix it up, probably into something pretty nice. And there was an extra bedroom for the other baby he and Christina wanted to have. But they were holding back on all of that for the time being. This lot, like so many others, was slated for redevelopment.

Knowing they'd eventually have to go, even though they didn't know exactly when, was enough to make Breton put plans on hold and withhold any kind of investment in the place, or its people. The closest thing they had to friends or family nearby were the employees at the farm store across the street, who'd gotten to know Emily as she'd grown. After a lifetime of being uprooted, Breton said he knew better than to attach to anything or anyone more than that. "You know those people that have had their heart broken too much and don't want to get close to anyone because they're afraid to get hurt again? It's like the community version of that," he said. "If I don't get involved, I don't feel as much loss when I have to leave."

As much as economists tend to be pro mobility, psychologists generally have a more mixed view. The kind of heartbreak and grief that serial movers like Breton experience has real consequences when it comes to mental health, quality of life, even longevity. Studies from University of Chicago psychology professor Shigehiro Oishi show that high "residential mobility," basically, moving a lot, can have lasting impacts on both individuals and communities. For instance, adults who moved a lot as children report higher rates of depression, lower overall life satisfaction, lower rates of well-being and less satisfying relationships than their peers who didn't move as much. This might be due to the fact that although frequent movers become very adept at socializing, their relationships with others tend to be more surface-level, viewed as almost a professional interaction. And introvert movers suffer more than extroverts, with higher rates of early death compared to their more outgoing peers—bad news for the more than 70 percent of Canadians who identify as introverts. Additionally, people who move frequently, especially at a younger age, develop a more individualistic sense of self and are less likely to see themselves as part of a collective whole. Zooming out to a population level, Oishi told me this can make it much harder to work together to solve problems that require collective action, such as solving climate change or even the housing crisis itself.

High turnover of residents can also make our communities less pleasant places to live, even for long-term residents. Oishi found high residential mobility is associated with higher crime rates and less willingness from residents to help each other out. High turnover even shapes how our neighbourhoods look and feel. Oishi's studies found the anxiety people experience when moving triggers "familiarity-seeking behaviour," meaning that communities with less residential stability are more hospitable to big-chain businesses. So, the next time that independent corner café in your neighbourhood becomes a Chipotle, it's worth pondering how much of the housing stock around you has recently been converted to Airbnb.

What's often missing in our discussions of mobility—and our experience of it—is the nuance of choice. The choice to continually move is freedom. Being forced to do so is an act of violence, even a violation of our human rights. That's why the United Nations has been careful to identify "secure tenure"—the choice to stay put, the time to put down roots—as a key component of international laws around the right to adequate shelter, which it defines in part as "not having to worry about being evicted or having your home or lands taken away." At the same time, people should not be forced to stay in living situations that are unhealthy, dangerous or limiting their prospects for the life they want. When it comes to mobility, choice is the key differentiator between the good and the bad; it's the difference between the glamorous-seeming life of a travel influencer and the desperate reality of a refugee; it's the distinction between someone happily rooted and attached to their home and a prisoner.

What's needed to restore mobility is more viable choices for more people, whether those are options for downsizing within your neighbourhood, buying your first home close to your family and friends or being able to take a new job or go to school in a booming coastal city because you know there will be housing available—and housing you can afford. It also means being able to stay put, if you want to, in a place where you've found a fulsome sense of home. This kind of choice used to be central to the North American experience, and it's this that's been whittled away in recent decades. As Appelbaum put it: "The freedom to choose one's city or community has become a privilege of class." And the more the topic of housing dominates our attention and determines our big life decisions, even those with the privilege to choose where they live may discount some important considerations.

---

"Seven hundred and eighty thousand!"

John repeated this figure throughout our conversation like a mantra, or maybe a tick. An energetic 60-year-old with close-cropped white hair and a slim build, John told me he didn't feel anywhere near his age, and I believed him. He spoke in the kind of breathless stream-of-consciousness you might expect from someone several decades his junior.

Maybe it was excitement. "Seven hundred eighty thousand dollars!" he blurted out mid-tour of the pristine marble-clad kitchen, open-concept living room and tempered-glass railings of the slim, ultra-modern four-bedroom house he bought less than a year ago for just "seven hundred eighty thousand dollars! Can you believe that?"

Throughout his life, John hadn't just climbed the property ladder; he'd scaled it, making calculated moves to increase the value of his properties at each and every rung. Though it hadn't always been a smooth progression. Originally from the Vancouver area, John got caught with a leaky condo in the 90s that ended up costing him $180,000 in repairs. Then came the townhouse he bought for $320,000 with the noisy neighbours that I got the impression he kind of wished he'd held onto. "Those places go for between $800,000 and $900,000 now," he told me. His last place before leaving the province was a townhouse in the Vancouver suburb of Port Coquitlam he bought for $240,000 and sold five years later for $550,000, more than double what he'd paid. That windfall allowed him to buy his dream home in a tony area of Edmonton. He didn't know anyone in the city and wasn't super keen on it as a place, but the house more than made up for that. It was everything he'd ever wanted: sleek, new and his. "This house, I never thought I'd be able to afford it in my life," he gushed. "I flew here and the houses were so cheap, I went for the max I could buy on my single income."

John's pride in his house was palpable, and it was clear that he'd landed in a more-than-spacious haven for him and his two ragdoll cats, Miiyu and Scooter. But when I started asking about the other elements of home, John's answers painted a picture of a life that seemed a little, well, thin. He didn't feel compelled to explore Edmonton much. It had a "weird" vibe and the roads were bad for cycling, so he'd cut back quite a bit on the hobby he'd always enjoyed. The dating scene was dismal, but that may have been more a function of his age. There were a couple of neighbours he chatted with on occasion, but not so much he'd call them friends. He'd had a job when he moved, but it hadn't worked out so he'd decided to take an early retirement. "I spend a lot of time in the house," he told me.

John was adamant these were just minor annoyances, maybe not even that. Nothing mattered as much to his quality of life as having a nice house with an affordable mortgage. He was genuinely dismayed that anyone would put up with the cost of living in places like Vancouver just to be close to the people they cared about or the things they liked to do. "I won't sacrifice my life just to say I live somewhere," he told me. "Like, in Vancouver a lot of people just sacrificed everything. And they really have nothing—other than, I mean, they got friends."

I am not in a place to doubt John's claims of being truly, deeply satisfied by realizing his real estate aspirations. I don't know him that well. But I did wonder if, like Breton, John's frequent moves had led him to live in a state of protective dissociation to dull the pain of leaving his community and friends behind. It is possible I'm projecting. As I mentioned before, my move to Calgary felt like it was more difficult than it should have been, which became a source of deep shame. That's because I thought I should be more like John, happy enough with my new house and the opportunity more affordability would bring me to cancel out the sting of leaving my entire life behind. I attribute this belief to how mobility is portrayed in our media and framed in our public discourse. Jet-setting social media influencers and TV shows like *House Hunters International* (which, to be fair, I sometimes binge obsessively) glorify the process of picking up your whole life and moving across the world. And it's just understood that moving from the city to the suburbs in order to settle down and start a family is a triumphant mark of maturity. Perhaps because moving is thought to be so instrumental to our economy, our general attitude toward it is, in my opinion, a bit flippant. Compared to other big life stressors like a job loss or a death in the family, the disruption of moving seems to be universally portrayed as temporary, short-term pain for long-term gain. It's only a matter of time until we get used to our new surroundings, find new ways to engage in our hobbies and make new social connections. It hasn't really worked out that way for me. Even all these years later, I still miss Vancouver and the person I was there. I miss going to the beach; I miss riding my bike under cherry blossoms; and I really, really miss my friends.

I've often felt kind of silly about this, like it's immature to be pining over friendship when there are more serious things, like finding a home where I can raise a family, at stake. Beverley Fehr, a psychology professor at the University of Winnipeg, assured me I shouldn't. A researcher and author of a book about how we form friendships, Fehr told me friends get short shrift in our society, taking a back seat to familial and marital relationships in terms of attention, understanding and priority. "There aren't the kinds of supports for friendships that we have for other kinds of relationships," Fehr said, noting that when a friendship struggles we don't go to counselling, and when we lose a friend we don't receive the same kind of compassion or understanding that we might in the case of a family member or spouse. "There isn't that same recognition of the grief that we can experience. That can be a lonely kind of grief."

Fehr's research shows that one of the biggest reasons friendships end is due to somebody moving away. We like to think that in the era of social media, instant messaging and video chats our friendships can bridge a physical gap, "but the reality is that people are more likely to respond to what's going on in the here and now," she said. "It's hard enough for most people to prioritize their face-to-face friendships given the other demands in their lives, and then if you are lacking that physical presence it becomes even more difficult." Of course, there are friendships that do stay strong despite the distance. Every time I see my Vancouver friends it feels like I never left. But Fehr said that without frequent in-person interactions we don't get the full benefit friendship confers on our lives, which is significant. People with close friends that they see in person often experience better moods, less fatigue and less stress than those who don't. Research has even shown high-quality friendships have a bigger impact on our overall life satisfaction than romantic relationships—they can even offset the negative effects of being in an unhappy marriage.

Another misconception about friends is that they're easily replaceable. While we seem to realize our parents and siblings are one of a kind, and we treat spouses similarly, people are often told we can always make more friends, especially in the case of a move. Except, it's not that easy. Unlike familial and sometimes even romantic relationships, friendships require a unique amount of effort, as well as a bit of luck and kismet, to even get off the ground. First, we need to be in close physical proximity regularly enough and long enough that we can notice each other and take a liking. After a bit of time, we might venture to go do something together, a shared activity we both enjoy. That's usually when we start to test the waters with a potential friend by revealing more personal details about ourselves and gauging how they respond. If you deem the person trustworthy with those more sensitive details and, this is key, they reciprocate, you may finally have a budding friendship on your hands. That's why so many of us make friends in school or work settings—places where we have the time to go through this complicated dance and cement a bond. But even this can prove insufficient for forming a friendship. Just like with other relationships, keeping a friendship afloat requires time, attention and a mutual willingness to work through strain and even conflict, so each one of us has a limit to the number of friendships we can sustain at any given time. Fehr calls this our "friendship budget." One of the reasons it can be so hard to make new friends in a new place, especially as you get older, is because people tend to have maxed out their budget on existing relationships. "You could move to a new place and become familiar with someone and you might even hit it off with that person," she said. "But if that person already has a full catalogue of friends, as the newcomer, you may not make it in."

This explains a lot. One of the things that's bothered me since moving to Calgary is a lack of really close, deep friendships. It's not that I don't have friends here; I do. They are some of the sweetest, most generous, most genuine people I've ever met. But with few exceptions, I don't have the kind of closeness I felt with most of my friends back home. It's not for a lack of trying. I've met people with whom I've felt a kindred connection, but we never seem to graduate to bona fide besties—you know, where you're texting all the time and sharing in-jokes. Mostly, the problem seems to come down to scheduling. Everyone is so dang busy these days and Calgary is such a spread-out city that it's hard to carve out the time necessary to nurture that level of intimacy. But there's a nagging question as to whether there's more to it than that. Am I trying too hard? Not enough? Do I smell? Fehr said I'm not alone in my questioning. When people are in situations where making new friends is difficult, like after a move or when attempting to break into an existing social circle, they often blame themselves. "The tendency is to think that there's something wrong with them—that they can't make friends rather than recognizing: this is a lonely situation."

And boy, are we ever in some lonely situations, so much so that social isolation and loneliness have been declared a public health emergency, as bad for us as smoking 15 cigarettes a day. Of particular concern is that we have fewer friends today than 20 years ago, and we spend considerably less time socializing with the friends we do have.

While the reasons for all this are complex and varied, I found it interesting that very little research seems to have centred on the relationship between loneliness and residential mobility. But evidence of a correlation isn't hard to find. All you need to do is talk to someone who's been displaced. When the writer Robert Caro interviewed some of the nearly 500,000 New York City residents, mostly low-income, many racialized, who had been forcibly uprooted by "urban renewal" efforts in the mid-20th century, he found himself transcribing one word over and over again: lonely. This corresponds with what surveys show us today. The

World Health Organization warns that "anyone, anywhere can become lonely or socially isolated," but it is much more common among low-income seniors, people with disabilities, racialized and visible minorities, Indigenous people, and LGBTQ2+ folks. All of these groups are more likely to be renters and thus at continual risk of housing insecurity and displacement, according to national statistics. Another group that also ranks disproportionately high on the loneliness scale are young people. Those under 35 across the income and education spectrum are more likely to say they are lonely despite being pretty well socially connected. This means they objectively have frequent interactions with people, but they view the quality of those interactions as poor. This is also the group most likely to be caught on one end of the mobility divide or the other—either cycling through roommates and short-term rentals or stuck in their parents' basements, feeling powerless to establish homes of their own. And then there are the lonely cries of new parents everywhere who find the village required to raise children is conspicuously absent. Considering how many of them are forced to move away from family and friends in order to find suitable housing in which to raise their families, it might not be that the village has disappeared as much as we force people out of it, right when they need it the most.

Shrinking household size, shifting demographics, technology and social media use, burnout, overwork and remote work—all of these have been variously flagged as contributing factors to our loneliness, and there's no doubt they all play a role. But we have been hesitant to dig into the relationship between these distressing trends and the ways our views on home and housing have changed. That may be because if we did, we'd be forced to confront an awkward truth Paul Kershaw believes keeps us locked in this pattern. "We are culturally addicted to high and rising home prices," he said. Like any addiction, it's hard to admit and harder to kick, even when the harm it causes becomes impossible to ignore. But with the right support recovery is possible. If it is an addiction we're facing, and it might well be, we may need to look beyond the traditional authorities within our housing sector for guidance. After all, realtors, financiers, developers and even many elected officials benefit from keeping us hooked. More valuable insight might be gleaned from fields like social work, psychology and addictions medicine. This makes me think of the work of journalist Johann Hari, who travelled the world researching the root causes of addiction for his book *Chasing the Scream* and came to a surprising conclusion. The opposite of addiction isn't sobriety, as many of us think. It's connection. In our search for solutions, this is fertile ground to explore. Intentional or not, our housing system has evolved to sow disconnection at every turn—from the physical design of our housing, to its legal and financial underpinnings, to our culture of competition and comparison. We're just so steeped in it that it's difficult for us to see. That is, until you encounter a different way of doing things.

6

# NEIGHBOURHOOD WELCOME

Before I show you what it looks like to create housing that truly connects people, I need to tell you what happened next in my housing journey because I've come to see it as a prime example of how our system subtly incites division within our communities. Even among those who are desperate to belong.

When I found out my rental house was destined to be bulldozed, I decided I was done with renting. I'd never harboured strong aspirations to become a homeowner, but facing eviction made finding a place I couldn't get kicked out of a burning priority. I am incredibly lucky I was in a position to even consider it.

I had some savings; I had some help from my parents (yep, I am that millennial); and I had really good credit. Even so, it would have been almost impossible for me to buy. Banks don't generally love to lend money to freelance writers with highly variable incomes. But by then I was part of a couple, giving me the extra bump of financial credibility necessary to purchase a home.

A few months after I finally ditched my toxic ex, I met Dave. The timing could not have been worse. I had just moved from Vancouver to Calgary and he had just done the opposite. Neither of us was in the market for a relationship, particularly a long-distance one. But we kept gravitating toward each other on a camping trip with mutual friends, and by the end of the weekend we were pretty much a pair.

The first year of our relationship was like a jet-set dream. We both worked remotely, so we were free to float back and forth between our two cities, each of us newbies on the others' familiar ground. We'd spend a week or so at a time together in Vancouver or Calgary, and then some time apart. It was all very glamorous and fun—for a while.

Dave had a much higher tolerance for being on the move than I did. Before we met, he'd spent the last decade or so bouncing all over the world, living in London, Paris, Uganda and Montreal. He'd wound up back in Calgary to regroup after a big breakup, and his move to Vancouver was sort of a reclaiming of his life, which he'd always envisioned in a big, bustling city.

The debate between Vancouver and Calgary was a continuous topic of conversation; we talked about it pretty much every day. To be honest, we still do. Our preference would have been to stay in Vancouver, and meeting Dave felt like a chance at a do-over for me, a ticket *home* to have the life in the city I loved with the partner and promising future I'd always wanted. But spending time in Dave's rented high-rise condo, I was reminded of what had driven me from the city in the first place.

His one-bedroom apartment had a killer water view and a convenient central location, but it was never going to work for us long-term. We both worked from home in jobs that required a lot of meetings and private space to hold them in. We knew we wanted to have a kid one day, which would require a second bedroom at some point. Then there was the fact that the floor-to-ceiling windows that gave Dave's place its panoramic view also turned it into a sweatbox for nine months out of the year. Dave dealt with this by working shirtless most of the time, but for many reasons this was not a comfortable option for me.

Staying in Vancouver would mean eventually having to find a new place and contending with that wicked housing market again. I was hesitant, still traumatized by the last time I'd tried to form a new household in Vancouver. We ran the numbers forwards and backwards, up and down, inside and out. No matter how we tried to skew the math, every time the answer came up: Calgary.

For Dave's part, if he was going to settle back in his hometown after living in some of the world's most vibrant cities he was going to have fairly exacting standards. Our neighbourhood had to be biking distance to downtown, be close to transit and have a walkable "main street" with coffee shops and restaurants and little indie stores. I was on board with all of that, plus I wanted to be walking distance to a yoga studio and a grocery store. Basically, we wanted to feel like we were in Vancouver, even if we couldn't be. We started looking in an old inner-city neighbourhood we both liked. It was surrounded by railways and decommissioned factories and was surprisingly diverse, in both its housing stock and its residents. There were million-dollar infills (brand-new houses built where old ones have been torn down), century-old character homes, two seniors' apartment buildings, a city-owned social housing development and even a rare housing co-op. It all made for a funky and inviting village-like atmosphere we were eager to join; we just had to find the right house. The million-dollar infills didn't fit our budget, and the century homes were cute, but I worried about maintaining hundred-year-old pipes and dug-out basements in a harsh Alberta winter. Then I found a listing for a 1980s split level that seemed to hit a sweet spot right in the middle. It had a cherry-red front door and cottage-like curb appeal, just like my beloved little bungalow that had been slated for demolition. I took it as a good omen.

I could tell we both loved it instantly because Dave and I were uncharacteristically quiet during the showing, trying, I think, to downplay our enthusiasm in front of the seller's realtor.

The house was super weird, and we loved that. To the great confusion of the guy who did our home inspection, there was no clear primary bedroom, just two equally-sized rooms on the back end of the house. One we would use as our bedroom, the other as an office for Dave. The kitchen was on the top floor, the uppermost of four levels, beside an asymmetrical alcove we agreed would make a good office for me. Off the living room on the "main" floor was a rectangular room with a skylight at the top of a vaulted 20-foot ceiling that had been grandfathered into the building code on a technicality as a bedroom. We thought it could make a good nursery when or if the time ever came. The basement had a wood-burning fireplace, original oak panelling and a mirrored wet bar that offered a speakeasy sort of vibe we thought we could turn into something cool. *And* it had a big backyard. Sure, it was completely overgrown, and the 40-year-old fence and deck were rotted beyond repair. Parts of the house were also covered in peel-and-stick industrial carpet tile, the kind of flooring you'd see in an office building, and the vanity in the main bathroom was original from the '80s and hit us at about mid-thigh. But these were all things we felt we could live with and improve over time. The potential to make our space truly ours actually made us excited. We got as far as the end of the block before deciding we had to make an offer. After a few heart-pounding days of back-and-forth it was accepted.

We moved in a few weeks before Christmas 2019. We were ecstatic to be a part of a community where we could put down roots. We'd moved in with the intention of forging the kind of long-lasting relationships with our neighbours that seemed increasingly to belong to a bygone era. We were willing to put in the work to be a part of the community.

Then we discovered that most of the owners on the block weren't interested in that.

We'd lived in our weird house for about three weeks when we got notice of a public hearing for a rezoning application, not just for a lot or two but literally our entire block—including our house. I sleuthed around online but couldn't find much information, so on a frigid Monday in January, Dave and I took the day off work and went to city hall to find out exactly what was going on.

We quickly discovered that there is no more awkward way to meet your new neighbours for the first time than while facing off on opposite ends of a development issue. This is how we learned that while we had moved in with the hope of meaningfully contributing to an existing community, most everyone else was on the way out. We'd bought with the knowledge that our block was zoned for duplexes and laneway houses, so we expected some redevelopment over the years. More neighbours! Yay! What we hadn't expected was that the other owners, mostly small-scale investor-landlords who owned two or three adjoining lots on our block, had gotten together to plot a collective cash-out. They had hired a consultant to draft a proposal to upzone the quiet street we adored to allow for a huge condo development that would more than quadruple the number of residences on the street and dwarf our house, walling us in on both sides.

My reaction? *Hell. No.* I fell into a full-on existential crisis. *Oh God, was I a NIMBY? Had it happened that fast?*

For those who believe we can simply build our way out of our housing crisis, the way most cities consult with the community on development proposals is often considered a hindrance to progress. In a situation where it appears that we need all the new housing we can get, they often argue, people who already have homes shouldn't have the right to block future homes for others—especially for selfish reasons such as wanting to preserve your light or privacy or the quiet, calm street where you envisioned your future child learning to ride their bike. There are times in my life when I've agreed with this stance, especially when the community opposes affordable social or non-market housing. But facing a potentially massive development right next door, I was glad to have the option to speak out.

I'd had personal experience being harmed by this exact kind of development before. I felt for all the renters living in the houses around us who would be inevitably displaced. I had just been that renter. Like the luxury townhouses going up in the place of my old bungalow, the housing proposed for our new block were not going to help them.

That day at city hall, I sat there shaking with nerves as one by one the landowners and their consultant spoke in support of a plan that seemed to me like nothing more than a pump-and-dump scheme. Their aim was to upzone the land to dramatically increase its potential value so they could either redevelop or sell to a developer for top dollar. It was as simple as that. They felt they were entitled to the money by virtue of having bought this land however long ago. Some even used the fact that they'd let their rental properties fall into disrepair as an argument in favour of demolishing them. I remember many of the city councillors agreeing that, yes, this was the only logical thing to do. These property owners had a right to realize the value of their investment, and a decision should be made based on that. Nobody talked about the renters who would be turfed from their homes, or that their landlords had purposefully withheld maintenance as they waited for the right time to sell. Nobody talked about the need for family-sized units or affordable housing or non-market housing in the neighbourhood. That would have been a very different conversation.

I remember feeling flushed and my voice quavering as I approached the podium to plead our case with an off-the-cuff speech. I told the mayor and council that we were new owners who had just bought our first house, who'd hoped it would be our forever home, who'd been blindsided by this proposal that seemed like it would totally change our street. We were clearly outnumbered so I played the only bargaining chip I thought we had—could we at least remove our address from the application? I remember feeling like I must be taking crazy pills, like we must be the last people on earth naive enough to buy a house to actually live in, when the mayor, with a wink in his voice, suggested I might want to reconsider that ask. If we joined up with the rest of the crew our brand-new home would be worth a bucketload of money, he said, probably several. And then who even cares what happens next door? Like the rest of them, we could just cash out and leave.

# PART 2: POSSIBILITIES

*A society grows great when old men plant trees*
*in whose shade they know they shall never sit.*

—anonymous Greek proverb

7

# VIENNA: A MODEL OF HOME

There is no shortage of reasons to visit Vienna, Austria. Almost smack dab in the geographic centre of Europe, the city has been home to more pivotal moments and prominent figures in Western history than any one place has a right to. Visitors can feast their eyes upon the baroque opulence of Schönbrunn Palace, home to the Habsburg nobility that ruled over much of Europe for more than 600 years, or indulge in the rococo trappings of the Belvedere, the former abode of Prince Eugene of Savoy, whose military brilliance served as inspiration to Napoleon. You can take in the art nouveau masterpieces of the painter Gustav Klimt, tour Beethoven's apartment, view Mozart's (alleged) grave and poke around the flat where Sigmund Freud pioneered the practice of psychotherapy. You can quaff traditional Austrian beer, soak it up with Wiener schnitzel and sachertorte (reportedly the world's "most famous cake"), then walk it off along the Ringstrasse, a study in Greek revival, Gothic and Renaissance architecture.

For all these reasons and more, locals told me, the city truly has no off season. It is beset by tourists year-round arriving via plane, train or boat on the famous Danube River. But in recent years Vienna has attracted a different class of visitor, drawn not to the grandeur of the city's imperial history but to its contemporary suburbs, sleek social housing developments, and elegant working-class apartment blocks harkening back to the early 20th century.

In a world besieged by soaring housing costs, Vienna has positioned itself as a beacon of hope. The city is proof positive that it is possible to buck the trend of financialized housing, and that doing so can actually net a city considerable clout. Vienna has topped lists of the world's most livable cities for nearly a decade straight, thanks in large part to its plethora of beautiful, accessible, centrally planned communities that are vibrant, diverse and, above all, affordable.

It's worth noting Vienna is not alone in this endeavour. Many places in the world have demonstrated progress on creating or maintaining affordable housing, even in big, exciting, in-demand cities. Tokyo, Japan, for instance, has managed to sidestep the global affordability crisis with average housing costs that are not only considerably cheaper than in comparable locales like New York, London or Hong Kong, but even lower than where I live, in not particularly large, not particularly exciting Calgary. With the average one-bedroom apartment in Tokyo renting for about C$930 a month (as of 2024), even minimum wage earners can comfortably rent in many areas of the city. However, this level of affordability has been achieved by methods that may not be palatable to your average North American. It's not unusual, for instance, for single-occupancy apartments to clock in at 250 square feet, or less. The city has also incentivized private development by virtually abandoning zoning restrictions, sacrificing green space, and preserving almost none of its historical architecture.

Singapore is another example of a place that has managed to shelter its citizens from the crushing weight of high and rising house prices, despite its reputation as one of the world's most staunchly capitalist nations. While the city-state has become synonymous with luxury real estate aimed at the global elite, that constitutes only a tiny sliver of its overall housing landscape. Most Singaporeans, over 80 percent in fact, buy their first homes directly from the government for a very reasonable sum, somewhere in the range of C$90,000 to C$525,000. Many are even eligible for additional housing grants of up to $80,000, though there are caveats here, too, such as the fact that government housing policies favour heterosexual, nuclear families, making it harder for LGBTQ2+ couples and families to access the system.

By far the most famous example of an affordable housing haven I have come across is Vienna. For years I'd been bumping into the city in my research. At conferences, in meet-up groups, and trawling the internet, Vienna was portrayed as a kind of promised land. It is a city where over half its residents live in subsidized, rent-controlled apartments; where social housing doesn't come with crime, grime and stigma but instead wins international awards as some of the most beautiful, innovative and environmentally sustainable housing stock in the world; a place that has somehow managed to strike the elusive balance between preserving its history and building for its future without displacing existing residents or inviting gentrification.

It only made sense that my search for ways to reimagine our own housing system to better serve human needs had to start in the city *The New York Times* dubbed a "renters' utopia." Still, I arrived with a healthy dose of skepticism. After all, the reason Vienna is often described in near-mythical terms as a "utopia," or "promised land"—is because what it has purported to achieve is widely reputed to be impossible in much of the rest of the world.

According to the natural laws of the universe—or at least of capitalism—a system that provides high-quality, affordable housing to all should bankrupt the government, hamstring the economy and disincentivize private industry and worker productivity. Such a bold, state-sponsored approach could only come at the cost of democratic freedoms, requiring the kind of unilateral control only a dictator, probably communist, could possess. And yet there stands Vienna, claiming to have cracked the code with a system it says is economically self-sustaining and incredibly politically popular—so much so that the party that brought it into being more than 100 years ago has been re-elected in Vienna's free and fair elections nearly continuously ever since.

And as more and more cities have become mired in the global housing crisis, Vienna has put considerable resources toward marketing its housing strategy as a possible template for solutions. The city's public housing agency, Wiener Wohnen, even has an international relations department explicitly geared toward coordinating visits for nosy journalists like me. In the orange bureaucratic cube that is the agency's head office, I met Veronika Iwanowski, the primary contact for my week in Vienna who introduced me to the city via an overview of its housing system. To my North American perspective, it really did seem like the stuff of dreams.

More than 60 percent of Vienna's 2 million residents live in some form of subsidized housing, whether in flats built and managed by the municipality or by dozens of limited-profit or non-profit entities such as housing co-operatives. And these are far from the depressing, isolated compounds that have tarnished the reputation of public housing elsewhere. The buildings are pristine, spacious and often designed to advance a social or environmental agenda. Biotope City, for example, is an urban forest with facades covered in foliage that mitigate the effects of climate change on the urban heat island and lend a lush, futuristic jungle aesthetic. In Aspern Seestadt, a new suburb on the outskirts of the 23rd district connected directly to downtown by a newly built subway, all the streets are named for women, an intentional move to balance out the institutional sexism ensconced in so much urban nomenclature. There's no skimping on maintenance to keep costs down, either. The city has an army of 3,000 employees dedicated to this task—as well as a network of well-organized tenant groups that have a direct line to the city to submit concerns, requests or suggestions. All this is key in avoiding the kind of neglect, abuse and stigma suffered by so many public housing complexes elsewhere in the world, Iwanowski told me. Putting people in beautiful, intentional homes they can be proud of inspires them to take care of their surroundings. "That's the thing with affordable housing. It has to be beautiful. It has to be climate friendly. It has to have a benefit for the people who live there and for the people who live in the surroundings," she said. "If it doesn't have that it's a different story."

On average, each resident living in social housing enjoys 35 square metres, or 376 square feet, of living space, with the typical two-person household sharing 70 square metres, about 750 square feet. The units are certainly not palatial, but they're not tiny either. To augment their more modest floor plans, Vienna's centrally planned communities are designed with plenty of green space and common amenities to meet residents' needs, such as meeting rooms, co-working spaces, bike storage, car parks and garden plots available for resident use. They are always serviced by public transit and come fully stocked with doctors' offices, daycares and essential businesses like grocery stores. Retail spaces are often available at a discount to local residents who want to literally set up shop. To prevent displacing long-term residents, Vienna's social housing developments are exclusively built in uninhabited areas, such as former industrial sites or farmland that is no longer in use. Meanwhile, the city's Gebietsbetreuungen Stadterneuerung, or Urban Renewal Office, helps people living around these new developments adjust to the change with on-site offices staffed with multidisciplinary teams including social workers, counsellors and urban planners available on a drop-in basis to answer questions and provide advice. These offices also host information and planning sessions to involve residents in the planning process for things like improvements to the public realm that serve both existing and new communities. When new developments are completed and people move in, the Gebietsbetreuungen Stadterneuerung office—marked by its jaunty GB* logo—hosts social events where new and existing residents can mingle, and when staff are convinced the newly mixed community is gelling nicely, the team and the office pack up to move to another community on the verge of redevelopment.

Rents in Vienna are capped by national legislation at a base rate of €6.67 per square metre (about 10 square feet), as of 2025, for municipal housing, pricing the average-sized flat at about €467 (about C$730) per month, though residents often pay a bit more because of taxes and operating costs. Rent is adjusted every two years and adapted to the Consumer Price Index (the measure of how much certain goods cost at any given time) to account for inflation. That predictability is a core feature of Vienna's housing system, which is predicated on the understanding that plentiful housing is only a first step toward creating good, long-term homes. To that end, all city leases are open-ended. Residents can, and often do, live in their flats for life and even pass them on to children or grandchildren. That doesn't mean they're stuck in one place. Those who need or want to move can apply to the city for another flat to suit shifting needs, with special considerations often given to divorcing parents, downsizing seniors, single parents, or multi-generational families that need to be kept geographically intact. People can choose which area of town they'd prefer to live in and can consider up to three different flats before being booted to the bottom of the list. Evictions are exceedingly rare, due to a combination of Austria's strong national tenancy laws and a litany of municipal programs—everything from emergency rent subsidies to payment plans to free counselling and free legal advice—provided by Vienna's Eviction Prevention Office.

Even as a fairly progressive person I found this all hard to comprehend. I just couldn't stop looking for the catch. Surely the city had to be grappling with continual cost overruns or plagued by unmeetable demand? Iwanowski nipped those doubts in the bud with a series of slides breaking down the financials. Vienna's annual housing budget of roughly €500 million (about C$781 million) is continually replenished, with about half coming from a national one percent housing tax distributed to all states in Austria (Vienna is a state). The other half comes through the repayment of municipal loans by those non-profit developers and the rent paid by residents. By law, all the money made through the system goes toward maintaining and creating yet more housing, allowing the city to continually procure more land. To discourage speculation, a lot of city-owned land is zoned specifically for social housing, which requires a minimum of 60 percent of units to be non-market housing, thus capping its value for private, for-profit investors. To continually raise the bar for quality and livability, the city holds an annual developer competition for its lucrative housing contracts, inviting firms to submit proposals that are judged against four pillars of criteria: architectural innovation, economic feasibility, ecological sensitivity and social sustainability.

As for demand, there is often a waitlist for housing, about 12 to 18 months on average, with priority given to those living in overcrowded situations, young people moving out of their family home for the first time and those with mobility issues in need of barrier-free housing. To get on the list you have to be an Austrian or European Union citizen or equivalent, such as a refugee who's been granted asylum, and have lived at the same address in the city for two years. At the time of my visit there were 15,000 people on the list, half of whom were already in a municipal flat and looking to change things up.

It all sounded reasonable enough, but still I had doubts. Wasn't a system like this ripe for abuse by people looking to take advantage of an overly generous state? Iwanowski's response made me finally realize how far I was from home, and not just geographically.

The philosophical underpinnings of North American public housing and assistance programs have evolved to reflect a kind of paranoia that has taken over our culture. We are so afraid of people abusing the system that we make it impossible to help most people in need, as if doing anything more than offering crumbs to the poorest of the poor will inevitably lead to societal collapse. As a result, housing subsidies are often only available for extremely low-income households, with cut-offs for assistance set far below what's required to pay market rents. Vienna takes the opposite approach. It's more concerned with maximizing gain than minimizing loss. Iwanowski explained that the city *wants* people to take advantage of its affordable housing—even those who have the means to pay private market rents. If housing is truly a human right, governments need to make it easier for people to obtain quality shelter, not harder, she said. "It's not just the poorest who need to be taken care of or who need to be helped and supported. It's everybody."

As such, the income cut-off for social housing in Vienna is set intentionally high, enough that roughly three-quarters of the city's population is eligible for a subsidized flat. A single-income household can earn up to €3,810 a month, about C$5,900, and still qualify for social housing, far above the average Viennese income of €1,600, roughly C$2,500. Two-earner households can bring in nearly €5,700 (C$8,900) per month. Once in the system there is no limit to how much a household can grow its income. It is never rechecked.

This leniency allows Vienna's housing program to capture households that often fall into the affordability gap, those that are not low-income enough to qualify for housing assistance but struggle to comfortably afford market rates. Having higher-income households living in social housing also creates economically diverse communities that prevent the ghettoization and stigma associated with public housing, Iwanowski said. This is a point of pride among Viennese. "If somebody tells you 'I'm from this or that district,' it's impossible for you to tell how much they earn because they can be living in a district where rich people have their mansions but there is also social housing there." She explained that high- and low-income households are intentionally placed in the same neighbourhoods, and often in the same buildings in social housing developments, with nothing to externally indicate the income disparity. These are often mixed in with market housing units. "So nobody needs to feel ashamed or hesitant to say their address."

The price tag for all this is undoubtedly high, but Vienna has done the math and found the upfront costs to be considerably lower than those incurred in cities reactively dealing with the fallout of unattainable housing—homelessness, mental and physical health issues, and crime. It's also a closed-loop system, meaning the money paid out comes back to the city instead of flowing into the pockets of private landlords and propping up ever increasing property values. "If we spent most of the money on housing allowances, that would then go to the private owners and that would be it," Iwanowski said. By managing housing itself, the city "can reinvest and really ensure that we continuously create a stable and affordable housing situation." The presence of a well-oiled, widely accessible social housing system provides effective competition to the private market, keeping market rents far lower than in comparable cities like Salzburg. Private landowners also benefit from the system, receiving financial support from the city to fix up aging buildings and bring them up to modern environmental and accessibility standards in exchange for keeping the rents stable for a period of time.

If it seems as if Vienna's approach is uniquely well-thought out compared to the floundering, often ineffective band-aids put forward in so much of the rest of the world, it's because they've been at this a long time.

---

My first glimpse of Karl Marx Hof, a public housing project completed in 1930, came from the back. A looming wall of russet bricks punctuated by grand arched tunnels through which I caught a glimpse of an open courtyard dotted with park benches and mature leafy trees still dripping with the remnants of a cold spring rain. I followed Iwanowski through one of the arches and she deftly handed me off to Max Schranz, a bespectacled graduate student in urban planning who was my tour guide for the afternoon. I bid Iwanowski goodbye and finally turned to see the building in all its glory. It *was* glorious.

At nearly a kilometre long, Karl Marx Hof in Vienna's 19th district is one of the longest continuous residential buildings in the world, home to 5,000 tenants in its heyday. But more than its size, what stood out to me were the design details positively dripping in pomp. Six brick pillars extended beyond the roofline, each hoisting a flagpole far into the sky, recalling the battlement of a castle, or maybe a fortress. I blurted this observation out to Schranz, who nodded as if to give me a gold star. That, he told me, was the intention behind this building and many of the "residential palaces" constructed during the earliest days of Vienna's social housing program. The period, known as Red Vienna, arose between the First and Second World Wars, coinciding with the surging workers' rights movements sweeping Europe at the time. Housing complexes of the era, such as Karl Marx Hof, were designed not just to give people shelter but to elevate the proletariat by evoking the grandeur and dignity of the bourgeois classes with their ornate design details. It was an ambitious move meant at once to advance the political agenda of a bold new government and alleviate a housing crisis so bad it earned Vienna the dubious honour of having the worst living conditions in all of Europe.

Vienna's housing system is a direct result of the devastation Europe suffered at the time, though it came into the war years already worse for wear. During the late 19th and early 20th centuries, the city experienced an explosion in population, growing from just over 400,000 to over 2 million people in a few short decades. The stress on the city's housing stock was profound. The Viennese working class crammed into decrepit "bassena" apartments named for the floor plans that saw whole families living in a single room with an adjoining kitchen. The only light and ventilation came from a dank interior corridor with four or more apartments sharing only one sink—one basin—and one toilet, which often wasn't plumbed.

In these dark, unsanitary tenements sickness ran rampant, with tuberculosis so common that it became known throughout Europe as the "Viennese disease." Such squalor did not come cheap. Market rents at the time were so high it was common for families to sublet to "bed lodgers," usually unattached men working the night shift who would pay to sleep in the family bed (often there was just one) during the day while the breadwinners were at work. By 1917, with the city now also reeling from the ravages of the First World War, the government of the day brought in rent control, which lowered housing costs but led to a loss of shelter for those bed lodgers whose supplemental income was no longer needed for families to make ends meet. With inflation rates soaring and little private development in housing on the horizon, the situation seemed poised to continue spiralling downward.

That is until the Social Democrats swept to power in the 1919 election, after running on a platform to revolutionize housing, and with it Viennese society as a whole. "They really set out to create a completely new time, to really change society and how people would live together," said Schranz. "They wanted to create a new person, a new human even."

Financed through a tax on luxury items such as domestic workers, gambling, horse racing and Champagne, the government set about creating thousands of beautiful and affordable worker flats, ensuring each had access to fresh air, light and sunshine. Features such as external windows became mandatory in each room, and balconies became commonplace. The campaign to uplift the working class didn't stop with housing. The program also saw the construction of schools, libraries and theatres, often built right into housing complexes or within a short walk, ensuring access to education and culture. Despite the pressing lack of affordable housing, the Social Democrats eschewed building to the highest possible density in favour of reserving green spaces where children could play and people could exercise. Public health campaigns touted the benefits of basic health care and hygiene, furnishing social housing with modern conveniences that were scarce in the aging private market stock. Vienna's social housing complexes were some of the first in Europe to boast things like laundry facilities, electricity and indoor plumbing—which remained absent in many private rentals in Vienna until the 1980s. The health, productivity and happiness of the Viennese quickly increased with the improvements in housing, and with it the city's reputation as a cultural and commercial powerhouse in Europe began to recover.

It wasn't all smooth sailing, though. Enamoured with the political philosophies of thinkers like Marx and Engels, the Social Democrats had strong ideas about how people should live their lives, which extended into their private abodes. The great iron gates at Karl Marx Hof, for instance, were drawn closed and locked every evening to dissuade residents from staying out late drinking in the pubs (though you could get back in "after hours" by paying a fee). The subject of interior design also became a strangely contentious issue in the formation of this new society.

Government-hired architects often designed flats with sleek and sparse furnishings in mind, envisioning a streamlined interior meant to encourage residents to concern themselves with acquiring knowledge and culture rather than material goods. They even went so far as to create model suites that they filled with minimalist pieces like convertible wall beds intended to demonstrate to "the working class how this new socialist human should live," said Schranz. But the residents themselves had different ideas of what it meant to live well. After generations spent living in precarious, dangerous, cramped conditions, the opportunity for the proletariat to furnish and decorate their living quarters to their own tastes was "something of a new kind of luxury for the working class." They weren't about to relinquish this new-found freedom to the opinions of architects and politicians, most of whom were bourgeois and had never wanted for worldly possessions, much less a home to display them in. To the dismay of the political elite, the interiors of Vienna's elegant social housing blocks were often chock full of heavy wooden furniture sets, chintzy lace curtains and purposeless knick-knacks cluttering every doily-covered surface.

Another unintended consequence of the improved living standard was that it problematically undermined the commitment to egalitarianism at the heart of the workers' movement. As housing costs went down, more families were able to live on a single income, relegating more women to the realm of unpaid domestic labour. In an attempt to bridge the widening gender gap, some buildings incorporated experimental technologies, like central vacuum cleaners, meant to lighten the workload for housewives. In one building, suites purposely lacked kitchens to prevent in-home cooking, with meals for the whole building prepared en masse in a central kitchen and delivered to individual suites via dumbwaiter. To the chagrin of harried parents everywhere, this model has unfortunately not withstood the test of time.

Other growing pains sprang from the technologies themselves. Laundry day was a source of great anxiety for the initial residents of Karl Marx Hof, who shared a state-of-the-art washing facility with assigned weekly access times. But many struggled to get the newfangled machines to complete the task within the time allowed and wound up carting half-soaked linens back to their flats, where they were banned from hanging them to dry on balconies, lest the visual clutter tarnish the building's carefully crafted façade.

Standing in the main courtyard of Karl Marx Hof today, still home to more than 1,000 people, there was substantial evidence that the overly intrusive aspects of Red Vienna's housing revolution had given way to a more relaxed approach. Many of the original suites had been combined to create bigger flats in line with modern expectations, Schranz told me, and the gates were no longer locked at night. Laundry liberally flapped in the breeze on a few balconies, and many brimmed with potted plants, plastic flowers, garden gnomes and other non-conforming bits of flair.

The poles on top of the building were bereft of the Austrian flags that would have broadcast the nationalistic fervour of the age. What remained, however, was a testament to the values that have endured. Four statues built into Karl Marx Hof's edifice depict the guiding principles behind Red Vienna's success. Each is a person, three women and one man, respectively representing four main elements: access to education, workers' rights, child and maternal welfare, and recreation and health care. A century on, the idea that positive social change and improving public health most effectively begins at home is still the driving force behind Vienna's housing policy. Only these days, it's advanced less through socialist ideology than through the liberal application of the social sciences.

---

Over in Floridsdorf, Vienna's 21st district, the design cues of the Wohnpartner Neighbourhood Centre definitely have not been borrowed from the ornate homes of the city's imperial elite. If anything, the building reads more like a gas station convenience store: cheap, utilitarian and fast to construct. But the forgettable exterior belies its incredible value. One lesson learned over the city's century of trial and error with social housing is that it's not enough to simply build a bunch of new apartments, beautiful as they may be. If you want something approximating an inclusive, egalitarian utopia to take root in new communities, you have to build the *social* infrastructure to support it. Wohnpartner's neighbourhood centres—open seven days a week and spread throughout the city—are an integral part of Vienna's commitment to social sustainability, offering a free, welcoming space where people in the neighbourhood can find support, connection and community.

The centre I visited in Floridsdorf was a big open space easily reconfigured to host a range of free, scheduled programs—language and fitness classes, homework clubs, craft circles and drop-in parent-and-tot coffee hours, to name a few. A stack of multilingual pamphlets sat by the door, offering info on upcoming events and local community resources; there was a rack of free donated clothing and other household goods, and a kids' play area set up in the corner. In the back was a kitchen for cooking classes and potlucks. It looked similar to your average North American community association hall except for one critical difference. Rather than being overseen by a band of time-stressed volunteers, it was staffed by a roster of social workers, sociologists and other professionals specifically trained to facilitate community cohesion.

In a city where the housing strategy hinges on bringing diverse groups together in close proximity, often for life, people need to get along, or at least figure out how to peacefully co-exist. This doesn't always happen organically. That's why Vienna established Wohnpartner in 2010, with an express mandate to support the city's pillar of social sustainability. Elizabeth Kunze, a Wohnpartner social worker at the Floridsdorf Centre, explained that social health isn't just a cornerstone of the city's housing policy but is also integral to overall public health. "In a large city, there's the risk of increased anonymity and isolation, which are, from a public health perspective, unhealthy and dangerous, especially for older adults," Kunze said. "The work that we do is preventative in that respect." For all the ways it is a positive outlier, Vienna is not immune to the rise of loneliness and isolation among its population. The impact of the COVID-19 pandemic accelerated this trend, precipitating the loss of many "third spaces"—intermediaries between home and work where people can gather and socialize, preferably for free. A key part of Wohnpartner's mandate is to fill that void, gently nudging people toward each other in low-stakes, casual settings.

"One of our core values is self-determination," Kunze told me. "So, a lot of our work is to empower residents to decide for themselves how and when and in what respect they want to become involved." A lot of this means supporting resident initiatives.

Many of Wohnpartner's programs are led or co-led by community volunteers, and they often take on a life of their own. A city-wide renters' choir started in one of Wohnpartner's centres, and several cookbooks have emerged from Wohnpartner's various classes, with recipes reflecting residents' diverse cultural backgrounds. From a social workers' perspective, the impetus behind these programs is often a little bit crafty, aimed at achieving more than one outcome. For instance, at a cooking class for men I attended, the group congregated around a blender, jovially daring each other to gulp down a truly revolting smoothie concoction containing kohlrabi, orange juice and other incongruous ingredients. When I caught the eye of Flo, the group's sociologist coordinator, he told me he intentionally starts the class with a culinary curveball in order to bring the students out of their shells. The gathering is as much, if not more, about providing a social outlet for men, a group at higher risk of isolation, as it is engineered to improve their competency in the kitchen.

Outside of its centres, Wohnpartner also has a role to play in facilitating competent, compassionate conflict resolution when disagreements among neighbours inevitably arise. As in many cities, noise is a continual source of acrimony among tenants in Vienna, particularly in its older municipal buildings. "Even just walking or washing your laundry too late at night or making schnitzel with barking dogs or kids playing in the apartments, the sounds of daily life can be overwhelming for some neighbours," Kunze said. That's something apartment-dwellers the world over can relate to. However, instead of leaving residents to resolve disputes on their own, or to call the police, people living in Vienna's municipal housing can call Wohnpartner. Often, this results in a visit from a social worker to help facilitate a resolution using non-violent communication techniques meant to inspire empathy and compromise instead of confrontation. A common approach on these visits is to have neighbours participate in a "perspective changing" exercise, wherein they go into each other's apartments so they can experience the noise of the offending activities for themselves. Very frequently this is enough to resolve the situation, but in more serious cases, like those arising from a long-standing feud, Wohnpartner can refer residents to a free legal mediation process where neighbours are guided through a formal process to reach a mutual agreement outlining future conduct.

Not only does the process help keep Vienna's social housing peaceful, it allows social workers a window into other areas where they might be of service. "A lot of the time complaints will direct us to an unmet social need," Kunze said. For instance, it may turn out that a senior who can't stand the sound of kids playing in the communal courtyard is estranged from their family and missing their grandchildren. Or they may be increasingly housebound and frustrated by noise as their mobility and health deteriorate. In such cases, Wohnpartner's social workers might take the intervention as an opportunity to invite the senior to tutor kids at the homework club, or facilitate some help with groceries, housework and outings in addition to addressing the initial complaint.

This expertise in bridging generational and cultural differences also comes in handy as Vienna's demographics change. About half of residents in municipal housing are immigrants, said Kunze, and Wohnpartner plays an important role in helping new and established residents to learn to live together, thereby reducing the likelihood of conflict arising from language or cultural barriers. "Our work is to sensitize different cultural groups to each other by sharing common activities like gardening or cooking."

---

Kunze had a rare perspective on how housing policy can not only shape people's lives but society as a whole. She's an American who wound up in Vienna on a Fulbright exchange, and the contrast between the way Viennese and American societies approach housing has been a subject of her studies. Back in Wisconsin where she grew up and started her career, the cost of housing was an "intransigent barrier" her clients, usually working mothers in essential fields like home care or health assistance, faced in every attempt to introduce stability in their lives. It was common for more than half their monthly salary to go toward rent, leaving little left over for their own needs or those of their children, who were disproportionately affected by the burden of housing insecurity. "Too often, kids will change schools or lose all their belongings, and often to enroll in social programs requires a permanent address. So, to be constantly moving and changing addresses due to not being able to afford the rent is a huge risk factor for social well-being." In Vienna, Kunze found evidence to support a theory she'd held for some time. "I started to think if housing can be a risk factor in one social context, it must be a protective factor in other cities like Vienna."

Unless you have moved overseas and experienced alternative ways of living first-hand, it is nearly impossible for the average North American to conceive of housing as a protective factor in our lives, much less the impact this shift in perspective can have on one's sense of home. A great irony of our housing system is that for all our talk of real estate or homeownership as a tried-and-true path to security, many of us spend our lives surfing wave after wave of housing-related anxiety, hoping not to be pulled under. *What if the building I live in gets sold? What if I can't afford my mortgage when it comes up for renewal? What if home prices collapse just as I'm about to retire and I lose all my savings? Crap. I'm losing money on that condo I bought as an investment.*

We are never more than a couple of misfortunes or miscalculations away from being un-homed, unhoused or otherwise unduly burdened by housing. We think of it as normal because it's all we've ever known, and it has rendered us nearly incapable of contemplating any other relationship to housing—even those of us who set out with that very goal in mind.

Even as I was on the ground in Vienna, I found myself continually butting up against my own mental barriers. I couldn't wrap my head around what it must be like to live in a society where most people just don't worry about their housing. For all the international attention Vienna's housing system has attracted, I discovered that the people who live there don't actually think about it all that much, and so they don't talk about it much either. Housing prices are not the topic of dinnertime conversation and a source of constant public consternation. You don't walk into someone's apartment and immediately wonder what the rent is. When I asked people how the city's housing system impacted their lives, many gave me a blank, slightly annoyed, stare. A key benefit of having great housing accessible for most is that it allows housing itself to simply fall off the radar, opening up social, emotional and mental space for literally anything else.

I started to wonder what effect that must have on life for people in Vienna: Was it just a little lighter overall? It certainly seemed so on the day I visited Sonnwendviertel, a newly completed social housing community in Vienna's 10th district built on the site of a former freight train station. It was a Saturday, the first sunny afternoon after a week of unseasonable rain, and it seemed like everyone was out in the big seven-hectare park that acted like a village green. In the middle distance from where I sat on the edge of a stand of mid-rise apartment buildings, kids shrieked with nervous joy as they clambered over the movable parts of an obstacle course. In front of them, toddlers dominated an open field, careening toward soccer balls like kamikaze torpedoes. A group of men hovered at the sidelines, ready to head off any head-on collisions. Beside me, women chatted with each other at café tables spilling out toward the grass from a porous bistro, some of them nursing a baby, and also a beer. Compared to the stressed-out parents I see where I live, it looked like a much easier environment in which to be a parent. Even the streetcar lazily rolling to a stop at the station in the middle of the park radiated a relaxed vibe.

Served by ample transit and with parking only at its peripheries, Sonnwendviertel was largely car-free, connected by a wide pedestrian mall that deposited people on park benches or in the doorways of local businesses like they'd been carried by the current of a lazy river. On the outskirts sat a GB* office—evidence that city staff were active in the neighbourhood to ensure it came together socially. The work seemed to have paid off. Without the constant din of traffic and the hypervigilance it requires, I could pick out snippets of conversation in Arabic, Balkan dialects and English interspersed with Austro-German. Women in hijabs pushed kids in strollers, and couples lounged on the benches, heads resting dreamily in laps, or holding deep, sustained eye contact and quiet conversation.

Eventually I wandered into a multipurpose space at the base of a housing co-op, where I met another Max, this one the 29-year-old co-owner of the coffee stand set up in the corner. Max was uniquely game to chat about the impact Vienna's housing system had on his life. He told me he'd been asked to participate in a panel discussion about that exact topic organized for a delegation from California due to visit the following week, so he was keen to practice his talking points. Max had grown up in the countryside but didn't like the nature of life in a small town where everyone knows your business and judges you for it. He much preferred the balance of living in the city, where you can be known to the people in your neighbourhood but also accepted for your differences. "Here, it's more of a playground of how people can be," he said. "You can kind of experiment with what is acceptable and what's not. And I haven't really found anything that's not acceptable—I mean, except to be very loud, that's kind of an Austrian thing."

Max lived a life that would seem fairly "experimental," even "alternative" to a lot of people, but the city's housing structures made it workable. He'd first discovered the community of Sonnwendviertel before he'd moved in, when he ran a business delivering fresh-baked bread via bicycle. He liked the vibe and the people, and the fact that it was virtually car-free made it safer and easier to do his deliveries. Eventually, he moved into a limited-profit flat just across the big park from his coffee stand. His two flatmates in the three-bedroom were his partners in the business, which they ran co-operatively as a social enterprise. Their flat was on the small side, only 775 square feet, but the building had a sauna and a rooftop garden and a big room you could book for parties. The rent was just €650 a month, total, (about C$1,000), which was what really let the coffee business thrive. The low cost of living meant the roommates had lots of resources, both temporal and financial, to put into the business, which was also partially subsidized by the housing co-op that ran the building where it operated. The residents there were mostly artists and musicians who saw the value of having a community gathering space on the ground floor, and the coffee stand was the perfect magnet to draw people in. "The point is not really to make money," Max said, adding he'd been cautioned to downplay that aspect in his upcoming speech to the Californians, lest it confuse or even offend an American audience.

Just then a small rush hit the shop and I could see the real value of the business as a social incubator. Two men spoke in English in the corner with such familiarity I was surprised when they ended their conversation with a "nice to meet you." A young mother wandered in and absent-mindedly let her toddler slip from her hip without breaking her gaze from the pastry case. Another young woman, perhaps in her late 20s or early 30s, sat alone at a table in the window, reading an actual physical newspaper and sipping a cappuccino. It suddenly dawned on me then that I'd barely seen anyone pull out a smartphone all day—people in Sonnwendviertel seemed exceptionally committed to making space for in-person connection to organically occur. As if on cue, someone from a workshop winding down in the back of the room came over and offered me a bowl of leftover cream soup that, though lukewarm, was delicious. The skeptic in me was still looking for downsides to Vienna's housing system, and maybe there are some that I didn't see. But on this day in this place, it really did seem fairly utopic.

However, by the time Max finished up with the rush, another question had sprung to mind: In a place where owning a house isn't perceived as the only path to stability and security, where it isn't portrayed as the epitome of adulthood or the highest form of proof you are a productive, morally upstanding citizen, what arises to take its place? In other words, what exactly is everyone in Vienna striving for if not owning a home of their own?

Max paused at the espresso machine, his eyes trained on the coffee grounds. After a beat, the corner of his mouth curled into a smirk as he pulled his slim shoulders into a staccato shrug.

"Fulfillment."

8

# BERLIN: A STREET FIGHT FOR THE CITY

The coolest apartment in the world sits atop an old bookbinding factory in central Berlin, behind a large metal door with a faded mural of a couple of city rats having a party. At least I think that's what they are. I'm still contemplating the image and trying to catch my breath after hoofing it up six flights of stairs when the door swings open to reveal an interior that looks like a design collab between Frank Lloyd Wright and Willy Wonka. Floor-to-ceiling windows bathe the place in natural light, to the delight of several dozen thriving plants wound around a crosshatch of exposed beams, industrial pipe and reclaimed wrought-iron banisters. These form the undercarriage of a layer cake of living spaces that spirals ever upwards like a human-scale cat tree. Up a central staircase of weathered wood, a stack of mezzanines strategically fold over one another to form little nooks and loft-like spaces variously outfitted as lounges or libraries. Behind them, often hidden from view, are sleeping quarters accessed through secret doors, screened in by grids of old, clouded windows or found by scaling a ladder and slipping into a pocket between two floors. It's worthy of a spread in an architectural magazine: equal parts whimsical, practical, elegant and cozy, all culminating in a showstopper of a rooftop patio boasting panoramic views of what,

I swear, is all of Berlin. I've never been one for having a lot of roommates, but in a place like this I can see how it could work. The creative design has been intentionally applied to allow for a gentle separation between public and private—essential considering this is home to 11 people, soon to be 12.

In the open-concept kitchen on the main floor, Dorna, an American expat with cropped strawberry waves, thick, black-rimmed glasses and a big round belly holding a baby who will be born any day now, is making a salad next to her partner, Sanja. "Come in" she beckons, directing my attention toward some of the less obvious features of the flat. She plops the salad bowl down on the countertop and punches a few buttons on a control panel concealed beneath its ledge. Some numbers appear on the tiles in front of the bowl, a reading from the built-in digital weight scale. "Notice nothing touches the floor?" I look down. Everything from the kitchen cabinets to that central staircase appears to be levitating. All of this is the work of Peter, Dorna and Sanja's septuagenarian flatmate, one of a handful of original tenants in the building who saw potential in a derelict factory decades ago and painstakingly transformed it into a unique and beautiful home.

The metamorphosis is an apt metaphor for Berlin as a whole.

If you were to cast a movie starring famous capital cities, Berlin would clinch the role of the comeback kid. Its current status as a hip global hotspot renowned for its nightlife, street life and eclectic urban character was not at all guaranteed given its more than tumultuous history. Berlin's most dubious distinction, of course, is as the seat of power for the Nazis during the 1930s and '40s and the central command post for the worst atrocities of the Second World War. As such, it was brutally, repeatedly bombed by Allied forces during the war, with much of its infrastructure and housing stock left in ruins. But it's actually the legacy of an entirely different conflict that has had the biggest impact on how Berliners live today.

After the fall of the Nazis and the end of Second World War, control of the city was carved up between the Allied forces, with the French, British and Americans jointly controlling the west side while the Soviets presided over the east. As the relationship between the Western allies and the Soviets soured in the post-war years, Berlin became the very emblem of the Cold War: a single city split into two countries and played as a pawn in an ideological skirmish between capitalist Western democracies and the Communist autocracies of the Soviet Union. In 1961, the political and economic division was made physical with the construction of the Berlin Wall, a hulking monument meant to stem the exodus of East Berliners fleeing to the West by essentially locking them in.

I was in second grade when the Berlin Wall came down in 1989, so I have only the vaguest recollection of something major happening in the news at the time. But for Berliners my age and beyond, it is impossible to overstate the impact the city's division and subsequent reunification has had on their concept of home and, in particular, what it means to "own" one's home.

When the wall came down, Berlin was all but abandoned as people flooded out from under the Iron Curtain seeking the political and economic freedom promised on the other side. Depopulation remained a huge concern throughout the 1990s as the city struggled to resuscitate its neglected infrastructure, jumpstart its economy and reconcile issues like duplicate transit systems and power grids that were both costly and confusing. Still, there were high hopes that Berlin would return to its former glory as a true capital city, not only of the newly reunified Germany but of Europe as a whole. Plans were set in motion to turn the city into a world-class cultural destination on par with

Paris and Vienna. Hefty cash injections promised to restore its museums, resurrect its great symphonies and build new and bold monuments atoning for its sins. By the early 2000s all of this was in doubt. Berlin remained underpopulated, economically crippled and rocked by leadership scandals alleging fiscal mismanagement and corruption. At one point the city was so broke it resorted to turning off its stately water fountains in order to save money.

A significant upside to all this, however, was that it kept the rents extremely cheap.

"For a very long time the landlords were like 'give us anything, it's better than it just being empty,'" Dorna told me back in her flat in the district of Kreuzberg. It was Dorna who defined home as a safe place to experiment at the beginning of this book, and she's far from the only Berliner I met who made that connection. Freedom to experiment with the shape, expression and management of their households, their housing and the use of public space has become a deeply held value among Berliners, a direct legacy of the citizen action that led to the end of the Cold War. As the scholar Quill R. Kukla writes, "We are used to hearing about the 'fall' of the Berlin Wall, it did not fall; it was dismantled by angry citizens who wanted to control their own mobility and who were insisting on their right of access to the *whole* city." This attitude persists today. Newcomers to Berlin are often initiated into a culture of almost mandatory participation in continually shaping and reshaping the city.

Rebuilding Berlin after the wall did not come with a well-financed, centralized housing plan like Vienna's. With the economy in shambles and the city's government embroiled in chaos, it was everyday citizens who took the lead on reconstruction, repurposing abandoned buildings and adapting redundant infrastructure to their needs. This is how Berlin came to be a modern mecca for misfits and fertile ground for flourishing subcultures.

Artists, anarchists, eccentrics, inventors, swingers, punks, ravers, LGBTQ2+ folks, DJs, immigrants and refugees—anyone whose identity put them outside the mainstream could find in the "broken" city a space to build community and carve out a safe haven. Over time, this informed the city's physical form and its decidedly DIY aesthetic. Imposing brutalist facades of Nazi-era buildings became canvases for street art preaching values of tolerance, inclusivity and anti-fascist, anti-capitalist rhetoric. Old Soviet power plants were transformed into world-renowned nightclubs showcasing the city's creative economy. With their bare hands, people turned defunct factories, dilapidated warehouses and bombed-out tenements into housing for every kind of domestic configuration, from nuclear families to queer feminist art collectives to radical anarchist communes with dozens of residents.

It's this evolution that is largely responsible for Berlin's story ultimately arriving at success. Today, the city is a shining star on the world stage despite the lingering odds against it. Compared to other cities of its calibre, Berlin is still quite poor. It doesn't boast extensive lists of corporate head offices that provide high-paying jobs for locals, and it hasn't, until recently, been a magnet for global capital. Berlin's primary draw is a cool factor it owes almost exclusively to the sweat equity, vision and commitment of its citizens. And it's this that Berliners fear is under threat as the city contends with a wicked housing crisis. Despite the strong sense of ownership citizens feel toward their city, few own any of it in the legal sense. Berlin is a city of tenants, and as its popularity has risen, so too have the rents.

By the mid-2000s, word was out about Berlin's burgeoning status as an ultra-hip city where you could easily live well as a working artist or simply working part-time. More people started to arrive. The government, slow to catch on to the city's shifting fortunes, was reluctant to take action on housing. Thus, it was poorly equipped to handle the influx of global capital and international investors who inevitably swooped in to snap up real estate in what they saw as an up-and-coming market. Since the early 2010s, market rents have been driven far beyond what typical Berliners can afford, trapping the city in residential gridlock. Anyone lucky enough to have secured a sweetheart deal on a rent-controlled apartment decades ago is refusing to move unless they absolutely have to. This has led to a situation not dissimilar to the one playing out in North America, where there's a generational divide. Older people who could or should be downsizing and freeing up space for a new generation are holding tight in their homes while growing families cram into expensive, cramped apartments meant for young wealthy singles. Meanwhile, tenant groups allege the concentration of corporate landlords in Berlin is increasingly putting renters at risk. They believe faceless monoliths are taking advantage of loopholes in tenancy laws to unfairly increase rents, evict tenants or force them out by withholding maintenance or cutting the heat.

By the time Dorna and Sanja, originally from Singen, a city in southwest Germany, moved to Berlin in 2017, the city's housing crisis was already in full swing. It took several months for them to find two rooms in a different shared flat—this one with nine roommates in all. This wasn't a problem. Dorna told me they enjoyed living in a large community. Even though she found the multi-hour meetings held each week to keep things running smoothly a bit excessive at first, she learned a lot about the interpersonal skills required for collective living. But the couple eventually ran into a roadblock they couldn't negotiate.

In a lot of ways, Berlin is a bit of a time capsule. Many businesses only take cash, Wi-Fi is definitely not a given and, from a North American perspective, at least, there's an alarming prevalence of people still smoking. Indoors. When Dorna became pregnant, her American sensibilities and concern for her baby's health collided with the habits of a few of her flatmates and their accepted German mores. "Germany has this weird cultural thing of, like, in the leftist scene, smoking is like a human right," she explained. At first, they struck a deal to limit smoking to the evenings, after Dorna was in bed. But as her pregnancy progressed she realized reaching an acceptable compromise with people who considered smoking to be part of their identity "just wasn't going to work."

In 2023, the couple was thrust into a frantic home hunt in a city whose housing stock was now also facing pressure from an influx of well-heeled digital nomads freed from any physical ties by the pandemic. Dorna and Sanja applied for more than 300 places and received an invite to view just 15. Ultimately, they were offered none. Finally, just a few weeks before their due date, they caught a break when a room opened up in the Wonka-esque flat just across the hall from where they already lived. Not only was it gorgeous and smoke-free, it was already home to two children. In fact, their kid would be the eighth to grow up in the apartment—if they were allowed to stay that long. Another layer of Berlin's housing crisis is that many of the spaces restored by citizens after the Cold War, such as the old bookbinding factory, are not protected by Germany's tenancy laws. With their multi-decade leases now coming due, many converted flats, including all the ones in Dorna and Sanja's building, were facing big rent hikes as new owners sought to capitalize on their increasing value.

The situation illustrates an important question at the heart of Berlin's response to its housing crisis. In a building—in a city—that is only habitable, much less valuable, because of the physical labour and emotional investment of its residents, whose claim to ownership should the law protect?

---

Back in 2021, a cluster of headlines coming out of Berlin caught my attention. The city had just passed a referendum calling on its government to expropriate—that is, nationalize—240,000 apartments that were owned by corporate landlords, mostly international REITs. The Deutsche Wohnen & Co. Expropriation, or DWE, initiative, which nods to one of the largest corporate landlords, Deutsche Wohnen, won nearly 60 percent of the popular vote, more than any political party in that year's state election. The referendum, it was said, was the real winner that day. Critics were quick to point out this wasn't quite the coup for affordable housing that activists all over the world were celebrating. The referendum wasn't legally binding, they noted, and the government that emerged was a right-leaning coalition of parties that had vowed not to act on the referendum results. Still. The fact that Berliners were organized enough to get a referendum on the ballot, much less get it to *pass,* seemed significant to me. I couldn't imagine any city in North America coordinating enough sustained effort to put the plight of renters front and centre in an election, much less galvanize a majority to vote in their favour. Whether the referendum was legally binding or not, I wanted to find out how Berliners managed to build a movement so steadfast and unwavering in its support for housing reform, and to see what lessons, if any, we could apply to our own housing crisis. What was it, I wondered, that made Berlin's tenant movement so powerful? Especially when, by comparison, escalating housing costs in North America are often met with anger but seldom citizen action.

Partly, it's a numbers game. Tenants account for at least 80 percent of Berliners, making the rising cost of rent an issue that touches almost everyone, at every stage of life. However, that alone doesn't explain the successes of its tenants' movement. In cities like New York, Los Angeles, San Francisco and Miami, renters account for between 60 percent and 70 percent of the population. The rate is generally somewhat lower in Canada, but renters still make up a solid majority in Montreal and Vancouver and are nearly at par with owners in Toronto, and yet those cities haven't seen anywhere near the organization of tenants that is the norm in cities like Berlin. Lisa Vollmer, a housing activist and researcher who has studied tenant movements, told me Berlin definitely owes some of its success in the housing fight to its unique history. "Berlin has a long tradition of protests," she told me. "So there's some resources that a movement can use, physical spaces to meet, knowledge about organizing political campaigns and stuff like that." There is also the fact that Germans in general simply have a much higher expectation of the state when it comes to providing basic necessities like housing.

One lingering remnant of Germany's politically divided past is that many people have living memory of growing up in a Communist country where state-funded housing for all was the norm. While there were many downsides to living under Soviet rule—restrictions on movement and free speech, and living under constant surveillance, just to name a few—affordable housing was a strong point. According to Vollmer, some households spent as little as 3 percent of their income on housing. It wasn't anything fancy, that's for sure, but it kept ideas of private homeownership as well as class divisions related to housing from taking hold in East German society. Some former East Germans I spoke to had downright fond memories of growing up in state-funded housing where neighbours cared for one another in strong, close-knit communities. But even Germans who grew up in the West are accustomed to much more state involvement in housing than is typically expected in North America, Vollmer added. "After the Second World War, the Western State always intervened in the market to more or lesser degrees," she said. "We have an expectancy of the state to do this stuff."

So does this mean societies without a history of Communist rule, substantial public protest and a wide-reaching social safety net are out of luck when it comes to fighting against the scourge of financialized housing? Not necessarily. Vollmer said although each city she's studied has its own approach to housing activism, there are a few rules of thumb she believes can be effective in any cultural context. While it's common in North America for housing movements to be led by policy experts or professional organizations, Vollmer said she found those most impacted by housing issues often do a better job at taking the lead. "You have to find affected communities that are suffering from whatever absurd thing the housing system is doing and then organize together with them," she said. "Usually the best analysis of the problem—and the best analysis of capitalism—comes from the regular tenant, from the regular neighbour. They understand the problem." Another critical point? "Also, it helps to pick a fight that you have at least some chance of winning."

Coming from a city where any form of rent control is considered deeply controversial, I found it astonishing that so many Berliners truly thought convincing the government to nationalize nearly a quarter-million housing units owned by corporate behemoths was a fight they might actually win. Even in the context of all of Berlin's history, it seemed like a stretch. That is, until I learned about the work Berlin's housing activists had been doing for over a decade before the headline-grabbing referendum. The movement to expropriate wasn't just some radical one-off attempt at getting the government's attention; it was a calculated step in a highly organized continuum of campaigns for housing reform that, though not without setbacks, had been progressively racking up wins.

Since 2011, tenant groups in Berlin have fought for, and won, a years-long rent freeze on all social housing in the city; convinced the government to buy back tens of thousands of units of publicly funded social housing it had previously sold to corporate owners; and successfully pressured Berlin's state government to implement a five-year, city-wide rent cap on all units built before 2014, accounting for about 90 percent of the city's rental stock. That last move suffered a blow when a court overturned the rent cap on a technicality, determining tenant legislation was the jurisdiction of the federal government, and not the state. But rather than give up, activists channelled the resulting ire among Berliners into support for the expropriation initiative. When the DWE referendum passed with a decisive victory in 2021, Berlin's state government convened an expert panel to investigate whether expropriation was even legal, a move many activists saw as a delay tactic. In 2023 the panel released its findings overwhelmingly in support of the tenants. It found that articles in the German constitution that allow for essential resources, such as roads and land, to be nationalized for the benefit of the "common good" can also apply to housing. What's more, it found expropriation to be an appropriate and prudent way to deal with the city's growing housing crisis. As of 2025, a new, legally binding version of the referendum was in the works thanks to a crowdfunding campaign that raised enough money for organizers to hire their own legal team.

Getting to that point has taken a mammoth effort. It required coordination among every tenants' union in the city (there are dozens), plus the support of hundreds of thousands of regular Berliners, many of whom were not politically active and weren't particularly interested in becoming so. It took years of highly organized and regimented meetings, striking committees and subcommittees, and thousands of volunteer hours poured into researching, organizing and strategizing. But before all of that, this movement and its incredible momentum started just like Vollmer said, with the simple act of neighbours talking to each other about the fact that the rent was too damn high and deciding to do something about it.

---

Not far from Dorna and Sanja's collective home in the centre of Kreuzberg sits an area known as Kottbusser Tor, Kotti for short. From an urban design perspective, there's not much in the built form to foster a sense of community—just the opposite. The centre of Kotti is a massive roundabout (the "tor," or *tour*, in Kottbusser Tor) where a constant stream of cars slices the area into four distinct quadrants and elevated U-Bahn tracks cut an imposing figure overhead. Compared to some of Berlin's other neighbourhoods, or even other parts of Kreuzberg, which feature leafy parks, narrow cobbled streets and pedestrian-friendly plazas, Kotti's narrow sidewalks, roaring traffic and distinct lack of green space don't exactly invite people to linger, and yet they do. Turkish cafés, smoke shops, greengrocers and electronics kiosks lining the sliver of pavement beside the road are busy with patrons, many of whom are more than mere passing acquaintances. Kotti residents seem to really *know* each other in a way that defies an urban environment clearly engineered for anonymity. As I chatted with people on the street, our conversations were regularly interrupted by hugs, handshakes and brief, enthusiastic catch-ups between passersby. Kotti wasn't always this way.

During the Cold War, Kreuzberg sat at the outer reaches of West Berlin, a peninsula of sorts pinned up against the wall and surrounded by Soviet territory on three sides. Its proximity to the armed guards and glaring searchlights of the "death strip," the space between the East and West sides, made the area an undesirable outpost where the most marginalized Berliners were all but banished. Turkish migrants, who began arriving in the 1970s and '80s at the behest of a West Berlin government seeking a source of cheap labour, were sent to the area, congregating in the unremarkable utilitarian high-rises ringing Kottbusser Tor. The buildings, constructed by the Berlin government as social housing, became symbolic of the neglected neighbourhood, which was a hotbed for gang activity and crime. When the wall was dismantled the all-but-forgotten area on the fringes of the city became prime real estate, sitting at the centre of the newly reunified Berlin. So, when the government started selling off its public housing at fire-sale prices during the 1990s, Kotti was one of the first developments to go. It wasn't long before the rents started to rise, pushing the poorest households out of the area and once again to the fringes of the new Berlin. But others managed to hold on, and those that did dug in for a fight.

Erçan Yasaroglu, a café owner, told me he had already fled a military coup in Turkey and survived an invasion in Lebanon before landing in Kreuzberg in 1982. The district was where he married, had his children and rebuilt his life from scratch. He worked as a social worker before starting his business, Kaffe Kotti, overlooking the tor, which served the dual purpose of deterring crime by putting more action on the street and providing a de facto living room for the high-density neighbourhood. The Turkish community in Kotti may not have physically built the buildings in which they lived, Erçan told me, but they'd built everything else that made the place desirable to real estate investors. They ran the businesses that brought the streets to life; they'd fought to clean up the neighbourhood, fought for better schools and cleaner water; they'd liaised with the police to get crime under control. They had an ownership stake in Kotti, and they weren't about to give it up to some faceless corporation looking to make a bigger buck. "It's a home and I don't want to leave my home," Erçan told me, recalling how he felt at the time.

By the 2000s, a different kind of resident had started to move in, taking the place of the poorer families who'd been pushed out. These newcomers, mostly Germans or wealthier immigrants, had been priced out of other parts of the city and found Kotti to be more affordable, at least at first. But as the rents continued to rise, they also started feeling squeezed. This is where Kotti's story diverges from that of so many other places facing gentrification, because it managed to eschew the silent but enduring rift that frequently emerges between established residents—usually lower-income immigrant groups—and the often whiter, wealthier new arrivals. It would have been so easy for people like Erçan to look at newcomers with suspicion and disdain, to blame them for changing the neighbourhood and driving people out. But that's not what happened. Instead of adversaries they saw allies. "We were all having the same problem, we were all having the rent issues," Erçan said. And so they started talking to each other about it. Up to that point, life in Kotti's apartment buildings was distant and impersonal. Residents told me most people didn't know their neighbours, but the common struggle they faced came to be an icebreaker. What became a cohesive and coordinated effort to fight the rising rents literally started with casual conversations in the elevator—"Hey, I just got another rent increase, how about you?" Slowly, it became a little more formal: knocking on doors; handing out fliers; holding meetings in the courtyard to compare notes on interactions with their landlords. One day, someone invited a lawyer who looked over eviction notices and helped people plan strategies to push back.

Eventually, the neighbours formed an official tenants' group, Kotti & Co., and approached the government to formally ask for help. When they were told that there was nothing elected officials could do, no laws on the books that protected the tenants, the next step became clear. "Well then, we have to change the law," Ulrike Hamann, a founding member of Kotti & Co., recalled. To do that, Kotti & Co. turned to the tried-and-true tactics that had served Berliners so well for decades: They organized an occupation.

---

*Gecekondu* is a Turkish word, meaning "put up overnight," used to describe the kind of hastily built shanties you might find in a slum. In Turkey, gecekondus (pronounced geh-che-con-doo) are a popular housing option for the poor, as there's a law that prevents structures built after dusk and completed before dawn from being torn down. With its cultural significance and symbolic importance, a gecekondu seemed like the perfect structure to shelter Kotti residents as they waited for the government to come to the table. In 2012, a little white building with a slanted roof made of corrugated plastic, recycled pallets and reclaimed windows went up on the southern corner of the tor. Kotti residents filled it night and day—and had quite a nice time doing it. You might think a protest for something as consequential as the human right to housing would take on a serious, even angry tone, but the mood in the gecekondu was anything but dour. In a documentary I watched about the occupation, the gecekondu had the air of a community clubhouse. People sat and drank tea and chatted while sitting vigil. Passersby popped in to ask what all the fuss was about and were met with friendly banter and an invitation to join the cause. People stopped by with food and gifts for the occupiers, or offered to pick up groceries and run errands for the people on shift. Many of the close ties I witnessed between people I met in Kotti were forged in the gecekondu during the occupation, when neighbours who'd never spoken to each other before made real and lasting friendships that cut across cultural, linguistic and religious lines. The growing sense of community made it seem pleasant, if not downright fun, to be involved in protest. It was also effective.

In the fall of 2012, after six straight months of occupying the gecekondu 24/7, the Berlin State Senate agreed to a conference with Kotti & Co., the outcome of which was the rent freeze on all social housing units across Berlin. But Kotti residents wanted more. Part of the deal when Berlin sold off these apartments was that there was a time limit on their designation as social housing. After a few years they would become just regular apartments, subject to the market. Kotti & Co. wanted to ensure their homes would remain affordable forever, meaning they would have to be removed from the market entirely. For the next nine years they continued to meet in the gecekondu, coming up with ways to continually exert pressure on the government to respond to their demands. In 2020, their patience paid off. Berlin's government bought 15,000 Kotti apartments back from private owners and put them under government control. It was a massive victory for tenant rights that showed the city what could be achieved with little more than persistence, positivity and community cohesion. Watching closely were the DWE organizers, who made note of Kotti's successes, as well as its mistakes.

As much as Kotti's win was celebrated, it also became a source of scandal due to the cost of reacquiring the buildings. In 2004, during a time of extreme financial and political vulnerability, Berlin's government sold an entire state-owned housing company, GSW, to a "consortium of private investors led by Goldman Sachs and Cerberus," according to an article in *Broadview* magazine. The portfolio of 65,000 homes, including the Kotti flats, fetched a price of €405 million, a pittance compared to what they were worth when the government bought them back in 2020 at the current market price. According to Hamann, the Berlin Senate paid €2.4 billion to reclaim just 15,000 of the units originally built as social housing using public and privately donated funds. Many Berliners found this egregious, and the public outcry served as a cautionary tale for the expropriation campaign to come.

As such, the details of the DWE referendum propose that any landlord with more than 3,000 units in their portfolio should be forced to sell them back to the state at a fair, though below market, price. They argue that the corporate owners have made their initial investments back many times over and have had long enough to profiteer off the backs of Berliners. Since most of the flats are already occupied, they have the potential to be financially self-sustaining. Rents can be put toward maintenance of the properties, with a portion devoted to paying back the government for the purchase over time. The DWE also plans to ensure expropriated homes will be administered by a public entity and managed primarily by tenants rather than by the government, thus ensuring they won't be sold again in future as political and economic climates shift.

This all adds up to a complex proposition, and not one easily conveyed to the general public, which makes it all the more impressive that the DWE campaign managed to engage almost the entire city by prioritizing some relatively basic concepts: inclusivity, joy, and, in true Berlin style, experimentation.

---

In the days and weeks leading up to voting day in 2021, Berliners told me you could barely catch a subway or cross the street without running into DWE campaigners in their signature purple vests, waving flags, holding banners and even sporting complementary yellow N-95 masks. But by far the most enduring images of the time are of a roving band of crop-top wearing, pom-pom shaking, hooting, hollering, chanting cheerleaders led, in part, by a woman named Berta Del Ben.

When I met Del Ben at a quaint Italian café in Kreuzberg, she was dressed in the ultra-casual style common in Berlin: loose jeans, beat-up trainers, not a stitch of makeup, brown hair pulled back in a low ponytail and a bike helmet tucked under one arm. She was far from the stereotypical image of a perfectly made-up cheerleader, but the more we talked, I could see that she had some things in common with that icon of American pop culture. Del Ben had a rare quality that can be such a difference maker when it comes to rallying people for a cause. She was light and funny, endlessly energetic, as well as deeply knowledgeable and super serious about the issue at hand. I found her inspiring.

Del Ben told me she'd been very politically active as a young student in her native Italy, but had burned out a bit by the time she moved to Berlin a decade earlier. So when she faced a €400-a-month rent hike "for nothing" six months after moving into the first flat she'd rented in the city—one owned by Vonovia, another REIT targeted by the DWE—she and her roommates simply parted ways and moved on. "We were not a strong community between us," she told me. When the pandemic hit, Del Ben, an actor and theatre professional, found herself out of work. With some time on her hands, she was intrigued by the growing referendum movement she saw taking over Berlin social media. When the campaign put out a call specifically looking to recruit people like her, migrants who were *ineligible* to vote in the upcoming referendum, she answered.

A big hurdle the campaign faced early on was that only German citizens could sign a required petition to get the referendum on the books, and only Germans could vote in the state election to support it. That meant almost a quarter of Berliners like Del Ben who didn't hold a German passport had no voting rights on an issue that affected them in the most intimate aspect of their lives. But that didn't mean they couldn't lend their support in other ways, and the organizers knew it. "I came in because there was a welcoming space for me," said Del Ben, who soon found many places to apply her talents to the cause. As a polyglot, she took on a role as a translator, both linguistically and culturally, between the German-dominated DWE organizers and the legions of non-German Berliners who wanted to get involved but didn't know how.

To harness the energy among expats and migrants, Del Ben helped organize a chapter of Right to the City, an international network of civil society and local government groups working to keep cities diverse and inclusive, particularly for marginalized groups. In Berlin, Right to the City wound up being the English-speaking working group aligned with the DWE campaign where non-German Berliners received an education in the particularities of the city's specific brand of political activism, but also brainstormed how they could be effective allies. Every idea, no matter how bizarre or how silly it might have seemed, was seriously considered. "We started with 'yes, we'll do it,'" Del Ben said, citing a version of the old adage "nothing ventured, nothing gained." Out of this process the idea for the cheerleaders emerged. "We reflected on the fact that, okay, we can't sign but we can scream. So let's scream."

It is not hyperbole to say this was a stroke of genius perfectly timed for the moment. Cheerleading was in the zeitgeist at the time, with a popular Netflix show about an elite Texas squad in everyone's pandemic watchlist, but Berlin's spin on the concept was also a cheeky nod to a history of "radical cheerleading" in protest movements throughout the late 20th century. Plus, the cheerleaders themselves embodied everything about the city the DWE campaign sought to protect. They were international, they were gender diverse, they were queer, creative, quirky and super DIY. They were a massive hit. As the campaign ramped up, the squad often led the evening news and regularly graced the front pages of the papers. They performed at some of Berlin's legendary nightclubs at the invitation of famous DJs who had joined the campaign. They rode a big yellow bus out the suburbs to make sure their message reached beyond the city's core. With a little bit of light twerking and catchy chants like "Hear our voice/Loud and clear/This is our city so we keep it cheap and queer!" they pulled off a feat the highest-paid political strategists in the world would die for. They made it seem cool, fun, maybe even a little sexy to get involved with politics. "The campaign exploded in that time," Del Ben told me. Literally hundreds of new people showed up to meetings every week to join in the effort. When they did, organizers were ready to put them to work with small actionable tasks that anyone could do, like heading out for an hour with a friend to collect some signatures. "The important thing was having a very complex project, but a very simple thing to do," Del Ben said. Equally important was keeping the mood light. The DWE was a very serious initiative aimed at a serious issue, but, as in Kotti, people found that their involvement in activism also offered a welcome chance to meet their neighbours and make some friends. "It's a fight but it's also about community, it's about being happy, it's about being together," Del Ben said. It was also about impressing upon Berliners, whether they had voting rights or not, that the city was for *them*, not for corporations that happened to possess some property deeds.

At its core, this is what expropriation is all about. It's a way to set in law the ownership Berliners already feel for their city and demonstrate with their actions. And it's an idea that has proven to be somewhat contagious. Since the referendum, campaigns to reclaim housing from the private market in some form have popped up in other cities such as Hamburg, Lisbon and parts of Spain. Meanwhile in Berlin, activists are still at work figuring out the next step for the DWE and figuring out how the movement can help people like Dorna and Sanja, whose commercial leases are trickier to protect. The gecekondu still stands as a symbol of resistance and a meeting place for further tenant action. Though housing issues are complex, requiring different approaches tailored to specific legal, political and economic conditions, my biggest takeaway from Berlin is that no matter the constraints, progress tends to start from the same place. For real change to happen, people have to *believe* that they have a right to the place they call home. They have to *believe* that the housing problems they face can be solved, even if all the solutions haven't been identified. In the end, that may very well be the biggest victory the campaign for expropriation has scored so far. "It's giving hope that it's possible to change things and it's possible to do it together," said Del Ben. No matter the eventual outcome, "Berlin can still be a place where we try."

# 9

# HARARE: HEADS HELD HIGH

Tendai wants a white kitchen. A white bathroom too. Soft-spoken, perhaps a little shy or maybe just suspicious of the foreigner in her midst, Tendai, a 45-year-old single mother of three adult children, comes alive as she walks through the partial footprint of what will one day be her dream home.

Over here will be the kitchen with raised cabinets and a built-in cooktop. White tiles will cover the floor and flow all the way up the walls, creating a clean, modern feel. It'll be the same in the bathroom, which will have a big bathtub with a view out the window and the toilet and a full-length mirror along the opposite wall. In a bid to save space and time through clever design, Tendai's opting to put a vanity in the corridor outside the bathroom; that way, she and her family can get ready in the morning without having to compete for space. Down the hall on the right is one of the bedrooms, with bare brick walls awaiting plaster and then a coat of cobalt-blue paint. Tendai hasn't decided on the colour scheme for the second bedroom just yet, but she's got some time to think on it. Right now it's just a concrete pad piled with pallets of red brick that will one day form the walls. The foundations for the dining/living room as well as her own bedroom and a second toilet room haven't been laid yet, but she's hopeful at least the frame of the house will be completed by the end of the year.

When it's all finished, this three-bedroom, detached bungalow will be something any new homeowner would be proud of. For Tendai, it will be an especially significant achievement, because she won't be upgrading from a rental apartment or a starter condo; she'll be trading in a literal shanty for a well-built family home she can pass down to her children.

If you Google "Dzivarasekwa," Tendai's community on the western edge of Harare, Zimbabwe, you'll see it referred to as a "suburb," or sometimes a "high-density residential area." Offline, however, it's described using entirely different language, as an "informal settlement" in official capacities, or more commonly, a slum—a word I would come to appreciate in new and nuanced terms throughout my time in Zimbabwe. Home to hundreds of thousands of the poorest residents in one of the poorest countries in the world, Dzivarasekwa's visual landscape is one of potholed dirt roads bisecting blocks of single-level structures as far as the eye can see. But slowly, parts of it are coming to resemble a middle-class suburb that wouldn't be entirely out of place in middle America. What's really impressive is that it's happening without any of the components we've been taught to think of as essential in solving a housing crisis, and in particular in providing more housing for the poor. There are no commercial developers or investments from private equity. No mortgages or bank loans. Most people in Tendai's position don't even have bank accounts. There are no handouts from foreign charities with white-saviour agendas, and there's been no major funding committed by the city or any other level of government for public or social housing. This is the work of a grassroots effort spearheaded and financed by the slum dwellers themselves.

---

Here's a little known fact about slums: As far as home goes, they have a lot going for them. If we think about some of the vital elements of home like belonging, familiarity, place and need, slums make a better home in many respects than your average North American neighbourhood. Many people who grow up in slums, defined by the United Nations as places that lack either clean water, sanitation, sufficient living space, durable housing or security of tenure, feel fiercely attached to and protective of their communities, where looking out for one another is a way of life. From Dolly Parton to Bob Marley to Brazilian soccer legend Pelé, the world is full of celebrities who grew up in communities without running water or electricity, but where cultural pursuits like music and sport fortified their spirits, honed their talents and set them on a path to superstardom. Slums are also hotbeds of entrepreneurship and innovation. Because they are often unable to access traditional employment and are largely ignored by regulators, slum dwellers specialize in launching businesses that cater to the community's needs—making bricks, giving haircuts, selling clothes or mobile airtime, sorting waste and recycling, doing renovations or building yet more shanties for the continuous stream of new arrivals. In many ways, these organically occurring, hyperlocal economies are exactly the sort of thing urban planners in more affluent areas try to emulate with trendy concepts such as 15-minute cities (the idea that communities should be planned so that people can access all their daily needs within a 15-minute walk from their house).

What slums lack—and this is, of course, the major issue—are havens in the form of safe, good-quality housing and the necessary infrastructure to support the health and safety of their inhabitants. In such places, people use whatever materials they can access to create rudimentary shelters that often become a defining local aesthetic. In India, corrugated metal shacks line the banks of polluted rivers around major cities; in Turkey, gecekondus made of concrete blocks cascade up hillsides. On the outskirts of Harare, simple rectangular structures about the size of a garden shed pop up in cornfields like companion crops.

Known locally as "cabins," they're so prevalent in Zimbabwe that you can buy premade timber versions on the side of the highway, ready to load onto a flatbed and set down next to the last family who, with nowhere else to go, figured their best option was to do the exact same thing. Cabins are meant to be a shelter stopgap on the way to something better, but it's not uncommon for people to live in them for decades, generations even, upgrading to sturdier materials over time. Tendai's is a typical example. The original timber cabin her family lived in when they arrived in Dzivarasekwa 13 years ago is now weathered beyond recognition, covered in shredded plastic and leaning precariously to one side. Despite the threat of imminent collapse, the building is still used as sleeping quarters for Tendai's adult son as well as storage for the building materials Tendai's been stockpiling for the new house under construction a few metres away. Beside it sits a newer cabin, this one made of brick, covered in creamy yellow plaster and divided into two halves. Tendai and her 18-year-old daughter live on one side, miraculously fitting a makeshift kitchen, seating area and bedroom into a space that's *maybe* 100 square feet. The other half is rented out to another family.

Like Tendai, most people living in Harare's slums improve their housing with every chance they get. They build extensions on their cabins and add roofs made of corrugated metal or install real glass windows with vibrant, coloured trim. They affix satellite dishes and solar lights. They dig wells for groundwater and plant maize and kale in neat rows around the edges, often selling what they don't eat. Despite their obvious poverty, many slums become well-organized, even cheerful-looking villages intentionally built to make an objectively bad housing situation as good as it possibly can be. So it's heartbreaking when, almost inevitably, the results of all this effort get swept away.

Zimbabwe, like much of the rest of the world, has traditionally met the persistent problem of visible urban poverty with a bulldozer. Raids on informal settlements are so common throughout Southern Africa that one community in neighbouring Zambia, where I also travelled, was actually called Chaisa, meaning "it is coming" in Bemba, one of the local languages. This is the warning neighbours would shout to each other when the police inevitably showed up in the middle of the night, sending people scattering into the dark. But it's not just the Global South that has a problem with slums, or a problematic history in dealing with them.

As we touched on earlier in this book, slum clearance measures were a central pillar of urban development in many North American cities throughout the 20th century. Low-income areas, mostly populated by racialized, immigrant or other marginalized groups, were expressly targeted to make way for "urban renewal" projects like freeways, parkways and other vehicular-oriented examples of "progress." These days, slum clearance initiatives are more opaque, commonly cloaked in the language of development and public safety, with rundown rental buildings or aging housing stock often sold off and redeveloped under the paradoxical argument that destroying what little affordable housing remains on the market will somehow fix the lack of affordable housing on the market. When some of these displaced people invariably wind up in tent cities, they often face violent removal at the hands of police acting on orders from city governments fed up with the blight. Whether in Harare, Mumbai, San Francisco, New York, Toronto or Edmonton, the justification for slum clearance, in whatever form it takes, is almost always the same: In a civilized society, you simply cannot have people erecting housing willy-nilly without any regard for private property or zoning or building codes. To allow such a thing would invite chaos and anarchy. Public order must be preserved, and besides, it's simply not safe.

Some of these criticisms are undoubtedly true, though all too often they are misdirected. Slums certainly do affect public health and safety—but the victims are far and away more likely to be the people who actually live there rather than those in more comfortable surroundings whose complaints often boil down to a profound discomfort with poverty. In overcrowded dwellings without clean water and sanitation, diseases like cholera, COVID and tuberculosis flourish. Without proper heat, ventilation or drainage, people suffer disproportionately from the effects of our changing climate: heat stroke and dehydration in drought-inducing heat waves and flash floods from heavy storms that wash away belongings, houses and sometimes people. In colder climes, frostbite and hypothermia haunt slum dwellers in the winter, when people also die in fires or from poisonous gases emitted from portable heaters. Without security features like doors that lock and windows that close, property and people are more vulnerable to theft, invasion, assault and vandalism, all the darker sides of human nature that our regulated housing stock is designed to protect us from.

In contrast to the 1950s and '60s, officials defending more recent slum clearance initiatives often claim they are simply acting out of concern for slum dwellers—it's just not right to have people living without access to proper infrastructure like sewage, roads and sanitation. However, the situation is rarely improved by a bulldozer's blade or a police raid. In fact, when police sweep through and clear out makeshift shelters, they often destroy critical items people need to get out of their predicament, things like prescription medications, identification, letters of employment, and personal items like photos of loved ones that remind people of their humanity and their self-worth. What's worse is that sweeps don't even work to solve the slum problem. Most of the time all they do is usher people off to find new places to congregate in much the same fashion, or to return within a few weeks or months.

The awkward truth is that removing poor people from the only homes available to them doesn't change the conundrum at the heart of our housing crisis. People with nowhere else to go will still have nowhere else to go even when you tell them they can't stay where they are. It's fine, noble even, to decide that as a society we won't tolerate people living in squalid and unsafe conditions. However, in North America at least, we have utterly failed at providing other options. Rather than devote legislative power to reducing the cost of shelter, many lawmakers concerned about the growing occurrence of tent cities and homeless encampments have instead opted to criminalize them. The result has not only been an increase in the problem, but also an inordinate amount of police resources wasted on arrests for offences like loitering and panhandling, not to mention an overburdened court system clogged with charges that essentially stem from simply being poor. It is very expensive to maintain systems that permit persistent poverty—though you wouldn't know that from the way we talk about them. Thanks to prevailing political and cultural ideologies that centre on fiscal scarcity, real alternatives, like the sort on offer in Vienna, are often seen as prohibitively costly, time-consuming and politically risky in an era where our collective responsibility to uphold the human right to housing has been recast as a drain on society. This is a particularly prominent narrative in countries throughout the Global South that are often contending with political corruption, economic mismanagement and the cultural scars of colonial violence. In these places, the capital and coordination required to build extensive housing programs is commonly accepted to be simply out of reach.

All of this is what makes what is happening in this corner of Dzivarasekwa so intriguing. The improvements here are rooted in an idea considered completely antithetical in the world of philanthropy and foreign aid. It's the idea that the most pressing thing holding the world's poorest people back from escaping cycles of poverty is not necessarily a lack of money but a lack of time.

---

Around the corner from Tendai, past a row of houses like hers in various states of construction, sits a glimpse of what the neighbourhood is on its way to becoming. A 1,600-square-foot three-bedroom half duplex is the first on the block to be completed. It's home to Joice, her husband and several of their seven children. A tall, broad woman in her 40s with high cheekbones and a regal countenance, Joice welcomed me onto her veranda, framed in decorative wrought-iron pillars and shaded from the midday sun by a brick awning, a mature tree and a tall fence of sugar cane growing along the boundary of her corner lot. A mid-size hatchback sat in the driveway, next to a tuck shop Joice owns and operates, stocked with household basics and snacks for sale, like the fresh doughnuts stuffed with lemon cream she makes every morning.

Inside the house, Joice flicked on a light, showing off the electricity that was recently installed as well as the slate-blue tiles stretching across the living room and down the hall. The house had been under construction for eight years, she told me, and the building process started only *after* more than a decade of saving and planning while living in a cabin much like Tendai's. Even now, there was work still left to do. The living room walls were unpainted and the bathroom, covered in striking dark-navy tiles, didn't yet have a door, but the place was livable, with indoor plumbing, a completed kitchen and a brand-new toilet. So how did Joice manage to go from a cabin to a future in this custom-built three-bedroom house? That's all thanks to what everyone in these parts simply calls "the federation."

Founded in Zimbabwe in 1997, the federation—short for the Zimbabwe Homeless People's Federation—is part of an international network of slum dwellers who pool financial and social resources in order to incrementally upgrade their communities and dramatically improve their lives. United by an international non-governmental organization (NGO) called Slum Dwellers International, there are federations in 18 countries across Africa, Asia and Latin America. Each federation operates in partnership with a local NGO that acts as a "technical partner," helping members to develop savings schemes that align with local customs, laws and economic realities, as well as supporting negotiations with municipalities and securing additional funding from values-aligned aid organizations. In Zimbabwe, the local NGO is called the Dialogue on Shelter for the Homeless in Zimbabwe Trust. Most people just call it Dialogue on Shelter.

There are a lot of moving parts to this system. In each country where Slum Dwellers International operates, the federation details are a little bit different, responding to local customs and conditions, but the core remains the same. The essence of the organization are small, women-led neighbourhood savings groups that pool money to pay for specific community projects.

To understand the power of these savings groups, and the work of the federations and their myriad affiliated groups, I found myself contemplating the phrase "time is money." Made famous by American founding father Benjamin Franklin, the aphorism is meant to caution people against the financial losses incurred by taking time away from waged labour and devoting it to other pursuits such as travel or leisure—basically the ethos behind our modern-day hustle culture. But anyone with a pension plan or any other type of investment strategy knows there are other ways time and money interact. Our financial markets, for example, are based on the principle of compound interest, which allows money to grow passively over time as more and more interest gets accrued. For people without access to formal employment or mainstream financial systems, however, time and money have a different but no less important relationship. Just as capital markets respond favourably to certainty, delivering higher returns and creating more wealth in periods of stability, people operate in much the same capacity.

Though he might not have put it in those exact words, a man named Jockin Arputham had a solid grasp of this concept when he started advocating for the rights of slum dwellers in India during the 1970s and '80s. A resident of the Janata Colony, an informal settlement of some 70,000 people on the outskirts of what is now Mumbai, Arputham knew that many slums operated under complex social orders that hinged on a high degree of collective responsibility and community accountability. Arputham saw potential in these social structures to form the basis of a system whereby slum dwellers could use their own resources to upgrade housing and infrastructure in their communities, and build businesses and livelihoods as well, if only they were spared the threat of constant eviction. In other words, if only they were given the time to allow these investments to grow. To demonstrate to doubtful authorities that slum dwellers were indeed capable of completing these projects, Arputham started organizing small groups of neighbourhood savers. These women-led groups of 10 to 50 households used their own money to upgrade their communities. They put in a clean water well here, a road there, and worked up to larger projects, including building proper housing compliant with modern building codes. Some 50 years later, these groups have essentially become independent financial systems tailor-made to serve the needs of their communities. Members contribute to multiple savings streams at once with money in each pocket earmarked for different purposes.

Joice in Harare, for example, belongs to a neighbourhood savings group made up of 20 or so households on her street. The money she contributes here goes toward a financial reserve from which she can take out loans to pay for things her family needs, anything from roofing sheets for her house to school fees for her children; what she spends it on is entirely up to her. When she pays the loan back with interest, normally somewhere between 3 and 10 percent, the pool of money grows. This process is repeated at the network, regional and national level to finance larger projects that have a wider reach. Joice also contributes money to her network, made up of all 12 neighbourhood groups in Dzivarasekwa, which collects money for projects that benefit the whole community, like construction of the site office where the federation members hold meetings and also rent out the space to make extra income. At the regional level, the money Joice and others contribute can be accessed by federation communities across the city in order to pay for infrastructure upgrades like water and sanitation. These loans are also paid back with interest, growing the funds over time. And then there's a national fund all 20,000 members of the Zimbabwe Homeless People's Federation contribute to for the primary purpose of buying land.

As I sat in the living rooms of people like Joice and visited the cabins of people like Tendai, I became increasingly puzzled. No one I met from the Zimbabwe Homeless People's Federation was, in fact, homeless. At least not in the way that we usually think about it, which is to say they were not unhoused. Nobody I met lacked a roof over their head or a space to store their belongings.

Nobody spent their days roaming the streets with their stuff in a shopping cart or slept under a tree or even couch surfed. This does happen in Zimbabwe, I was told, but those people were not the target group of the federation. What made members identify as homeless was that they were initially renters.

Talking to people about what it means to be homeless in Zimbabwe raised many of the same issues that routinely plague the one-third or so of Canadians who at any given time do not own their homes. Tenant protections were not well-enforced and disputes required a lengthy resolution process routed through an overburdened, under-resourced public office. Landlords commonly implemented illegal rent hikes or had overbearing rules such as limitations on overnight guests or visiting family. If tenants made personally financed improvements to their rental cabins, like adding a satellite dish or solar panels, it could result in conflict or eviction. Some people told me of situations that sounded eerily similar to some of those I encountered as a renter in Vancouver—where tenants were forced to abide by curfews or were expected to clean or otherwise perform domestic labour for their landlords. Like in Canada, virtually the only way out of a life of precarious housing and toward stability and autonomy was to somehow become a landowner. As Joice put it: "When you have land you are free."

So when the City of Harare agreed to permanently allocate 408 plots in Dzivarasekwa to the federation in 2007, just two years after it had embarked on a brutal eviction campaign displacing slum dwellers across the city, there was much rejoicing. The land was part of a pilot project called the Harare Slum Upgrading Project, a partnership between the City of Harare, the federation and Dialogue on Shelter, the local Zimbabwe NGO, that would finally see informal settlements included in municipal planning with an eye toward improving rather than destroying them. The city guaranteed security of tenure to the federation as they built up the area, taking payment for land only after construction was complete. Joice and Tendai were among more than 2,000 people in Harare to benefit from the land. Recipients were selected by federation members from networks across the city based on their savings history and their good standing within the organization, but being among the lucky few to get a plot was just the beginning of a long and arduous effort. The portion of Dzivarasekwa allocated to the federation was completely undeveloped. "There was no roads. There was no water. There was no sewer. No houses," said Joice. As part of the pilot program, the city supplied engineering oversight for infrastructure projects, but not the labour. "The community were the ones who were doing the job," Joice said. "Especially the women, we were trenching for the sewer and the water because mostly the men [were at] work." Once the basic infrastructure was in place, federation members could start living on the land, most in those little two-room cabins built with materials paid for through the federation's funds. Only once their temporary housing was in place could they start work on the real thing. "We started planning: As poor people, what type of a house can we afford to build?" Joice said. What followed were several group brainstorming sessions, with community members sketching out ideas for houses they felt were both attainable and desirable. The city engineers helped them choose a few designs and provided architectural drawings that local builders, mostly trained by the federation to do the work, could follow. The city also relaxed the zoning in Dzivarasekwa to allow for duplexes in an area technically zoned for single-family homes. Finally, almost a decade after the federation was first allocated the land, construction started on the first demonstration houses, which were built incrementally with loans from the savings groups for every specific stage. "You will be given a first stage [loan], from box up to slab level. Okay then you pay back," Joice explained. "After that you will be given from slab level to window level, you pay back. After that, from window level up." And so on it went.

---

If the process of providing small, low-barrier loans to the world's poorest citizens sounds familiar to you, it's probably because at first glance this seems similar to microfinance, a movement that promised to eradicate world poverty that was all the rage a couple of decades ago. Popularized by Bangladeshi economist Muhammad Yunus and based on his belief that "credit is a human right," microloans were celebrated as a panacea for the urban poor by providing hard-to-come-by capital they could use to start or expand businesses, increase their income and improve their lives. It didn't quite pan out that way. Today, microfinance is big business in many developing countries where the financial institutions that specialize in microloans are often multinational conglomerates publicly traded on the stock market. This means their ultimate allegiance is to shareholders, not the populations they serve, despite the fact that many still receive funding from international aid organizations financed by taxpayers. A 2021 investigation by Bloomberg revealed that many of these banks have come to operate in much the same manner as the predatory lenders and loan sharks they were invented to replace in that they threaten and terrorize people who cannot repay their debts. In countries such as India and Sri Lanka, there have been well-documented waves of suicides among borrowers—most of whom are women—who found themselves in arrears. Meanwhile, a litany of academic studies have found that even among the majority of cases where debts are repaid, microloans haven't managed to transform people's lives as originally hoped. More often than not, the money is used to cover shortfalls for daily expenses, like food or rent, not invested in long-term projects that can permanently improve a family's economic situation.

In contrast, the federation system advocated by Slum Dwellers International is hyperlocal and community-based, with support available when people need help. Loan recipients are vetted by federation members, with those with the most consistent savings habits—therefore those who demonstrate the most likelihood of being able to repay—getting first priority for large loans such as those needed to buy land. If for whatever reason people cannot repay their debts, they are dealt with by the community. Though rare, there have been cases where people have misappropriated funds or defaulted on loans. In those cases people are required to take on lodgers in their home or leave the community temporarily and rent out their house until the debt is repaid. There are also strict protocols federation members follow. There is no political talk, no religious affiliation and members must keep meticulous track of the money. In countries like Zimbabwe where the banking system is rife with risk due to chronic hyperinflation (the government has a tendency to "revalue" currency without warning, essentially wiping out the value of people's accounts), money is kept in cashboxes guarded by treasurers who do not have access to the keys. When the boxes are opened and the cash is counted, every single person in a savings group must be present. And because the system is non-profit, all the interest paid by federation members goes back into the community to pay for more housing or community projects, or help people with other goals.

While relying on your neighbours to finance loans and appraise your financial situation might sound like a recipe for disaster in the North American context, federation members I spoke with said the shared responsibility of managing money quickly creates a sense of trust that is virtually unbreakable. In countries with essentially no social safety net and where the government cannot be relied upon to provide even the most basic services, community savings networks are the best, and in some cases the only, option many people have to provide peace of mind and plan for their future. Many people even choose to add additional savings schemes on top of the four tracks the federation manages to help shoulder other expenses. In Dzivarasekwa, for instance, there is a grocery fund to buy bulk items like cornmeal, a staple of Zimbabwean cuisine, for the community, and a health savings account people can draw from to cover emergency medical expenses. Other communities I visited had funds to cover school fees for all the children, or to pay for funerals. In aggregate, all these savings schemes, plus the security of tenure and the community cohesion they engender, creates a foundation upon which the urban poor can not only improve the condition of their day-to-day lives but elevate their position in society, which has generational impacts.

In some countries where the federations operate, many women aren't easily able to start bank accounts or take out loans without a male relative's permission. Traditional marriage laws in many countries, including Zimbabwe, also mean women often don't have a right to property, even the marital home, in the case of divorce or the death of their husband. But by forging their own financial system, the federations create pathways toward financial independence and long-term security for women and their children. And by participating in federation activities, whether tallying savings, calculating interest rates or conducting community surveys, women like Joice, who are smart and capable but never had a chance to complete their education, regularly become pillars of their communities. In all, Joice told me she'd been able to borrow, and pay back, about US$4,000 to construct her home. She'd also been able to put one of her daughters through university, and build two successful businesses—a bakery and the tuck shop—she runs with her husband, all the while gaining skills, confidence and status as a national leader in the federation. "I can do something like someone who went to school," she told me, beaming.

---

To be honest, when I first arrived in Zimbabwe and started speaking with federation members, I felt slightly unnerved. The way people spoke of the organization was so reverent and relentlessly positive that it struck me as a little cult-like. But the more time I spent with members and the more I saw concrete evidence of what they were able to do together, I started to realize this might just be the real deal: a method for tackling world poverty that actually works. But if so, I wondered why I hadn't heard more about it. While Slum Dwellers International has won a number of awards in humanitarian aid circles, with the Dzivarasekwa Slum Upgrading Project a showpiece of the organization, it hasn't received nearly the mainstream attention, nor the funding, of a dubious system such as microfinance, whose celebrity endorsers include Hillary Clinton, and whose inventor was awarded the Nobel Peace Prize in 2006 (Arputham was also nominated in 2014).

The reason? In short, discrimination. As Lisa Vollmer in Berlin pointed out, when it comes to problems like precarious housing and wealth inequality, the people with the most insight are often those most affected by the problems. But, as a global society, we're still not used to taking advice from people who don't come with the qualifications or affect we typically associate with "experts." Despite some efforts to level the playing field and give airtime to people with "lived experience," poor people are still often excluded from conversations about how to solve the poverty they live with every single day. They are even less likely to be consulted if they are part of a racial or ethnic minority, and even less so if they also happen to be women.

This is a barrier federation members and their advocates have to continually overcome.

When I met Sheila standing in front of her four-bedroom detached bungalow on a quiet leafy street, she wore a Cheshire cat grin I would soon learn was a fixture on her face and a T-shirt that read *Know Your City*, a slogan used by federation members who collect local census information. With its tidy landscaping and burgeoning high street with butchers, bakeries and pharmacies in proper brick buildings, I never would have guessed that Crowborough, Sheila's neighbourhood, was once a shanty town akin to Dzivarasekwa. This is another area where federation members were able to buy land and build their houses over decades, but Sheila's journey to get here started long before she was granted even the hope of her own plot of land.

Like a lot of the women I met in Zimbabwe, Sheila was forced to leave school early. Her family had come to the city from the country, finding rental housing in Mbare (pronounced mm-bar-eh), a slum in the centre of the city. Sheila reached seventh grade before her parents asked her to drop out of school to care for her younger siblings so they could work. When both parents died not long after, it seemed Sheila's role as a caregiver was set in stone. By her early 20s she was married with children of her own. But like Joice, joining the federation as it was getting established in Harare opened up a different path. As we chatted in her sunken living room, featuring periwinkle walls, velvety brown couches and a pass-through to a kitchen rimmed in floor-to-ceiling cabinetry piled high with pots and pans, Sheila, 59, told me the biggest barriers in getting the federation off the ground weren't necessarily financial. When she and other members from Mbare first approached Harare's city council hoping to get support for their first project, they weren't just dismissed—their very existence was denied. "Our city fathers, they were not accepting that here we've got slums," she recalled. "When we went there they said, 'What is this? We don't have slums here.'" Sheila and the others were galled but not deterred. They simply called the mayor to the window, out of which Mbare was clearly visible. "These are the slums," Sheila remembered telling him. "That is where we are coming from."

Several decades on, Sheila is now a leader with the federation. She's worked side by side with city officials, even leading delegations of local politicians on tours of other slum upgrading projects in South Africa and India. They are partners now, almost colleagues. But back then, it took years to get their attention and respect; years of showing up at city hall month after month as a group of women with their handwritten savings ledgers and census data in hand. Slowly, their persistence started to pay off. "They began listening, first with one ear, then with two," Sheila recalled. But what really sealed the deal was the toilet.

Mbare is a different kind of slum from Crowborough or Dzivarasekwa on the outskirts of Harare. Mbare sits in the middle of the city, its residents mostly living in dilapidated mid-rise "hostels" originally built as lodging for single migrant workers, or in crowded public housing flats financed by international charities, some by the late Princess Diana herself. Like on the outskirts, it's not unusual for families of 10 or more to live in just one or two rooms, but the community has the added benefits of electricity, indoor plumbing and a central location, making it a perfect home for Harare's biggest produce market.

Each morning, scores of shoppers arrive to stock up on groceries for their families or to resell through their own businesses. Back in the early 2000s, the market had a problem. There was no public toilet anywhere that anyone could use. This made for an uncomfortable shopping experience, but for vendors the situation was much more dire. Faced with either going home or to a local business far away to answer nature's call, many vendors had no choice but to leave their stalls for a prolonged period of time, leaving their stock vulnerable to theft. There was also no private area in the market vendors could go to count their cash away from prying eyes. Federation members who lived in Mbare and worked at the market knew the problem intimately. So, their first proposal to the city was to build a pay toilet as proof they were not only capable of spearheading the project, but that they had the insider insight to make it really count. And so it was that a single, strategically placed piece of unglamorous infrastructure ended up doubling as a crime-reduction tool.

Once the toilet was installed, theft in the market went down and vendors were left with more money to take home at the end of their long, gruelling days. This, Sheila told me, is the real value of the federation's approach. As much as governments, aid agencies and well-meaning philanthropists would like to solve poverty overnight by giving poor people better housing and a higher quality of life, effectively achieving that goal is actually less about what you add to people's lives than what you take away. It's about effectively identifying and removing the barriers people face while they work to improve their own lives, Sheila said. "We say we have subtracted the poverty."

This insight is why the federation model has succeeded where so many others have failed, said Patience Mudimu, director of Dialogue on Shelter for the Homeless in Zimbabwe Trust, the local NGO that supports Zimbabwe's federation network. It's also its Achilles' heel. While these networks of neighbourhood savers are far from the first entities aimed at improving the slums, they are some of the first to do it through a consistently bottom-up approach.

But that can be a tough sell for funders used to a top-down way of operating. "Fundraising initiatives are very proscriptive: Do it this way, do it that way," Mudimu told me. That approach can make projects go faster and look better on paper, but in practice, it often results in wasted money, materials and opportunity.

To illustrate this point, Mudimu told me of another attempt to bring toilets to one of the federation's communities. Dialogue on Shelter had worked with an outside aid agency to deliver supplies for dozens of eco toilets to be constructed in front of people's homes, only to have them sit there untouched for months. When Mudimu asked the intended beneficiaries why they hadn't completed the projects, they seemed a bit confused. Shouldn't the aid group come and finish the project *they* had clearly started with *their* materials? "So that's the mentality, 'This is donor-funded, I'm just a recipient,'" Mudimu said. "Whereas the federation, they are not beneficiaries of a process, they are active participants. They influence the change they want."

Because federation members, not funders, get to decide how and where they use their money, the model is often deemed too unwieldy for many aid organizations, Mudimu said, adding that even in humanitarian circles many people don't trust the poor to make good decisions about how best to improve their lives. A few organizations, like the Gates Foundation for instance, have come on board as major funders of the Harare Slum Upgrading Project and contributed millions to augment the federation's savings. But for the most part, convincing people in powerful organizations to let go of their hubris and relinquish control is no easy task, even though evidence shows that empowering people to solve their own problems can literally mean the difference between a single toilet accomplishing more than anyone thought was possible and piles of unused supplies rusting away in the sun. "Supporting people is not bringing them to your agenda, but aligning your support to their agenda," Mudimu said, in an echo of Lisa Vollmer in Berlin.

When it comes to housing, we see this play out all over the world, with similar repercussions. As I was being ferried along the highways feeding into Dzivarasekwa, Crowborough and other informal communities in Harare, I couldn't help but notice large tracts of identical square houses, with all the trappings of a master-planned suburban development. They were postage-stamp perfect, if a little small, with pitched roofs and paved sidewalks—all they were missing was the white picket fence. When I asked who the houses were for, the answer sounded eerily familiar. A local bank had built these cottages in a bid to make a dent in Harare's housing crisis, but they were mostly empty, either too small or too expensive to meet the needs of the city's legions of precariously housed people. "The product that is on the market does not suit or is not afforded by the people who are in need," Mudimu told me.

It made me think of all those tiny condos for sale in Toronto and Vancouver that nobody looking for a place to actually live in seems to want, or to be able, to buy. When I mentioned this to Mudimu, the conversation took a *very* interesting turn.

One question I'd been scared to ask ever since arriving in Harare was about the use of the word "slum." To me it just seemed so harsh. I spent my whole time in Africa feeling like I had to apologize every time it left my mouth. Without meaning to, I'd frequently revert to the less offensive sounding term sometimes used by the federation: "informal settlement." I wondered if "slum" was a politically charged word that had been reclaimed by community members with lived experience—something that was okay for them to say but not for me. When I brought this up, Mudimu gently chided me for my sensitivity. "I think the West is very good at hiding negativity," she said, adding that it wasn't unusual for people from outside these communities to bristle at the term. Even the city officials in Harare insisted on using "informal settlements" in their official negotiations.

Slum Dwellers International, the organization uniting all the networks of savers across its 18 countries, intentionally chose that term in part because it is a little provocative, Mudimu told me, but mostly just because it's honest. "I think sometimes people want to hide world urban poverty through nice names, or through a nice lens," she said. Politically correct alternatives like "informal settlements" or "precarious communities" tend to gloss over the extent of the problem. More than a billion people worldwide live in slums, according to the UN, with that number expected to grow by an additional 2 billion by 2050. And though polite, imprecise language might make people in high-powered bureaucratic institutions feel more comfortable, it doesn't help the people experiencing extreme poverty get out of it. Calling a spade a spade, or in this case a slum a slum, is necessary to get everyone on the same page in looking for solutions. "The slum dwellers are just claiming the truth," Mudimu said. "That they live in slums."

Of course this raises another question: When does a slum stop being a slum? There's the simple answer: When essential infrastructure, quality housing and security of tenure are in place. But Mudimu pointed out that you can look at slums another way, which is essentially as a measure of poverty. And poverty is essentially a measure of deprivation. When you have a population that is consistently deprived of the opportunities and standards of comfort enjoyed by the majority in a society, what creates slum conditions can be found in the difference between what most people have and what some people cannot—although those gaps are a lot trickier to identify. Communities like Crowborough, where Sheila's four-bedroom bungalow sat on a well-manicured street, seemed miles away from Dzivarasekwa's dirt roads and timber cabins, but some people there still lived in overcrowded conditions or faced income challenges from having to move so far out of the city in order to afford the land, Mudimu said. Sometimes what makes a slum a slum doesn't have anything to do with the physical condition of the neighbourhood or its buildings, she told me, but the hidden challenges that eat away at people's ability to live in dignity and comfort behind closed doors.

So, if you're a renter afraid to request repairs lest it lead to a renoviction, or who can't control your own heat; if you're holding off on having a child, or another one, because you can't afford a big enough space; or if you're forced to change your job or skimp on groceries to make car payments because you've been pushed to the edges of the city where the buses don't run, "that," in Mudimu's opinion, "is a slum."

Hearing this was a little bit jarring. I'd come to Africa expecting to find solutions we might apply to what I thought of as Canada's rather contained slum problem—our tent cities and homeless shelters and First Nations reserves without clean water. I had not expected to discover the problem might be much wider-reaching than that. By Mudimu's definition, some middle-class renters, and even some homeowners, would qualify as slum households. I could never, ever imagine us as a society talking about that possibility in such bold and controversial language, or really talking about it at all.

One of the features of market-based capitalism and its emphasis on individuality is that it silences people by shaming them when they can't afford or are not served by what the market provides. For instance, if you can't afford a secure, family-sized home where you live and work, or if you can't fathom raising a family in the 300-square-foot shoebox you *can* afford, that's on you. Maybe you should have saved more, or been more creative, or more flexible. And no matter how badly the market misses the mark on meeting our housing needs, we are encouraged to be thankful instead of critical. You might live in fear that your building will be sold and you'll be evicted, but be grateful that you have a roof over your head for now. *Don't you know there are people that have no shelter at all? Think of the people sleeping on the streets! Heck, think of the people in Africa!*

With this patterning in the back of my mind, I found it eye-opening to meet people like Joice, Tendai and Sheila who refused to be held hostage by shame. They refused to reduce their standards to fit others' expectations of what should be "good enough" given their economic status. I'll admit I was one of them. I was genuinely surprised at first to discover their ambitions for their homes were a lot like mine. They wanted enough space for their families to live comfortably, land they could stand on that they would not get kicked off of, and the freedom to pick out paint colours and tile patterns and customize their houses until they felt like their own. They were not aiming small, for generic "tiny homes" or "micro-lofts" or some other twee equivalent. They were not going to accept what amounts to slightly upgraded cabins—and why should they?

The federation members I met seemed to understand what so many people in our culture don't: that their poverty was the result of an unjust economic system and a failure of leadership, not a failure of their character. From their perspective, living in a slum wasn't shameful, but it was unacceptable. This is what fuelled them to work so hard to create change. By the same token, they didn't see renting as being inherently shameful either, as we tend to do; the problem was that in Zimbabwe, as in many parts of Canada, it just wasn't a very dignified way to live. And at the end of the day, dignity is what everybody wants and deserves in their housing; it's what so many housing programs and policies the world over say they aim to provide. But dignity isn't one-size-fits-all. It's not something you can legislate or donate or mass produce for the market. What I learned in Africa is that dignity and agency have to go hand in hand. A dignified home is not determined by a design or even a price point. It's defined by your ability to define it for yourself.

# PART 3: PROGRESS

*Never doubt that a small group of thoughtful,*
*committed citizens can change the world;*
*indeed, it's the only thing that ever has.*

—Margaret Mead

10

# HOME FEELINGS

A few years after we bought our house in Calgary the city had indeed started to resemble Vancouver, though not in a good way.

Fleeing soaring housing prices and seeking more space, people from all over the country flocked to Calgary during the pandemic and the years following, for exactly the same reasons I had. They wanted familiar urban amenities but without the crippling housing costs in other parts of the country. Calgary's housing stock just couldn't keep up. The impact on the city's most vulnerable was, of course, pure carnage.

By 2023, experts estimated as many as 300 people a day were accessing the shelter system for the first time. Food bank usage surged and emergency services were overwhelmed. One in five Calgary households was said to be in core housing need, meaning they couldn't afford the housing they had without sacrificing other necessities. There were more people sleeping in underpasses and in doorways and more tents pitched in the woods along the city's winding river pathways, even out in the suburbs. Online, neighbourhood message boards filled with pleas for housing from renters facing renovictions or whose landlords had listed their homes for sale in order to capitalize on the hot market. In a province with no rent control, many of those spared from eviction faced rent hikes so high they were forced to move anyway.

Even my peer group in Calgary, all professionals and most firmly ensconced in the upper echelons of the middle class, was feeling the strain. Those with the means to buy a place felt compelled to do it right away, despite record-high sale prices and surging interest rates, before the opportunity simply vanished forever. My social network scattered in search of housing. Among those priced out of my particular neighbourhood were a lawyer, two teachers and a university professor.

Only this time, I watched it all unfold from my secure perch on the property ladder. By virtue of good luck and good timing, we had managed to buy a house ahead of the pandemic and thus were spared from its wildly distorting effect on the market. If we'd waited even a year before starting our hunt there's no way we would have been able to buy the house we had. At the rate prices were rocketing up in Calgary, I doubt we would have even been able to afford to rent it. Good luck and good timing. This was the only difference between enjoying the luxury of standing on solid ground and churning in the water trying not to drown. This was the backdrop against which I set out on my travels, and against which I returned with a new perspective on what we could be doing, or doing better, to create meaningful and lasting change.

The common denominator between Vienna, Berlin and Harare is that their response to their respective housing crises were all grounded in an understanding of home as something far greater, far more valuable and far more expansive than mere housing. Whether cognizant of this or not, their approaches prioritized those foundational elements we talked about in chapter 3: familiarity, haven, heaven (belonging), space, place, need and time (stability).

Vienna pretty much had it all. The central gift its system gives to its citizens is time—security of tenure through open-ended leases, predictable rent increases and a high income cut-off for subsidized housing mean people can stay in their homes as long as they want without having to worry about losing them. Knowing they are building communities and infrastructure meant to last for generations, Vienna ensures social housing developments meet a diversity of needs throughout every stage of life, with businesses, services, transit and third spaces that enable multi-generational, mixed-income communities. The city fosters belonging and familiarity among residents with organized and robust social programming, and its legions of social workers protect people's havens by helping neighbours deal with conflict in a respectful and constructive way. By giving each social housing development a unique architectural perspective—a personality, if you will—Vienna's system helps residents develop a sense of place, an attachment to the geographic and physical characteristics of their unique communities that in turn informs the culture. Finally, the relatively short wait times for housing and the wide variety of housing types ensures households can upsize or downsize their housing as their space needs change without having to leave their community and without losing their sense of home.

Berlin's approach was rooted in the interplay of haven and heaven. What made the city so special after the Cold War is that it became a destination for people who didn't feel safe in most other parts of Europe, or other parts of the world. It was a city where people could create their own havens out of the rubble to suit their specific needs. In Berlin, it didn't matter if you were an anarchist punk, a polyamorous nonbinary sex worker, a refugee, or some combination of all three. More than in almost any other city in the world, you could fashion a home that made you feel safe and free to be yourself if you were willing to work at it. The activists I got to know put it to me this way: Berlin's civic identity is being a place where a multitude of identities can find safety and belonging. The desire to keep it that way was the driving force that brought people together across race, class, gender, language and political lines in their fight against the homogenizing forces of financialization.

In Harare's slums, places where safe and secure havens were pretty hard to come by, slowly becoming familiar with neighbours and developing a sense of belonging and trust were the catalysts for the federation's ability to amass the financial capital slum dwellers needed to buy their own land, which ultimately bought them time. Without the spectre of eviction or slum clearances, federation members could work toward developing the other elements of home as their resources and capacity allowed. I found it really poignant that their individual houses were often the last thing to come. They prioritized digging trenches for utilities, and building community offices they could use for meetings or to rent out to other groups to create shared income. They started businesses to bring in the goods and services people needed to do all this work. Doing all of this together deepened their sense of community and rooted them in a place—they developed an attachment to the land that at first was strange and unsettled but eventually became familiar ground. Only after doing all of this did Harare's federation members finally turn their attention to building the housing they'd dreamed of—the personal havens they'd been lacking all this time.

The thing that really stood out in all of this? The actual built form of housing was kind of inconsequential to the end goal, which was to create the *feeling* of home. Whether in Red Vienna's "residential palaces" or its ultra-modern new developments like Sonnwendviertel, whether in Berlin's collective flats built from salvaged materials or its rundown social housing from the '70s, whether in Zimbabwe's timber cabins or the finally finished bungalows complete with plumbing and electricity, I met people who had a strong and deeply felt sense of home.

So what would it look like if we were to chart a similar path? If we were to build a housing system on top of a foundational understanding of home, so that the dwellings we produced were designed to prioritize human happiness, health and well-being rather than profit? Well, first we'd have to tackle the cultural attachment to the system we have and the way we've been doing things for a very long time. We'd have to redefine what it means to have a "good" home and realize that housing that nurtures a sense of home doesn't always look the way we think it should. We'd have to get familiar with some new ideas and new ways of doing things. And we'd have to approach this all with the utmost sensitivity and compassion and offer lots of support along the way. Because home, at its core, is a feeling. So, if you're going to help people shift their long-held beliefs and understanding of home, it is going to be *very* emotional.

---

In the spring of 2024, Calgary City Council held a marathon public hearing—the longest in the city's history. At issue was one small slice of a comprehensive affordable housing strategy passed the previous fall in response to the housing crisis. The hearing centred around a proposal to do away with the single-family zoning that applied to nearly 70 percent of Calgary neighbourhoods and make it easier to build housing forms like duplexes, fourplexes, row houses and townhouses. Urban planners and developers call these types of housing the "missing middle" because they fill the gap between single-family homes and large high-rise apartment towers that have dominated our cities, and because we haven't been building them in nearly the numbers we need. (Small, low-rise apartment buildings would also fall into this category, but they weren't part of the discussion in Calgary.) In considering this change, Calgary was part of a trend. Throughout the 2020s, dozens of places—Minneapolis, Toronto, Vancouver, Halifax, Edmonton, Oregon and California, to name a few—have done away with a practice known as "exclusionary zoning" that basically made it illegal to build anything other than single-family homes in most residential areas. These reforms have been heralded as a huge win by pro-housing, Yes In My Backyard (YIMBY), groups who see this change as critical to enabling more affordable housing options. It's also based on a belief that so-called gentle density, such as duplexes and townhouses, are more palatable for suburbanites who fear their idyllic, quiet neighbourhoods will become overrun by high-rise towers bringing thousands of new residents. There's just one problem: People still hate it.

In almost every place zoning reforms have been passed they have done so in the face of overwhelming opposition. Calgary was no exception. The city's public hearing lasted 12 days, beginning at nine in the morning and often going until well after nine at night. The vast majority of speakers were vehemently opposed. Of the 700-plus people who showed up to speak, 458 were against, 227 were in favour and a mere 51 presented themselves as "neutral." That was on top of more than 6,000 written submissions the city received, nearly 90 percent of which were against the idea. In the end, council passed the "blanket rezoning" anyway, in a 9–6 vote that was celebrated by city progressives. But many of the dissenting councillors voiced concerns that going against such overwhelming opposition could derail any gains the city stood to make. One councillor worried that people who spoke up would feel ignored, further eroding the already waning trust in city government. Others reflected the widespread belief that developers would be the only ones to benefit from the new rules, with the housing likely to be produced as a result set at prices few would consider affordable. "It'll increase the supply of duplexes, of row houses, they're selling for $600,000, $700,000, $800,000," one councillor told the local news.

He wasn't wrong. Newly constructed missing middle housing seldom sells at prices low- or even middle-income earners can afford. There are some very good reasons to build it anyway. New townhouses and duplexes may be pricey, but they're vastly more affordable than new single-family homes, and they can be much more environmentally sustainable. Plus, increasing density in established neighbourhoods is a financial necessity for cities, which are straining to pay for extending services to new communities sprawling out from the peripheries. Done well, gentle density can revitalize areas in decline, bring in new families with kids to attend local schools, invite more diversity and give aging residents housing options to downsize within their neighbourhoods. By almost any measure, mixing in missing middle housing is a prudent approach for mature neighbourhoods, particularly when replacing single-family homes that are nearing the end of their lives.

Still, as I watched the public hearing, I also worried the city's decision might ultimately do more harm than good. The hearing was an intensely emotional affair. On the pro side, council heard from people with lived experience of homelessness, students who had to choose between tuition and rent, young families concerned about their children's futures, all maintaining that any and all new housing could only be a good thing. Speaking against were mostly homeowners in established neighbourhoods, positively distraught by what they saw as an attack on their property rights, their neighbourhoods and their very sense of home. On both sides, people frequently struggled to speak through their tears. But when all was said and done, all those feelings—especially the overwhelmingly negative ones borne by the majority—were simply left hanging in the air.

Within months of the rezoning decision, those feelings had calcified into a stubborn and spiteful resistance. One group of Calgarians launched a court challenge to overturn the bylaw, arguing the city did not conduct a fair hearing on the issue. When a judge sided with the city, the residents took the case to appeal. Meanwhile, homeowners in some neighbourhoods began banding together at their own expense to put restrictive covenants on their properties that would prevent even future owners from ever building multi-family housing on the land. Calgary was also not alone in this trend. In California, a court challenge undid the state's move to end single-family zoning in several cities, and in B.C., residents in Burnaby, a Vancouver suburb, have also turned to restrictive covenants to sidestep provincial legislation aimed at boosting density.

This kind of hyper-organized pushback from well-resourced residents has become par for the course in the process of city building. So much so that progressive urban planners and elected officials often consider it part of the job to push through changes that might be unpopular now but that they believe to be prudent for the future. After all, this is how cities have operated for millennia. Buildings go up, buildings come down, people adapt, life goes on. Eventually, even the haters get used to it. They might even come to like it.

It may not be as simple as that.

Urban development pressure and people's emotional well-being is something that, unsurprisingly, hasn't seen a lot of study—emotions still being a taboo subject for "serious" science—but a team of Canadian researchers started looking into it when they stumbled upon the connection by accident. Julie Karmann and her colleagues started the Interventions, Equity, Research, and Action in Cities Team, or INTERACT, in 2017 with an intention to study people's reactions to urban design and development in the context of public health. They thought they'd be looking at things like whether people walked more in places with better pathways, or if people living in transit-oriented neighbourhoods had stronger social connections. But they soon realized they couldn't get a full picture of people's behaviour if they didn't first understand the emotions behind it. Emotions are "a driver to the behaviour," Karmann told me on a Zoom call with some of her colleagues.

The researchers found that not only do people have strong feelings about urban development and neighbourhood change, but these feelings had a big effect on how they interacted with new amenities, infrastructure and people in their communities. Essentially, no matter how nice that new public plaza or retail space is, "if people see the change in a negative way it is likely that they won't use the intervention you put in place," Karmann said. This means a lot of expensive public infrastructure meant to improve communities can actually make people feel more isolated and alienated, especially if they don't trust the process by which new additions to the neighbourhood arrived. Nowhere was this more pronounced than in people's reactions to increased housing density.

In one study, the INTERACT team measured Montrealers' reactions to urban change, paying special attention to the emotional impacts of condo developments because they were so pronounced. While study participants generally felt positive about new public infrastructure in their neighbourhoods, like better transit or more bike lanes, their feelings about new condos were overwhelmingly negative. "Massive real estate condo operations perceived as transforming the whole neighbourhood generated fear, irritation and pessimism," the study states. While "smaller and individual condo developments were mostly linked to disappointment," often over the loss of public green space or even private homes that residents had found added to the beauty and appeal of their neighbourhood. These negative emotions had knock-on effects for things like neighbourhood cohesion and social connectedness. Established residents in these areas had a tendency to regard newcomers as "others" rather than as a part of their community. "We observed that people are getting, like, suspicious of each other," Karmann said. "It's like the people from the condo are different from the people that are out of the condo." This was true regardless of whether the newcomers were of a higher or lower socioeconomic status than established residents. The researchers also found the pessimism conjured up by condo developments really did erode people's trust in city officials and the public consultation process. Many felt the city did not take the feedback or concerns of residents seriously. This, in turn, fed a belief that officials and planners were more concerned with maximizing developer profits and greasing the wheels of their own career aspirations than in addressing the city's affordability issues. "People do have in mind that this is all about money and power," said Karmann.

Finally, the INTERACT team discovered that the presence of new condo developments was so entwined with negative feelings that it took on an almost mythical status in people's minds and tainted perceptions of any and all new housing, regardless of size or ownership structure. "The actual nature of housing change was not always aligned with what people perceived," the authors wrote. "New or transformed housing that were not condos might be labelled as a 'condo' development, with the negative emotional charge that came with it."

This might explain why people's feelings can seem so disproportionate to the changes actually being proposed, and why, for instance, a walking tour of missing middle housing forms organized by the City of Calgary ahead of its public hearing had to be cancelled after staff received racist threats of violence. We are so emotionally tied to our homes and so fearful of losing them that the prospect of a duplex going up next door to someone in the suburbs can provoke a level of fear and anxiety that seems more proportional to a high-rise. I am no exception.

---

After falling off the radar during the pandemic, the proposal to massively redevelop my street resurfaced, this time bigger and even more intimidating. The consortium of landlords was now asking to be able to build up to five storeys and add 180 units on one side of us, in the space currently occupied by a handful of duplexes and single-family homes. On the other side, a string of four rental houses hit the market and were sold in a land assembly to a developer with a rumoured reputation for dirty dealings. Living on a block facing such immense redevelopment pressure brought on a similar anxiety to the kind I'd felt living in the rental bungalow that was slated for demolition. Logically, I knew it was different. I knew we weren't going to get kicked out of our house, but that didn't make me *feel* much better. If everything around us was going to change so drastically, rendering our street unrecognizable, would it still feel like our home?

Already we were struggling to feel rooted. Despite finally having the chance to do many of the things I'd been longing for my very own house in order to do—putting in a vegetable garden, planting a tree, renovating a bathroom, becoming a mom—something just didn't feel right. The soaring home prices on our street and the increase in speculation certainly boded well for our financial future, but it also felt like it undermined our present.

Our mailbox filled with flyers promising no-hassle, commission-free help to sell our house. A neighbour, inquiring about the landscaping and renovations we'd done, reacted with visible disappointment when I confirmed that, yes, they were for our benefit and not for boosting the resale value. We were, in fact, hoping to make this our "forever home." One afternoon, an upmarket sedan snaked down our street containing a man in a suit too nice for a Sunday who was going door to door. "Excuse me, ma'am, have you considered selling?" he said as he approached me on the driveway, where I was playing with my son. "We have a buyer lined up and all ready to go." It was all I could do to stop myself from screaming at him to get off my fucking lawn.

A conversation with Charles Marohn helped put my feelings in context. "Your neighbourhood has become prey," he explained to me after I told him about the saga on my block and my growing sense of being pressured to move along. As the founder of Strong Towns, a U.S.-based advocacy group, Marohn has made it his mission to encourage North American cities to pivot away from the postwar pattern of sprawling "suburban experiments" and embrace more financially and socially sustainable forms of urban development. One of the key challenges he continually butts up against in his work is the deep-seated belief that our neighbourhoods don't need to change, especially out in the suburbs, which have been largely exempt from any kind of development or densification for virtually their entire existence. "The game that we've set up is that every neighbourhood is locked under glass, like sealed under glass, it never changes," he said. That is, unless you live in a neighbourhood like mine, one that's working-class and inner-city. Those neighbourhoods face relentless development pressure, so much so they often become unrecognizable in a matter of years. Part of the pattern of suburban-style development is that "there's this game that goes on to figure out the neighbourhood that's going to get screwed," Marohn said. "What is the neighbourhood that's going to take all the change for the entire community, right? And the trick is you don't want to be in that neighbourhood. So, the incentive is for everybody to show up at every meeting and oppose everything. And the neighbourhood with the least amount of enfranchisement, or the least amount of power, is the one that gets exploited, so the place with the most renters or the poorest people." These neighbourhoods end up shouldering more than their fair share of the disruption that can come with rapid, large-scale densification such as construction, noise, gentrification and displacement.

The Strong Towns antidote to this predator-and-prey cycle is to gradually "thicken up" existing neighbourhoods with incremental development and gentle density—exactly the kind of thing Calgary and many other cities are trying to do. The idea is that if everyone shoulders a little bit of change, no neighbourhood should ever get "screwed" and cities should be able to evolve slowly, economically and fairly over time. It's a well-reasoned, rational approach designed to bring some fairness to a system of city planning with a history of favouring the wealthy and the white. But people aren't rational. Especially about their homes.

Findings like those of the INTERACT study underscore a fundamental human truth: Change is hard. Many of us experience changes to our homes—real, perceived or merely suggested—as an existential threat. They disrupt those fundamental elements of home like familiarity, belonging and place attachment. Shifts in the physical and social characteristics of our neighbourhoods can trigger a sense of being "un-homed," whether we are literally vulnerable to physical displacement or simply feel as if our neighbourhood is no longer for us. It can even affect our sense of self. "How I see myself is related to the place where I'm living," Karmann, the researcher, told me. In short, it's perfectly natural to get our backs up when we *feel* like our homes are under siege. Whether they actually are or not is irrelevant.

So what are we to do? Change is inevitable and necessary. City planners and elected officials simply cannot be held hostage to legions of freaked-out citizens dug so deep into their feelings they're incapable of listening to reason. But they can get better at meeting them where they are.

---

Throughout her more than 20-year career in urban planning, Teresa Goldstein noticed a pattern. Almost every time she was at a public hearing or an open house, people would pull her aside and pour out their feelings—anger, fear, grief, entitlement—about whatever change was on the horizon for their communities. After she spent some time listening, she'd get a version of the same feedback. "I would always be told that it was a time when they really felt like they had been heard. Like someone was listening to them, even if I wasn't agreeing with what they were saying," Goldstein, Calgary's director of community planning, told me in her office at city hall. It's worth noting that she has taken a fair amount of flak for her habit of lending a patient and compassionate ear. Colleagues have often suggested Goldstein is too emotional, or derided her approach as "spa talk," she told me. But she's kept at it because it's effective. The act of just listening, not as part of an official feedback process, but as one human being talking to another, seemed to help diffuse people's negativity and pessimism, so much so that she decided to study the phenomenon while pursuing a Ph.D. in urban planning. Her dissertation, called "Bringing Back the Love," argues that reorienting the planning process to operate from a place of empathy can create better outcomes for people and for cities.

Generally, the markers of success for urban planners are rooted in tangible things like deadlines and deliverables meant to satisfy goals informed by hard data on demographic shifts, population projections and, of course, city budgets. But in her research Goldstein found that planners can indeed do their jobs more effectively if they tap into the "softer, less rational, emotional connections that people have with their communities." However, planners aren't really trained for that, despite being just as likely to deal with intense emotions in a community meeting as they are with building permits and development applications. "When we were in planning school, we were not taught engagement," Goldstein told me. "We didn't go to university to be negotiators."

To be fair, planners working in the public sector already have a job many people would consider next to impossible. Before they can make any given decision or recommendation they must weigh myriad competing interests, from elected officials looking to please their constituents to the demands of industry, community groups and environmentalists, all while working with a limited amount of highly scrutinized public funds. On top of all that, as the first and often only point of contact for feedback on proposed changes, they can be on the receiving end of a fair amount of vitriol. In this context, asking planners to take the time to lean into individual emotions—one person's grief over the loss of some trees or another's distaste for a certain design element—can seem like a complete waste of time and city resources.

However, Goldstein found her empathy-oriented approach actually helped the planning process go smoother and faster. In pilot programs she ran as part of her research she found there was more community involvement, higher satisfaction with the outcome and reduced time required for planners to collect and integrate community feedback. There were fewer instances of planners being sent back to the drawing board for multiple revisions, and she even found the approach helped some people accept changes they didn't particularly like, which could reduce chances of people, say, launching costly lawsuits against the city in the future.

Too often, the first contact planners make with their constituents comes when seeking feedback for proposals that are already well into the city's approval process, Goldstein said. Additionally, there is little transparency about how that feedback is considered and what other factors go into the final decisions, such as the competing pressures cities face or how a particular neighbourhood fits into the bigger picture. This approach is a recipe for breeding distrust, said Goldstein. "If I'm talking with you now and you're telling me that you really want this to be orange and it becomes blue at the end, if I haven't gone back to that community to give them an update on why it turned from orange to blue, of course they're mad at me," she said. "So I've often felt that there's this missing step in our profession."

In her dissertation, Goldstein talks about the Calgary communities of Chinook Park, Kelvin Grove and Eagle Ridge, older residential areas that had been losing population as their residents aged. As a result, the Chinook Park elementary school was at risk of closure because there weren't enough families with kids moving in. When a community survey done by a private firm revealed that the residents' top two concerns for the neighbourhoods were a fear of increased density and the closure of the school, it was clear most hadn't realized that the two issues were directly related. The city could have used this insight as an opening to help people understand the connection between building more diverse housing options and saving the school, but instead "the school was already at risk of closure, and city administration was already in the community proposing increased density," wrote Goldstein. "The importance of connecting the dots was underestimated, leaving people caught trying to piece each of these areas together themselves."

A major conclusion of Goldstein's research, echoed in the findings of the INTERACT team, is that cities need to move away from top-down, paternalistic approaches to planning and more toward a process known as co-design, where community members are regarded as equal partners in shaping their communities. This doesn't mean letting random people or special interest groups set the agenda, but it does mean giving residents some control over how they want to help the city meet its goals.

The thing that planners know that most of us mere mortals don't always consider, Goldstein explained, is that cities are built on trade-offs. In order to get the things we need and want the most, we have to compromise on other things. You want more kids in the neighbourhood? You need to make more housing available for families. However, problems arise when cities don't include community members in determining which trade-offs are acceptable or which compromises they're willing to make. In Chinook Park, it could be that concerns about increased density come down to fear of increased traffic and parking availability—as they so often do. A co-design approach would see the city work with residents to identify places for traffic calming measures, add signals to crosswalks, maybe put in some separated bike lanes and more walking paths, or improve transit access so people don't have to drive as much, as a way of addressing those fears.

But implementing principles of co-design doesn't always have to be so hands-on. In her research, Goldstein experimented with some simple ways to create more physical touch points where residents could reach the city with suggestions and concerns about their neighbourhoods. She placed suggestion boxes throughout neighbourhoods in the shape of Little Free Libraries and sent out workbooks in the mail that got a surprisingly high rate of return. She even put a speakers' corner–type booth in a few locations where people could record videos. But there's more to it than dropping a suggestion box on a street corner and hoping for the best.

If you want thoughtful, constructive input you have to ask thoughtfully crafted questions. Rather than asking people *whether* they supported a proposed change, Goldstein started asking people *how* they could envision necessary change unfolding. *How could you stay in your community forever? How can we attract more young families to the neighbourhood? How can we keep the school open?* These kinds of questions helped people connect the dots about why change might be necessary and coaxed them to reframe it in the context of collective gain rather than personal loss, she found. They also encouraged people to start thinking of how people who are different from them might experience the neighbourhood, now and in the future—because it's not just planners who need to hone their empathy skills.

Another co-design technique Goldstein tested out was a rather involved working-group model where volunteers worked with a planning team for several weeks to identify priorities and trade-offs for a new community plan. By all accounts it was a successful process, except for the fact that it fell victim to a common issue cities face when conducting public consultation. It's a well-known fact that people with the time and resources to devote to an intense planning process tend to be whiter, wealthier, older and own more property than other stakeholders in the community, and that can skew the input in their favour. To correct for this bias, Goldstein and her team had participants go through an exercise where they imagined the impact of changes on different "neighbourhood personas," like renters, seniors, immigrants or future residents. It was a valuable exercise, but it's no replacement for having those people actually sitting at the table. In the future,

Goldstein said she'd like to see the city offer things like stipends, childcare and transit passes to reduce barriers to participation for all people in the community. Not only is this essential if the goal is to come up with plans that accurately reflect a diversity of needs, but it also points to another important way to transform our housing system into something more human and humane.

While it's necessary to rework how we plan our neighbourhoods, we also need to revisit how we relate to the people we share them with.

11

# GOOD NEIGHBOURS

Recent history has not been particularly encouraging of neighbourliness.

For most of human history, maintaining relationships with the people around us—our neighbours—was not exactly optional. We depended on our neighbours for survival in times of war, famine, drought or other periods of strife and scarcity. We relied on a community effort to keep roofs over our heads, to build houses and raise barns, to raise children and develop the infrastructure needed to support our livelihoods. Most cities began not by virtue of some grand centrally planned strategy, but by neighbours organically riffing on what the person next door did. Not everyone got along all of the time, but this interdependency forced people to work through conflict in a way that isn't required of us today. And we are poorer for it despite being richer than we've ever been.

The introduction of modern creature comforts and an exponential increase in personal and collective wealth in the latter half of the 20th century saw our homes—as in our houses, our neighbourhoods and our cities—redesigned in a way that encouraged self-sufficiency and individualism rather than community. Close quarters in tenement buildings or boarding houses with shared kitchens and bathrooms gave way to single-family houses set far back from the street behind expansive private lawns. Private automobiles replaced public transit or even walking as a primary mode of transportation. Streetcar tracks got ripped out in favour of smoothly paved roads engineered for cars. Sidewalks got much narrower, or disappeared entirely. Eventually, front-drive garages replaced front porches as the most prominent design detail of the new houses in ever-expanding subdivisions. We could now come and go from our dwellings without ever encountering our neighbours, save, perhaps, for a cursory wave from behind a shield of glass and steel.

Along the way, we began to place immense cultural value on the qualities enabled by this shift in built form. Privacy, seclusion and separation from those around us became defining characteristics of a "good" home, thus recasting the role of the neighbour in our culture. We became less likely to see them as critical resources essential for survival and more as curious strangers, if not outright impediments to our peace, quiet and privacy. As the sociologist Robert D. Putnam wrote in his famous book *Bowling Alone*, published in 2000, the decline in church attendance, dwindling involvement in labour unions and even the phasing out of neighbourhood bowling leagues and community dances throughout the 1970s, '80s and '90s further eroded opportunities to get to know those around us. In this century, megaplex movie theatres and shopping malls have been stripped of their status as both commercial and community hubs as more of us opt to stream and chill at home while compulsively scrolling through things we can buy online. Even the reliable din of the dinner rush at many local restaurants has been muted as tables intended for people to gather around become platforms for takeout containers awaiting a silent parade of app-enabled couriers. Inside our private abodes, space to accommodate our vast selection of screens now takes precedence over in-person human connection as a chief design consideration. The rise of the internet and mobile devices has changed our daily habits and how we move through our neighbourhoods as well. Many of us, myself included, purposefully plug into a podcast or browse social media in order to *avoid* having to make small talk with the strangers in our midst. Then came the pandemic, accelerating our growing social anxiety and justifying our latent sense of stranger danger with an actual physical threat.

As we reconfigure our cities and towns to allow more housing to be built closer together, much of the resistance we bump up against is due to the fact that the skills we need to be good neighbours and live happily in closer proximity have essentially atrophied. Adding to the problem, no doubt, is the fact that we are just so damn busy trying to meet the demands of living in a 24/7 attention economy that we haven't much energy or capacity to rebuild them. Between answering after-hours Slack messages from our bosses, getting our kids to soccer practice and rushing home to catch up on the side hustles many of us need to make extra money, there's little time to chit-chat with that new person who moved in across the street. Forget forging a relationship that would make us feel comfortable enough to knock on their door and ask for a proverbial cup of sugar.

In the era of Amazon and Instacart, running out of baking supplies is hardly the emergency it might have been half a century ago. Our lack of neighbourly connections might seem a little sad but largely inconsequential to our lives. Nothing could be further from the truth. Multitudes of studies show that good connections with our neighbours have an outsized impact on our health, safety and happiness. People who spend more time socializing with their neighbours live longer, have higher life satisfaction and are more optimistic than those who spend less time with neighbours or none at all. More than that, neighbourliness has proven to be the glue that holds our society together. In addition to being happier and healthier, people who spend time with their neighbours are more trusting of people overall, a vitally important tidbit in an era where we are more skeptical and fearful of each other than ever. One study I looked at, from the U.S.-based Institute for Family Studies, directly compared the number of Americans who spent social evenings with their neighbours over the last 50 years to the number of Americans who believe others can be trusted during the same time period. The trajectories of the two graph lines are essentially identical: a steady, precipitous decline.

Insights like this have led a growing number of experts to argue that reclaiming neighbourliness is essential if we are to overcome the radical polarization that has come to characterize modern politics and patch together our tattered social fabric. As *Atlantic* writer Derek Thompson points out, another way to think of our neighbours is as the village so many of us lament has gone missing from our lives in the last decades. Its disappearance hasn't just made us feel more isolated and alone; it's eroded our ability to form a functioning society. "The village is our best arena for practicing productive disagreement and compromise—in other words, democracy," he writes. The power of neighbourliness can be boiled down to the simple fact that we generally don't get to choose our neighbours, so getting to know them gives us a rare opportunity to practice building relationships with people we might not encounter in any other way. In fact, sociologists classify neighbourly relationships as "bridging" relationships, as in, they bridge the divides between different groups in society. In a world where our social lives are increasingly bifurcated between the known quantities of our immediate households and the special interest echo chambers of the internet, talking to our neighbours is one of the only ways to develop tolerance, understanding, even appreciation for people whose politics, religion or world views may, at first, seem utterly incompatible with our own. "That is something that we need a lot more of in this world, to find those kind of slow, safe, low-stakes ways to get to know people who are fundamentally different than us," Michelle Hoar, project director with the Vancouver-based Hey Neighbour! Collective, told me. "It's kind of an important muscle."

It's also a muscle we'll need to intentionally strengthen if we are going to successfully shift toward more compact forms of housing without negatively impacting our quality of life and our experience of home. Given the economic, ecological and social need to move away from single-family homes as the dominant form of housing in North America, urban planners and developers have attempted to coax us into closer proximity by pitching a vision of community. Knowing the change will naturally be met with resistance, they try to sell it with renderings for new, high-density housing developments that tend to feature healthy, happy people in a pristine and bustling public realm. Condo buildings advertise party rooms and gyms and rooftop gardens as collection points where we can gather and get to know our neighbours. These buildings often have names that include "Village" or "Commons," chosen specifically to conjure fantasies of reclaiming a yesteryear when we naturally offered each other friendship and support. The inference is if you give up an element of home our culture has come to prioritize above almost all others—space—you get belonging in exchange.

Reality doesn't always live up to the hype.

Shoving people into smaller spaces and closer proximity doesn't necessarily lead to strong neighbourly bonds. As I saw in Vienna, Berlin and Harare, creating tight-knit communities in this day and age often takes a fair amount of intention and effort. Without that, attempts to close the physical gap between neighbours can actually lead to people feeling *more* isolated and estranged.

That turned out to be the case in Vancouver, when a 2012 survey from the non-profit Vancouver Foundation identified a perplexing trend: As the city was densifying in response to its housing crisis, people reported feeling less connected to their neighbours—especially those who lived in high-density housing. Since then, a growing body of research has found a correlation between living in high-density urban environments and increased rates of social isolation, due to factors including a lack of secure tenure in rental buildings, poor architectural design, a dearth of green space and limited access to nature, and stigma related to cultural values that equate high-density housing with lower social status. All this is leading to what researchers have termed the "emerging asocial society"; that is, a society in which people aren't just lonely but have actually lost the motivation or skill necessary to engage in healthy social connections. This has profound implications for individual health and well-being and for the health and well-being of our cities.

"As things stand, this will bring increased trends of urban alienation, asocial and antisocial behaviours, loneliness and social isolation, marginalization, nuisance and exacerbated vulnerabilities," warns one 2022 knowledge synthesis on the topic.

The Hey Neighbour! Collective, an interdisciplinary group based out of Simon Fraser University's Morris J. Wosk Centre for Dialogue, was formed in response to these findings, specifically to investigate what can be done to encourage better social connections as cities become more dense. Step one is helping people understand why they need to know their neighbours, and what neighbourliness even is. While it's wonderful to form close friendships with the people around us, to the point where we feel confident asking them to watch our kids in a pinch or think to drop off some soup when we know they're sick, it's not actually necessary to get to that level of intimacy to see benefits, Hoar said. Just becoming familiar with our neighbours is often enough. As more of us live alone or in smaller households away from extended family and friends, our neighbours can fill the gaps in our support systems, just by virtue of their proximity. For instance, if you regularly see that senior down the hall, you might think to check on them in a heat wave; or someone else might pop by to see if you're okay when the power is out after a storm—both scenarios that are getting much more common due to the wild weather effects of climate change. "The reason it matters that we know our neighbours is that they are the ones that are right there when we might spontaneously need them," said Hoar. Knowing the people around us are looking out for our well-being, and vice versa, helps communities become much more resilient in the face of challenges posed by everything from economic uncertainty to an unstable climate, she said. It also makes living in apartment and condo buildings a much more pleasant experience. Becoming familiar with our neighbours can lead to what Hoar calls a system of "mutual support," which can increase our sense of purpose and belonging where we live. That can't happen if we aren't afforded the opportunity to get to know our neighbours in a positive context, and our housing often works against this goal.

Despite the promises of many multi-family buildings, a majority are not designed in a way that intentionally encourages good interactions between neighbours. "What we see in a lot of buildings that have poor acoustics, few social spaces and no kind of social programming is that people's only experience of their neighbours is like 'this person parks too close to my car, or this person makes a lot of noise on Sunday morning,'" explained Madeleine Hebert, senior housing specialist with Happy Cities, an urban planning, research and engagement firm that works closely with Hey Neighbour! From there, it's easy to default to disliking all the unknown people we almost never see but who nonetheless still manage to infringe upon our private space. However, these impediments can be overcome with a bit of strategy. Our outward ambivalence toward the strangers who live among us often masks a deep longing for human connection, Hoar and Hebert's research has found. Most people actually yearn for closer connections with their neighbours. They're just not sure how to make it happen.

Hey Neighbour! and Happy Cities have found that creating an environment conducive to neighbourliness doesn't actually take all that much, but it does take someone or something to get the ball rolling. A pilot project Hey Neighbour! ran with Concert Properties, a B.C.-based property management firm and developer, put in place a social connectedness coordinator in five rental buildings. This person's job was to support and empower resident-led activities that could encourage neighbourliness in high-density housing. Ideas ranged from doggy dates for canine residents and their humans to online speed-friending during the pandemic. The most effective interventions, however, were exceedingly simple. Placing a puzzle out in the lobby that people could noodle with when they had time to kill; putting up a bulletin board in the laundry room where people could post recipes; and other "light-touch," almost passive, interventions gently nudged neighbours toward each other by puncturing the veneer of anonymity that can shroud life in a big building. Those safe and somewhat distant entry points into considering the humanity of their neighbours opened the door for more in-depth and in-person interactions. Surveys after the pilot program showed that most participants met three or more new neighbours in the process and that they'd be more likely to ask a neighbour for a small favour in the future, a small but significant step in the right direction. Residents also said they felt safer and more connected in their buildings after the project, while building managers reported less conflict between residents, lower turnover and less property damage.

Of course, another way to rebuild our capacity for neighbourliness is to design housing in a way that explicitly encourages it. It makes sense that if decades of separating people into single-family homes has made a lasting imprint on how we relate to our neighbours, we might be able to undo that with housing designed to do the opposite. This is not a consideration that typically gets factored into most design and development processes, Hebert, a former architect, told me. Nor is it generally a factor included in our building codes or our housing policies.

I found this hard to believe in an era where it seems like so many new condo buildings, especially higher-end ones, feature trendy community amenities like rooftop barbecue stations or game rooms as a rule. But Hebert's research into the link between design and social connectedness found those spaces are often under-used and seldom configured in a way that invites residents to use them together. These spaces usually need to be pre-booked, sometimes for a fee, and for security reasons they're often tucked away in parts of the building that are hard to access and even harder to see. She found this keeps them out of sight and out of mind for many residents. When these amenity spaces do get used, it's often as an extension of people's personal space—a place to host private events that don't fit in more diminutive urban abodes—not to gather with neighbours in the building. But a lot of architects and developers with good enough intentions may not realize this, Hebert said, because it is not common practice for them to go back and assess their work once buildings are complete. "As architects and planners, we kind of walk away from our projects and we don't really take the time to understand, okay, what's actually happening in these buildings after we leave?"

In the course of her research, Hebert did actually go back to several completed multi-family buildings to observe how real people in the real world used the space in daily life. What she found was that "community" spaces like gardens or party rooms really need to be accessible and visible to a majority of people in order to build familiarity between residents. Common rooms located off the lobby with an open-door policy and, better yet, some programming, had more potential to draw in people for a board games night or some other casual event. Community gardens were best placed on the ground level, like in a courtyard, and combined with other leisure spaces like children's play structures that encouraged a multitude of uses by multitudes of people rather than just those with a green thumb. But it doesn't even take expensive purpose-built amenities to encourage social connection through design, Hebert found. Sometimes it just comes down to more thoughtful placement of standard fare. Laundry rooms, Hebert discovered, hold untapped potential to encourage socialization when they are placed on the main floor of a building rather than in a dank basement. Add some seating and a few kids' toys outside the door, and laundry day suddenly turns into an opportunity for people to sit and chat with their neighbours while they wait for the spin cycle to finish. Hebert's research also found that parking garages, bike storage lockers, even the little nooks in front of elevators could all be configured in ways—think simple, cheap additions such as a few chairs, a bookshelf, or a bulletin board—that encourage people to form connections. Meanwhile, corridors with natural light led people to linger a little longer and carry on conversations with neighbours at the door when compared to hallways awash in fluorescent light.

Considering the amount of public money that goes into supporting the housing sector, the fact that architects, planners and developers—people whose work has so much influence over the way we live our lives and our broader culture—don't have to make sure their work lives up to expectations amounts to a glaring lack of accountability. Clearly, not all condo or apartment complexes are categorically impersonal, and nor is it impossible to form a strong sense of community within them. I certainly know people who love their condo communities, and I've seen people living in the most utilitarian of buildings—like Kotti's social housing in Berlin—build an incredible sense of belonging and mutual support with their neighbours. But it does seem that when these connections occur, it is often in spite of the built environment rather than because of it. The neglect of social considerations in architecture and design has gotten even worse as we've attempted to build our way out of our housing crisis by emphasizing quantity over qualities that encourage positive interactions with our neighbours and thus nurture a more robust and holistic sense of home. This is especially true of projects meant to be "affordable" or aimed at lower-income households, Hoar and Hebert have found. Booting social considerations to the bottom of the list or reserving them only for high-end housing isn't just contributing to the sense of loss and resistance so many people feel as our cities densify but it's also a wasted chance to meaningfully address some of the biggest social and public health issues of our time, said Hoar. "We are pouring a lot of money and human energy and materials and resources into buildings that should be lasting, you know, up to 100 years, maybe even longer," she said. "So if we're not spending the time and maybe a tiny bit of extra money to make these as livable and as health promoting as they can be, we're missing a massive opportunity—and we're baking in the negative impacts of poor design."

There are some ways around this. Happy Cities and Hey Neighbour! offer training on socially connected design to architects, developers, municipalities and housing providers all over the world that are well attended and well-received. But mainstreaming the idea of social connectedness in housing design will likely come down to policy and legislation. Socially conducive design guidelines could be factored into municipal bylaws or provincial building codes. Social well-being requirements could be attached to funding for publicly supported housing projects, along with things like unit count and environmental sustainability requirements that are already mandated. We could even follow the lead of countries like Denmark, which has had a national architecture policy overseen by its ministry of culture since 2007. Options to actively rekindle neighbourliness abound—at least in high-density communities with a high degree of government oversight and planning.

Things get a little trickier out in the low-density, single-family-dominated suburbs.

---

When I meet Adam Schwartz at a coffee shop close to my house in Calgary, he suggests I get my London Fog to go. We are going on a treasure hunt.

You may not be familiar with the word "placemaking," but you've probably seen some examples of it in your city, or even in your own neighbourhood. Little Free Libraries, a roundabout-turned-wildflower garden, a picnic table that mysteriously appeared in a park that was just begging for a spot to sit. These are examples of placemaking, also known as tactical urbanism, which usually take the form of cheap and cheerful interventions spurred by regular people who saw an opportunity to make their neighbourhood a little more pleasant, a little more social, and went for it.

Until I met up with Schwartz, I wasn't aware of just how many of these citizen-led gems I interacted with on a regular basis. On our walk, he pointed out a mini skate park and basketball court opposite a popular brewery. Known locally as Gopher Park, it's a spot where I often see people shooting hoops when the weather is nice, but I hadn't known it was the brainchild of someone who lives in my neighbourhood and got a bit of funding from the local business improvement association. We passed under an area previously known as the "dark, dingy underpass" that had just been livened up with a new mural designed by two local artists and painted by more than 100 neighbourhood volunteers. This too was a community-led effort funded in part by the organization Schwartz works for, ActivateYYC, which offers grants of up to $5,000 to individuals or groups that want to take neighbourhood improvements into their own hands. "It's always just kind of been about giving citizens the chance to lead projects, rather than, you know, people waiting on government to act for them," Schwartz told me, noting it's a controversial approach.

We've been conditioned to turn to our city governments to deal with everything from a wonky garbage can to more bike racks to that menace of a fence on the local sledding hill. After all, it's the city's job to ensure our communities are livable, functional, safe and inviting. That's why we pay property taxes. But Schwartz takes a slightly different stance. While private citizens should not be solely responsible for every public space or amenity, he said, when it comes to the potential for that vacant field to become a community garden or a pump track, city governments or other bureaucratic agencies aren't always the best entities to lead the charge. For one, they're often extremely risk-averse, operating within a bureaucratic structure that's been developed to minimize liability, so it can take years for them to approve what a handful of determined neighbours can do in a few weeks or months. And sometimes when cities or their affiliated organizations do get involved in "activating" public space, it doesn't quite hit the mark.

To illustrate, Schwartz and I ambled up the block to a surface parking lot that got a makeover a few years back with the addition of some pastel paint and large-scale sculptures reminiscent of emojis. There's some seating and a ring of scaffolding that, several years after the fact, I've come to realize is a permanent part of the transformation. It looks . . . interesting, but it's not really clear what the space is supposed to be. According to a wordy sign hanging near the entrance, the space, called ParkPark, was designed to combine the ethos of a parking lot and a recreational park with an intention to become a "community gathering" place with a "layer cake of uses." I'm sure the idea seemed great on paper. In practice, I've only ever seen it used as a gathering space for cars, probably because nobody wants to shoot hoops or play ball hockey in a place where they have to constantly worry about hitting, or being hit by, a bunch of vehicles. As we contemplated a lonely basketball hoop barricaded behind a row of mid-size SUVs, Schwartz told me this project was spearheaded by a city-led agency responsible for urban renewal that had contracted a Winnipeg-based architecture firm to do the design, which apparently had won a bunch of awards. The point here? We don't always *want* professional entities leading the charge on meeting hyperlocal community needs.

This is where the potential of placemaking—the DIY grassroots version of it—is helpful. Not only does it draw on local expertise to improve the places where we live, it organically builds trust and connection between neighbours. Schwartz said the projects funded by ActivateYYC are intentionally inexpensive and low-stakes, at least financially, but they do require people to take a social risk, and that's the magic of it. To spearhead one of these projects, you have to stick your neck out a bit for the betterment of the community and have faith that your neighbours will respond in kind. At their core, placemaking projects are an invitation for neighbours to work together in a way that feels comfortable and safe, leading more people to proactively contribute to the good of the greater community. For instance, if that basketball net at ParkPark gets torn down, probably no one does anything other than maybe alert the city. If it gets torn down in Gopher Park, however, someone probably takes it upon themselves to replace it. Seeing that, maybe someone else decides to repaint the court lines when they start to fade, and someone else starts up an annual round robin tournament. Placemaking has a tendency to spiral out in positive ways, Schwartz said, leading to organic connections and accountability among neighbours. This might all sound sweet but superfluous to our housing problem, but there is a connection. Because if neighbours can organically come together to paint a mural or make a park more usable in service of the community, they can also work together in the creation of more and better homes.

---

The idea of empowering neighbours to directly collaborate on solving the housing issues in their communities without as much, or any, intervention from city governments is one that's gaining traction in many corners of the urban planning and development fields. Strong Towns, for example, posits that "neighbourhood developers" can bring a level of sensitivity and local insight to their projects that large-scale corporate or investment firms lack by design. As the theory goes, a developer who lives in the same community where they work has an emotional investment in that place—a.k.a. a sense of place attachment—as well as personal relationships with their neighbours—a sense of belonging—that they likely want to maintain. These emotional ties serve to mitigate the influence of profit and greed that leads to impersonal, insensitive development choices that don't actually serve the needs of the community—for example, building luxury housing instead of affordable family-sized rentals, or places for local seniors to downsize.

This is largely the same philosophy that encouraged Alkarim Devani to attempt to revamp the approach to small-scale development with a "citizen-led redevelopment platform" called mddl. Launched in 2024 as part of the Canada Mortgage and Housing Corporation's Housing Supply Challenge, essentially a national competition for new ideas to fund and build more housing, mddl was one of 18 semifinalists to receive a $1 million start-up grant and later among nine finalists that received a $3 million prize. In 2025, mddl was named one of four winning "game-changers" selected to split a further $15 million in prize money. Government endorsement aside, Devani was convinced from the outset that mddl could revolutionize the way we build housing in the majority of Canada's neighbourhoods.

For much of his career, Devani has positioned himself as a developer with a conscience, a local kid born and raised in Calgary to immigrant parents who understands the struggle for the Canadian dream of homeownership. Through his family-run property development firm, RNDSQR, Devani specialized in building missing middle infills and purpose-built rentals in established inner-city areas. I've interviewed Devani a few times, and he's always struck me as someone who genuinely cares about his city and its future. Still, he's no stranger to the skepticism and stigma that automatically arises as soon as the neighbours find out someone among them has sold (out) to a developer. No matter how local, or how sensitive that developer tries to be, there will always be people who are convinced their neighbourhood is being sacrificed for the sake of a greedy corporation, and an acrimonious rebellion ensues. So, Devani started thinking about a solution. How about removing professional developers from the equation entirely by empowering regular homeowners to *become* the developer?

Along with colleague Darlene Jehn, Devani came up with the idea for mddl, which aims to share the tricks of the development trade with "property owners, independent builders and everyday Canadians." Their educational programs, called mddl School, offer introductory training to any interested party that might benefit from learning about what it takes to turn a single-family lot into a fourplex, or something like that. It sounded interesting to me, so I asked if I could go.

The day I attended mddl School, Devani opened with a talk about his "why"—people he'd worked with like Murray and Eilish, two seniors who'd redeveloped a property to accommodate renters, or the father of a son with a developmental disability who would at some point require a live-in caregiver. It's everyday people like these who Devani thinks should be driving the change in residential neighbourhoods now open to additional density thanks to moves like Calgary's blanket rezoning.

"What are we afraid of? Financialization of housing. Developers taking all our money," he told me when we caught up in a spare moment. "So how do you make those comments when it's like, 'Oh, that's my neighbour. They've owned that house for 30 years.' You're gonna go villainize someone because they need a fully accessible suite and they need to tear down that existing house but they want to stay in their community? They can't afford to live in that house anymore because it's too big? Those are the things that I think are important that we're not talking about."

I totally agree with Devani. We don't talk nearly enough about the myriad reasons someone might want or need to change their housing, or how we can help them do that without losing all the other things that create a sense of home for them and their immediate neighbours. Only, we didn't really talk about that at mddl School either. Despite Devani's vision of turning ordinary people into developers to help solve the housing crisis, there weren't a lot of "ordinary" people in the room on the day I attended mddl School, shortly after its launch. The room was mostly full of development industry–adjacent folks like architects, realtors, non-profit housing providers, even a utility company and a start-up that sells shares in real estate online for as little as a dollar. I learned a lot that day; I just wasn't convinced any of it was going to combat the influence of financialization to the degree that Devani seemed to hope.

Throughout the day, we were guided through a mock process of redeveloping a property, with sessions led by various industry experts. We learned about what pitfalls to look out for when selecting a lot (pro tip: avoid areas that need to be rezoned or that are obstructed by power lines); we got advice about managing construction and obtaining financing; and we worked together in groups to select a site and decide on a design. At the end of the day, it didn't seem like a program designed for homeowners looking to redevelop their own property for the benefit of the community, but for those looking specifically for a property to develop for profit, just like a commercial developer. We were encouraged to make our decisions based exclusively on the bottom line, with most groups selecting their design based on what they could build for the least amount of headache and the highest return. There was no dialogue about designing for specific needs in the community, adapting current residences for multi-generational use or encouraging social connection or affordability. And despite a cursory mention that it's best practice to get the neighbours on board before you submit your development proposal to the city, there was no guidance on how exactly one might go about doing that.

To be clear, I think Devani's drive to empower normal citizens to leverage their own resources—both financial and social—to create more of the housing our communities need is absolutely the right idea. I just thought it hinged on the wrong incentive. As much as enabling every homeowner out there to become their own developer *might* help create more of the sensitive, missing middle housing we need, it could also just be another way we hammer into our cultural DNA that the primary value of housing is financial. We've already seen this through the rise of platforms like Airbnb, which were originally conceived of as a way for people to make extra income by renting out parts of their houses while sharing their little corner of the world with others. But it ended up cannibalizing entire communities as people hoarded housing in popular markets—snapping up leases or inexpensive condos—in order to build lucrative vacation-rental empires. I worried mddl might unintentionally end up creating some similarly undesirable outcomes.

When I voiced my concerns to Devani after the workshop, he was receptive but quick to volley back. His goal with mddl was to allow more people to *participate* in the housing sector, he told me, not to reinvent the whole thing. He wasn't opposed to working with non-profit or affordable housing providers; in fact, mddl School had waived its $750 fee for non-profit groups—and also for me. But with housing more expensive to produce than it has ever been, there are limits to what the market can do, he explained. Some people coming through his program might have more of a social conscience than others. They might choose to forego the highest profit for the greater good, but that's entirely up to them.

Most people need more than altruism to motivate them to take on the risk, cost and stress of building housing in our current climate, Devani said, and money is the most powerful motivator we've got. "It's weird to me to think that there will be a world in which we don't financialize real estate," he told me. Places in Europe, like Vienna or Berlin, with a better social safety net and an entirely different social and political history—they might be able to do things a little bit differently, he said. But here in free-market, capitalist North America? "I don't know how that happens."

And that's just the crux of the whole thing, isn't it? We've been doing things the same way for so long our imaginations are bound up in a trap. Because we have almost exclusively relied on the market to produce housing for generations now, we are fixated on finding market-based solutions. Even many so-called innovations are essentially a wash, rinse, repeat of the same old market economics, which rely on one thing—profit—as the central motivating factor. The big, hulking elephant in the middle of almost every living room on this continent is the fact that profit is not an essential element of home. In fact, its corrupting influence actively works against even the most well-intended efforts at solving the crisis in our midst.

I would love to believe I could sit down with the other landowners on my block and hash out, neighbour to neighbour, a plan for redevelopment that everyone could live with. Without a culture shift around how we value property and housing, however, I have my doubts about how well that would go. The presence of profit, whether explicitly discussed or just hanging in the air like a phantom, undermines efforts at building trust and collaboration by planting seeds of doubt about people's intentions. This skepticism is something that surfaced in the INTERACT study where people doubted their city governments truly had the community's interest in mind. I also heard it echoed by city planners in Vienna, who told me all of their efforts to build trust and community cohesion hinged on people knowing that all of the changes they were asked to endure—even ones they might not like—would be in service of the public good. "You have to be able to make an argument that development will be good for the people who live there; if it's only maximizing money for private development then it's much harder," one city employee told me.

But in North America, most people simply cannot conceive of a housing system that doesn't revolve around profit and private wealth, except possibly in the abstract. Beautiful and plentiful non-profit housing might exist in a land far, far away, but not here, not for us. We all know we can't have nice things.

I'm not saying the market has to disappear, but it can't continue to be basically the only game in town.

It reminds me of the story of the two wolves—you know, the one that may or may not be an ancient Cherokee proverb that's become a staple of internet memes? A young boy goes to his grandfather for help because he feels like there are two wolves at war inside him. One is filled with anger, hate and greed; the other embodies generosity, selflessness and a desire to live in harmony with all. When the boy pleads with his grandfather to tell him which wolf will win, the grandfather replies, sagely, "The one you feed." Except, that may not be the end of the story. According to some corners of the internet, the grandfather actually tells the boy he needs to feed both wolves, because that way they'll begin to balance each other out. We've been feeding the greedy wolf for such a long time we've forgotten there's another one sitting right there.

Maybe it's time we threw it a bone.

12

# BUILDING FOR THE VILLAGE

From the outside, the only indication the six-storey, slate-grey building on Vancouver's Quebec Street is different from any other condo on the block is in the name, Little Mountain Cohousing, carved into a concrete slab near the entrance. It's only once inside that you start to get a sense of what those words actually mean.

Walking through the front entrance, the first thing you see is the common room full of long dining tables and a large kitchen capable of cranking out food for each of Little Mountain's 25 households, which happens here about three times a week. In between the community meals, cooked by a revolving roster of residents, the room is open to anyone, any time, whether for a game of cards in the evening or a quiet place to get some work done during the day. When I visited on a sweltering August afternoon along with my partner Dave, the floor-to-ceiling glass doors were closed to keep out the heat, but on cooler days they open onto a grassy courtyard with a clear view of the children's play gym on the other side. As if taking a page right out of Hey Neighbour! and Happy Cities' socially connected design guidelines, there's a laundry room right next door to the kids' area, and across from that an oversized purple couch and some well-loved patchwork pillows that animate what would otherwise be dead space in front of the mailboxes.

"When we moved in, somebody had this sofa that didn't fit in their living room, so they just plunked it down here trying to figure out what to do with it," Lysa, one of Little Mountain's residents and our tour guide, told me. "It's become a very popular spot just to hang out. The kids build forts."

In a standard condo building, dumping a couch in the lobby, even temporarily, is more likely to net you a fine from building management than praise from your neighbours, but this isn't your typical condo—at least not entirely. Legally speaking, Little Mountain Cohousing, named for its neighbourhood in central Vancouver and the process by which it was built, is just a strata corporation like any other. The residents here bought in with their own money and they are free to leave and sell at any time, listing their units at the current market price. Only most are not inclined to do so after all the effort it took them to get here. What makes this a cohousing development is the fact that Lysa and her neighbours designed, financed and managed construction of the building themselves, working together for years before they'd even found land or broken ground. Their express aim was not to make money but to create a socially connected, environmentally sustainable, multi-generational home for themselves and whomever might come after.

As we continued on our tour, Lysa pointed out all the ways these intentions were baked into the building's bones. In addition to all the common areas on the ground floor, Little Mountain boasts a soundproof music room off the parking garage as well as a workshop for the many makers and musicians among them. These options took precedence over more standard amenities like a gym, she explained, because in their planning process they realized that fitness centres are a dime a dozen but studio space for artistic pursuits is much harder to come by. They also put in a guest suite, a small shared office and a rooftop garden where people freely pilfered food from planter boxes overflowing with late-summer produce.

On each floor, the usually empty nooks in front of elevators or outside apartment doors had been kitted out for communal use. One was set up as a place for kids to do homework, another as a craft corner and another as a library. On the sixth floor, Lysa showed us a multipurpose room with a gorgeous wraparound deck featuring stellar views of the neighbourhood. People sometimes gather here for Friday drinks, and the teens and older kids use it for sleepovers, she said. "If you look next door and at the building across the street, they have all those rooftop decks and those are private. The developers put those in because they can charge a premium for those suites," Lysa said. In contrast, "You'll see that all of our best spots are the ones we kept for everybody." This small but significant divergence in priorities illustrates the difference between housing built for the market and housing built by, and for, a community.

---

Amid all the hand-wringing about what to do about our persistent, ever-worsening lack of affordable housing, we tend to fall into a false dichotomy. Most of the solutions on the table come from one of two places: the market, or the government. Both are problematic, though for different reasons. As we've seen throughout this book, the for-profit housing sector has never lived up to its imagined potential to provide every Canadian with a stable and dignified home. In fact, market economics have actively worked against that goal by perverting our values and contorting our conception of what a home is. Our over-reliance on the market is what got us into this mess. It is not, by itself, going to get us out.

Then, you have government, which has proven to be a rather fickle partner in our quest to ensure everyone is appropriately housed. Governments are the most obvious entity to turn to for leadership in solving our housing crisis. They have access to great gobs of money furnished by the taxes we all pay, and they can provide preferential financing. They have the power to create new laws and set policies that influence our values and our culture. They have a mandate to serve the people—even the ones who didn't vote for them.

Governments are also famously unreliable. All it takes is a shift in political ideologies or a change in ruling parties to decimate systems and organizations that rely on public funding. Let us not forget, the critical shortage of affordable housing in Canada today is due in large part to the decisions of successive governments to end funding for non-profit housing in favour of other political priorities—for example, shoring up a private, for-profit housing system that continually requires public resources to keep the whole thing afloat.

But there is a third option. A vast middle ground between public and private on which we can build not just housing but a *housing system* that puts human health, happiness and connection front and centre; in short, a system built on the foundational elements of home. There is an overlooked stakeholder group that is inherently motivated and perfectly capable of leading this charge. Us.

In my travels and research for this book I have learned that regular people, people like Lysa and her neighbours, like you and like me, are the biggest untapped resource we have in overcoming our housing crisis. What we lack are the right tools, education and, importantly, policies and programs necessary to strengthen our social muscles and build the capacity to work together on a scale that could truly transform our housing landscape, and by association, our lives. Except for experimental concepts like mddl, which run the risk of encouraging people to think and act more like corporations than as part of a community, very few of the programs and pathways meant to solve our housing crisis are aimed at equipping and empowering people to create the homes they want and need.

"It's like our ability to create housing for ourselves, in many ways, [has] been taken away from us," Ronaye Matthew, a cohousing consultant who worked on Little Mountain, told me. "Because, really, the only people who know how to do it are conventional developers, and they're doing it for profit." Having spent decades working for a conventional developer herself, Matthew hit a point where she no longer wanted to contribute to what she called "the cycle of greed." That led her to pivot toward a more community-focused way of building housing. Rather than taking a cut of the sales, as most developers do, she charges a flat fee for her expertise guiding cohousing groups through the development process. She helps them navigate city bureaucracies and construction contracts, as well as find suitable land and even recruit members to join in the process. The projects she works on are non-profit developments, where the end price reflects only what it cost to build. That's in contrast to the business model of conventional developers, which make a profit by selling dwellings for more than it costs to build them. While many developers do strive to produce well-built housing under the conventional system, Matthew said, at the end of the day, the focus on profits supersedes virtually every other consideration. By and large, our system is not set up to support or incentivize any other way of creating housing. Fortunately, people are figuring it out anyway.

All across the country, grassroots collectives of tenants, homeowners, activists, and even realtors and developers like Matthew are proving that we are all capable of building, maintaining and protecting good homes for ourselves and for the people around us, no matter our cultural background or political history. What's more, they are showing that we needn't rely on the promise of profit or a distant potential payday to inspire people to invest their financial, social and emotional capital into pursuing this goal. They are demonstrating that when it comes to our homes, we can be motivated by an innate desire for a safe, stable, socially connected place to live that is encoded in our DNA.

With the right set of policies, incentives and positive social pressure, I believe we can build on what these groups have started. We can shift our culture away from the harmful narrative that casts housing as a commodity to be traded on a whim and toward a culture that rightly comprehends it as a human right, a critical piece of social infrastructure as essential to our quality of life as education and health care. Reclaiming the ability to create homes for ourselves, in collaboration with our neighbours like we have done for tens of thousands of years, is how we can begin to diminish the hold that forces like financialization have over our institutions and our imaginations. It is by working together and getting back to a reverence for home as a holistic entity, as an end in itself, that we get to a place where all the resources we're pouring into solving our housing crisis actually get the job done.

We can do this by establishing a robust housing sector that empowers communities to take the lead in creating the housing they need. This approach is called collaborative housing, and many experts—as well as international organizations such as World Habitat, a global NGO aimed at supporting safe and secure housing, and URBACT, a European organization dedicated to sustainable urban development—have identified it as having unique potential to make real headway in addressing the global housing crisis.

Also known as community-led housing, this model intentionally casts a wide net, allowing for flexibility and experimentation that results in many different forms of housing. But in general, collaborative models have some core qualities in common: They put resident and community needs ahead of profits; they include some form of ongoing collective or co-operative management of the housing; they're designed in a way that promotes social connection while respecting individual privacy; and they transcend the distinction between private and public ownership, often drawing from both public and private resources to make them affordable, environmentally sustainable and socially responsible. Put simply, collaborative housing generally grows out of, and is led by, communities who share something in common. Collaborators might be drawn to a certain neighbourhood, city or region; they might connect over a shared aspect of identity, like being single parents, seniors or LGBTQ2+ folks; or they might have a common need, like affordable family housing with secure tenure.

In cohousing, one form of collaborative housing, what unites people is generally a desire for more meaningful social connection, Matthew said. But cohousing shouldn't be confused with trendy market developments that also promise community and access to communal spaces, often under the similar-sounding moniker of co-living. In true cohousing, residents are involved in the *process* of building, which is as important as the product, said Matthew. "One of the things that supports cohousing to work, where our common spaces get used a lot, is that we actually get to know each other in the development phase," she said. By the time people move in together, they already have some of the elements of home—familiarity with each other as well as an established way of working together, and a community to which they belong. This makes it a lot easier to adjust to what, for many, is an unfamiliar form of housing with way less private space than they might be used to.

Downsizing from, say, a 2,000-square-foot single-family house to a 600-square-foot condo is a lot easier when you have a guest room you can book for visitors, or neighbours that you know who might be out of town and willing to offer up their suite to your guests. You don't need as much room for kids to run around in when there's a play gym and the building is full of other adults and families that you trust. And you don't need to dedicate precious kitchen space to infrequently used items like an Instapot or food processor when you have the option to borrow one from the common kitchen as needed. But the biggest boost to quality of life in cohousing comes from the fact that your neighbours, as Michelle Hoar from Hey Neighbour! said, are right there when you need them.

I got a glimpse of what this looks like in practice on my tour of Little Mountain when Lysa ran into a neighbour in the lobby who'd just come down from meeting the building's newest resident, a baby who was less than 24 hours old. As they discussed plans to drop off meals and other ways to support the family—doing small chores and helping care for the family's older child—I felt a pang in my heart. My own postpartum experience was one of profound loneliness and isolation, a feeling I'd initially chalked up to the unfortunate timing of giving birth in a pandemic, but one that has persisted as the parent of a precocious preschooler whose sleep schedule traps me and Dave in our house every evening after 7 p.m. While we tend to collapse in front of the TV every evening after our son is asleep, often lamenting our lack of a social life, parents at Little Mountain regularly come downstairs with the baby monitor to visit or play cards, said Lysa. And the benefit of having multiple neighbours and generations under one roof goes in many directions. "It's kind of fun for those of us that don't have kids," said Lysa, who added she loves living alone in her two-bedroom townhouse unit, but couldn't imagine doing it without the community just outside her door.

Obviously, cohousing is not always a seamless experience. Not everyone is particularly fond of each other and conflicts do arise, but it's not necessary for everyone to hold hands and sing "Kumbaya" in order to make it work, Lysa explained. No one is ever required to socialize, but they do need to commit to learning how to effectively participate in collective decision-making and conflict resolution—something of a dying art in this world. For that reason, many cohousing groups hire facilitators to help them set the rules of engagement for their community, which normally work on consensus models. It's kind of like a privately financed form of Vienna's social worker–led interventions.

Cohousers also tend to have a positive influence on the people who live around them. After a Halloween street party got rained out and wound up in Little Mountain's common room, some people who lived in a condo across the street were inspired to make changes in their own building, Lysa said. "The people were like, 'Oh my god, you guys actually use your space.' They had this amenity room at the front of the building that nobody was using, so now it's full of toys and they have a kids' playroom." Another strata nearby took a cue from Little Mountain's frequent community meals and started organizing monthly potlucks for the building.

Though cohousing has existed in some form since the 1960s, most prominently in Europe, it's still a relatively unknown housing model in Canada. Even so, demand for this way of living is high. Little Mountain has more than 800 people on a list to be informed if one of its 25 units, ranging from studios to four-bedrooms, ever comes up for sale. Supply, however, is infinitesimally small. There are fewer than 25 completed cohousing projects across the country, and many frequently fizzle out in the planning stages because building cohousing is exceptionally difficult. There is almost no guidance, government support, funding or programs available to help groups navigate the building process.

Many municipalities are supportive of cohousing—once they understand it, Matthew said. But they don't have the tools to treat these grassroots initiatives as distinct from conventional, for-profit developers. As a result, these non-profit, self-financed groups are left to compete with deeper-pocketed players when bidding on land and are usually charged the same fees, taxes and levies as corporate builders. Because of this, and because cohousing is generally built to a higher social and environmental standard than conventional buildings, the end cost is often not any cheaper than new market housing. Sometimes it's higher. But advocates argue cohousing could easily be made more affordable with the right policies and support in place.

While cohousers don't generally come to their projects for altruistic reasons, their values around community make them receptive to implementing affordability measures when they're available, said Matthew. Cities frequently offer incentives to conventional developers, such as waived or reduced developer levies, density bonuses (building slightly more than the zoning allows) or fast-tracking permit applications in the hope that lowering the cost of building will result in more affordable housing. Often this is met with middling success. I've lost count of the number of times I've seen the "affordable" units planned for a market-driven development decreased substantially or dropped entirely when shifts in things like construction costs, interest rates or density constraints cut too deeply into the profit margin. But without profit to consider, cohousers simply pass any savings on. Matthew gave the example of Driftwood Village in the City of North Vancouver, another project she worked on. The city allowed the group to reinvest into its own project $1.6 million it had paid to the city in development fees, reducing building costs and allowing for eight of the 27 units to be sold at 25 percent below market price. The group then attached a covenant to those units, meaning they will always be sold at 25 percent below market price. "The expectation is, if you get a lower price for [building], you want to make sure that you can pass that benefit on to future generations," said Matthew.

Another way to reduce the cost of cohousing is to combine its community-led design approach with other forms of housing that have a proven track record of producing more deeply affordable homes.

---

As we touched on briefly in chapter 3, co-operative housing has a long and successful history in Canada, forming the backbone of our "golden era" of social housing from about the 1970s to the 1990s. For such a short-lived period it's had a lasting legacy—30 years after funding for new co-ops was cut, more than a quarter million people across the country still live in them, and as with cohousing there is high demand. Many co-ops are at full capacity with substantial waitlists that can be years long.

Part of what makes co-operative housing so desirable is its collective ownership structure. Unlike renting, where housing costs go toward the profits of a landlord who makes the rules and calls the shots, co-ops are collectively owned, self-managed and democratically run. Members vote to elect a board and have a say about everything from how much their housing charges should be to what they get spent on. Like cohousing, there's no profit margin on most co-ops (a scant few are "equity" co-ops where members buy in and get some of their investment back when they leave), so housing charges can be kept much lower than in market housing. To give an example of just how much lower, friends of mine who live in a two-bedroom townhouse in a Vancouver co-op paid just over $1,300 a month in 2025, compared to the average market rent of about $3,500 a month for the same kind of place. Plus, co-ops often feature shared common spaces like meeting rooms, gardens and playgrounds, and there are no leases. Members can and sometimes do live there for life. By law co-ops can never be sold or become privatized—though some exist on leased land, making them vulnerable to eventual redevelopment. In general, co-ops are an extremely pragmatic option for public housing investment. Government contributions—the tax dollars that go toward the capital costs, land purchases or financing of co-ops—can be recouped in part or in full once people move in and start paying housing charges. And when lower-income people living in co-ops receive subsidies from the government to help pay for their monthly housing costs, that money gets reinvested in running the co-op instead of lining the pockets of a private landlord.

For all these reasons and more, calls for a substantial reinvestment in housing co-ops have been wailing in the wind for years. Recently, we've made some progress on this front. In 2024, the federal government unveiled a $1.5 billion fund for the construction of new co-op housing, enough to build about 3,000 additional units over seven years. It's something, but far short of the 12,000 to 20,000 units produced *each year* during our golden era. When you consider the $115 billion (and counting) budget for our National Housing Strategy, most of which is earmarked for market-oriented solutions, we could be devoting a lot more resources to bringing co-ops back in a big way. But we wouldn't have to build all new co-ops from scratch. In fact, there are some very good reasons we should not.

Depending on where you live in this country, it costs about $500,000 to build a new unit of affordable housing. Saving one that already exists by removing it from the market—essentially buying it for conversion to non-profit housing—costs about half that. According to a 2022 analysis by housing expert Steve

Pomeroy, from 2016 to 2021 Canada lost more than twice the amount of affordable housing units built each year through housing programs. And that was an improvement on the previous five years, from 2011 to 2016, when we lost an average of 64,000 affordable housing units annually, compared to just 4,000 new ones created each year. Faced with a mammoth backlog and a dismal production rate, building our way out of our affordable housing crisis isn't just an unlikely prospect, it's mathematically impossible. Confounding efforts to address the housing crisis through new construction—which by itself is slow-going and expensive—is the fact that older, cheaper housing often gets demolished to make way for new buildings. Other times, affordable rental buildings are sold and renovated so the new owners can justify charging higher rents. It's only in the last few years that governments have started to pay attention to this fact. There are now a few fledgling funds aimed at preserving affordable housing, mostly by helping non-profit housing providers buy existing rentals and turn them into social housing. But there's another population that could benefit from a publicly funded boost in buying power. Tenants.

It's long been an unquestioned truth that every Canadian renter aspires to one day be a homeowner. And, as we discussed in part 1 of this book, the vast majority of housing policies and a substantial amount of money over the last century has been aimed at enabling Canadians to do just that. But heavily subsidizing private homeownership has also helped to keep the cost of housing artificially high, contributing to the housing crisis. We're now at a point where, for the first time in decades, the growth of renters is outpacing buyers, and many Canadians will have no choice but to remain renters for life. In response, some tenants in this country are taking a cue from places like Berlin and redefining what it means to take ownership of their homes.

---

In December 2022, Emily Power was browsing Realtor.ca, a real estate listing service, when she made a discovery every renter in this country dreads. The building she lived in, 272 Caroline Street South, in Hamilton, Ontario, was for sale. In a city where affordable rental buildings were being snapped up by corporate landlords at an alarming rate, Power feared the worst. An acquisition by a real estate investment trust or a large multinational company would surely mean rent hikes and renovictions to follow. But she also knew that this outcome was not preordained. As a community activist who'd studied urban planning and worked for a non-profit affordable housing provider, Power knew she and her neighbours could fight back if they worked together. She started knocking on doors and invited them to a meeting where she shared the news the building was for sale. "At that point, it was more of a 'how can we support each other?' You know, distributing like a Know Your Rights package and making sure people knew about how to access the local legal clinic," she told me. But then it morphed into something different. As they started batting around ideas to preserve their homes, the tenants hit upon a solution that, though a total longshot, seemed worth pursuing: Could they fundraise to buy the building and turn it into a co-op?

A tenant-led co-op conversion was basically unheard of in Canada at the time. There were no formal pathways or programs to follow, and no dedicated funding they could apply for to help them along. Conversations with the regional and national co-op housing federations were encouraging but offered no practical guidance. "We were on our own to figure most of that out," said Power. Remarkably, they did. In November 2024, less than two years after Power first found out the building was for sale, the Caroline Co-op was born. Power and her neighbours are hopeful their story will inspire other tenants to follow in their footsteps. "People need to get organized as working-class people," said Power. "This is how we're going to solve the problems that we're up against in all areas of our lives."

For Caroline Street, organizing was the first step toward success. Once they found out the building was for sale they formed a tenants' association and wrote a letter to their landlord saying they knew their rights and planned to fight back publicly against any attempts to push them out. Then they sent similar letters to executives at companies they'd discovered had made offers on the property, which essentially scared them off. "They rescinded their offers," Power said. That gave the tenants some time and leverage with their landlord, who agreed to take down the listing while they tried to raise the money to put an offer together. After being brushed off by the Canada Mortgage and Housing Corporation—the federal entity that's supposed to fund and encourage housing innovation—Power kept reaching out to financial and philanthropic organizations, and eventually found some surprisingly receptive partners.

A local credit union, FirstOntario, agreed to give them a mortgage to be repaid through housing charges, and Newmarket Capital, an impact investment firm with a social justice agenda, provided a "significant" grant and a low-interest loan to cover the down payment. The local community foundation and other donors also kicked in some money for closing costs. Altogether, Caroline Street raised around $5 million to cover the purchase and repair of the 100-year-old building, which has 21 units ranging from one to three bedrooms. The City of Hamilton also partnered with the co-op to provide some housing subsidies for lower-income members. In a city where market rents averaged around $1,600 for a one-bedroom (as of 2025), housing charges at the co-op ranged between $700 for smaller units and $1,500 for larger ones. That money goes toward paying back the mortgage, with some left over for maintenance and contingencies, according to the co-op.

Their success proves that co-op conversions are not only possible but could make a big impact on our housing crisis if they were to happen at scale. A few relatively simple policy changes could get the ball rolling, Power said. For instance, cities like Montreal require landlords to disclose to a public registry when they put rental buildings up for sale, while Washington, D.C. and San Francisco require that tenants are given first right of refusal to buy rental buildings that go on the market. Steps like this, combined with programs and pathways tenants can follow to access funding and support toward conversion, could help save thousands of units of affordable housing while preventing displacement and keeping communities intact. As with cohousing, going through the process of creating a co-op can even build a sense of belonging. Power said she and her neighbours didn't really know each other at the outset of their journey, but now they're a team. They have Christmas parties and game nights and get together to watch Jays' games in someone's apartment. And, in a way, it's allowed them to participate in the cultural rite of passage that is homeownership in Canada. Co-op members don't own their homes outright—they can't sell them for a profit when or if they move—but they do get many of the major benefits of homeownership, like stability and autonomy, that are so often denied to renters. "I do have a greater say over how my housing charge is being spent, and I do think that's empowering," Power said.

This brings up another issue baked into our housing system that unnecessarily drives up costs. When it comes to housing for renters, lower-income people or other marginalized groups, there's this idea that someone else always needs to be in charge, like a landlord, a social services organization or a government-run housing agency. Implicit in our valorization of private homeownership seems to be a belief that anyone unable to achieve that goal for whatever reason is fundamentally flawed. Basically, we think of renters, poor people and other marginalized groups as being incapable of managing their own housing.

The Caroline Co-op and almost every other co-op in the country prove that's just not true. There are specific situations where a third party is necessary to support independent living—for example, when people have certain disabilities or acute mental health concerns—but in many cases, it just adds overhead. The value of private landlords in particular is questionable. In our current system, landlords are thought of as essential to maintaining and managing our housing stock; that's why housing policies allow them to make a profit. While some undoubtedly do make good on that promise, countless others certainly do not, as the Caroline Co-op members discovered in the process of buying their own building. According to Power, disclosures during the sale revealed their landlord was making between $70,000 and $80,000 a year in profit while neglecting critical repairs that added up to more than $500,000 the co-op ended up paying for. That profit was on top of the massive windfall the landlord got from the $4.8 million sale on a building he bought for $975,000 in 2008. "Why should a landlord like him be trusted to manage the housing stock?" Power said. "We can manage our own affairs. We can manage our finances responsibly. We can make decisions collectively."

And if neighbours can work together to manage a building, they can manage a neighbourhood as well.

---

When I met Andy Bond for coffee in a part of Vancouver where the city's tourism and poverty meccas frequently and awkwardly collide, he told me he'd never seen the area in worse shape. "There's no denying it. It's bigger, it's messier," Bond said. "I think there's just a general feeling the population has shifted. There's just been more violence. The drug situation's made people more desperate, and people really feel fed up." It was late summer in 2024, and Bond was in a good position to gauge how the area was faring. He'd started working in the Downtown Eastside (DTES) in the 1990s as a front-line worker for a prominent non-profit social services agency that operates housing for the city's most vulnerable—those with extreme mental health and addiction issues. He later ended up as the organization's executive director before burning out and moving away from Vancouver. But during COVID, which absolutely rocked the DTES and amplified its poverty, a group of resident-activists reached out to ask whether he'd consider moving back. They wanted him to help launch something called a community land trust.

In the wide-ranging universe of collaborative housing, community land trusts, or CLTs, are the ultimate container in which many forms of community-led initiatives can combine to form a sustainable ecosystem. With a mandate to acquire and steward land for the benefit of a specific community, often a neighbourhood or region, CLTs build portfolios of property that are insulated from both the forces of the private market and the instability of government. "Community land trusts view land as something that should benefit the actual people who live and work on that land," Nat Pace, network director of the Canadian Network of Community Land Trusts, told me. As such, CLTs are structured as community-owned non-profit corporations with elected boards that include people from the neighbourhood, especially tenants, and those from surrounding communities, as well as professionals with expertise to advise on management and growth.

A key focus of CLTs is in creating and sustaining affordable housing in perpetuity, but they can also focus on other aspects that a complete community needs, such as childcare centres, arts venues and commercial spaces for small businesses. The revenue generated from these endeavours is reinvested in the CLT with the aim of becoming financially self-sustaining and continuing to grow. Canada's largest CLT, Toronto's Parkdale Neighbourhood Land Trust (PNLT), started with a single community garden it acquired in 2017. By 2025 it had grown a portfolio of 86 properties, including a total of 206 affordable rental homes, and had plans to acquire or build hundreds more.

It's an example Bond, executive director of the Downtown Eastside Community Land Trust, told me he hoped to emulate.

With frustration around the state of Vancouver's Downtown Eastside at an all-time high, it was clear that both public and private solutions to the problem had failed to make much of a dent. At issue was what to do with the single-room occupancy, or SRO, hotels that are the dominant form of low-income housing in that part of town. Generally three- or four-storey walk-up buildings originally built as short-term lodging for port workers in the early 20th century, SROs feature small rooms, typically about 10 feet by 10 feet, with shared bathrooms and minimal or no cooking facilities. Due to their small size and age (most are over 100 years old), SROs are usually the last housing option available to the lowest-income people in Vancouver, who rely on government shelter subsidies to pay the rent. And the number of affordable SROs is dwindling.

With Vancouver's property market continually soaring, private owners of these buildings have taken to selling them to investors, who generally renovict low-income tenants and put their units back on the market as "micro-lofts," charging more than double what someone relying on shelter subsidies receives. Other buildings have been so neglected that they're simply unfit for habitation. Since 2020, a number of SROs have been condemned by the city, while some have been gutted by fires that have claimed lives. An attempt to preserve at least some affordability in the area saw the provincial government commit to buying SROs a few years back, but that plan was scrapped amidst a series of public scandals related to their management and persistently poor condition. After that, the premier declared SROs an unfit and undignified form of housing the government would no longer support.

Fair enough, said Bond. The problem is there's just not enough alternative housing for everyone who currently lives in one. New, affordable options take years to come online, and for every SRO building that gets condemned or gentrified in the meantime, more people just wind up sleeping in doorways or in encampments in public parks, he said. From there, some might get approached by social workers and placed in supportive housing run by agencies like the one he used to work for, but they don't actually require the specialized services they provide. "They're not struggling as much with active addiction and mental health issues," Bond said. They just don't have the money for any other type of housing. Not only does placing these people in supportive housing take space away from those who need it, Bond added, it's an expensive model, costing anywhere from $500,000 to $1 million per building per year to operate.

This is where Bond said the CLT can help fill the gap. While some SROs are undoubtedly decrepit hellholes, others are still in reasonably good shape. The CLT's mission is to acquire the buildings that are still habitable, or could be with a little work, and support residents to manage and maintain them, similar to a co-op.

So far, the DTES CLT has access to one building, a former boarding house called Keefer Rooms that the provincial government agreed to purchase and renovate in 2023, with the aim of letting the CLT operate it for two years after renovations were complete. Bond told me he hoped that at the end of that time they'd have proven the CLT was a viable model of community-led housing and the province would hand over ownership and perhaps help facilitate the purchase of more buildings. In the meantime, they were fundraising to buy another SRO without the help of the government.

In addition to affordability, dignity and self-determination, giving marginalized and vulnerable people some power to shape their communities is central to the CLT model. That means the housing and other community assets CLTs steward might look and operate very differently from the accepted "best practices" of government or social services organizations. For instance, SROs may seem undignified or unacceptable in the eyes of the government, but many DTES residents don't mind living in them as long as they are clean, safe and stable, and they can work toward improving them over time, said Bond. "Some of these tenants have lived in this one building for over 15 years and all they want is to know that it's not going to be sold to a developer and that their rents aren't going to go up a lot," he said. And like other forms of collaborative housing, the process of figuring out what works for a specific community—with their input—can have positive impacts that extend well beyond housing.

The first community land trust, New Communities Inc., emerged out of the civil rights movement in the United States in 1969, when Black tenant farmers in Georgia formed a farming collective as a way to claim land and build wealth for a population that had been largely excluded from property ownership. Today, CLTs continue to be an important tool to address societal inequities perpetuated by racist, classist and ableist land use policies. Not far from the Downtown Eastside in Vancouver, the Hogan's Alley CLT is working to revitalize the city's historically Black neighbourhood, which was demolished to make way for a never-completed freeway starting in the 1960s. In Toronto, CLTs have been established in Kensington Market, an eclectic community of artists, immigrants and independent food merchants, as well as in the city's Chinatown—two culturally important neighbourhoods that have been under siege from gentrification and development pressure. Across Canada, several CLTs have been established to serve the interests of Indigenous groups who view collective ownership as a way of reclaiming sovereignty over land stolen through the process of colonization. In the Downtown Eastside, some also see the CLT as an avenue toward decolonization and healing for the area's large Indigenous population. "The land was here first. It is not property to us," Norm Leech, one of the CLTs board members, and a member of the T'it'q'et community of the St'át'imc Nation, told me. "The land is a relative. She's our ancestor. Our great, great, greatest grandmother." A spiritual relationship with land is central to Indigenous ways of being, Leech explained, so giving people an active role in deciding how land should be used for the good of the community can be a really powerful way for them to reconnect with their culture. What's more, learning to work collectively within the organization helps people acquire new skills. For some members, getting involved with the CLT has helped them learn to deal with emotions like anger in a constructive way or to cope with disagreement and reach compromise, said Leech, who is trained as a trauma counsellor. "Without telling people, you're kind of in therapy," he said.

The same sensitivity to local contexts and lived experience that give CLTs so much potential to improve Canada's poorest communities also holds the same promise for its richest.

---

About 20 minutes southeast of Banff National Park sits a town with a real estate market that rivals Vancouver's and Toronto's. For most of its existence, Canmore, Alberta, was a backwater coal town that fell on hard times when the last mine closed in 1979 and languished in obscurity for nearly a decade after. But when nearby Calgary hosted the Winter Olympics in 1988, tapping Canmore to host some of its events, the town's fortunes turned around almost overnight. After its debut on the world stage as an undiscovered mountain gem, Canmore rolled out the red carpet for visitors, clearing the way for the construction of hotels and short-term rentals without paying much heed to permanent housing for locals. Now, almost 40 years later, there's next to no place left for Canmore's permanent population of 16,000 to affordably live. "We have no property ladder here," Donna Houston, a Canmore realtor, told me as we walked along the creek in the centre of town. "We've watched the property ladder actually disappear." Canmore's stunning mountain scenery and proximity to world-class nature reserves and ski resorts have made it a favourite destination for investors, remote workers and wealthy people seeking part-time pieds-à-terre. But the money they've brought to the town has pushed the price of land, and therefore housing, out of reach for paramedics, ski instructors, bartenders, artisans and everyone else it takes to keep the town's economy afloat. That's what inspired Donna and her husband Ryan Houston, also a realtor, to start the Canmoreland CLT.

Between the mountains, the train tracks, the highway and the national park, there's just not much room for Canmore to expand, and what little undeveloped land there is in town is exorbitantly expensive. One site, consisting of six privately owned lots right in the middle of town, could be worth anywhere between $30 million and $50 million on the open market, the Houstons estimate. But, they argue, it would actually be more valuable than that—priceless, even—if it was owned by the community. It's not just affordable housing that Canmore lacks, the Houstons say, it's affordable studio space for the artists whose work fills the galleries on the main street, and the makers behind the jewellery and crafts that fill the gift shops. Canmore also needs a year-round market to showcase their wares, a conference centre, and an Indigenous welcoming space—a place where local Indigenous people can engage in cultural practices. All of that could fit here, along with a substantial amount of affordable housing, if it was owned and developed by an entity like a CLT.

But so far the Houstons haven't had much luck selling people on the idea. Not many people in town know about Canmoreland or understand what a CLT is and why it's needed, they say. Plus, as realtors, they face a lot of skepticism about their intentions—when it comes to affordable housing aren't they on the dark side? But the Houstons argue it's precisely because of their profession that they've been able to identify where and how a CLT could be most effective. "We're here in the present moment," said Donna. "We're with the people, we know exactly what they're going through. We know exactly what they're looking for."

As ridiculous, even offensive, as micro-lofts might be for people looking for long-term city homes, the Houstons say they've seen a demand for something similar in Canmore, where many young people come for just a year or two specifically to spend most of it playing outside in the mountains. "We joke because it's like there's no such thing as weather here. It's just a different layer of clothing," Ryan said. Whether it's 30 degrees above zero or 30 degrees below, "you're outside." Priced right, dormitory-style self-contained units could work great for lifties, restaurant servers and hotel housekeeping staff who are generally in town on temporary work visas, freeing up the houses they currently rent for families. There's also a huge need for missing middle housing for teachers and postal workers and civil servants—people whose love for Canmore goes beyond its status as a vacation destination.

The 2024 wildfire that wiped out a third of Jasper, another Alberta mountain town, proved just how quickly a tourism economy can literally go up in flames, the Houstons said. If that happens in Canmore, the town will need a population committed to helping it recover—not just to bring back the tourists but because it's their home. This is a situation the Houstons are more familiar with than most. They fled their previous home in Fort McMurray in 2016 when a wildfire swept through the northern Alberta city. After bouncing around the province for a few months they arrived in Canmore with their two young sons to stay with some friends. What they found was a haven they hadn't realized they'd been missing. "It saved our lives coming from Fort McMurray," Donna said, and not just because they found an escape from the flames. Canmore's slower pace of life and immersion in nature helped them heal from the trauma of the fire, and realize they didn't want to go back to the corporate treadmill they'd been on in the oil and gas boom town of Fort McMurray. In Canmore they had more time to spend with their two sons, now 17 and 20, and it's because they are the parents of two young men seeking to leave the nest and finding few options that they see the need for the community to take ownership of its future. "Most people raise their kids here with the idea that their kids are never going to live here," said Ryan. And as much as they stand to gain financially from perpetuating Canmore's hot real estate market (higher housing prices mean bigger commissions for realtors), they've realized the personal cost of doing so is just too great. There are other people in town, like them, who share that opinion, said Ryan, and with some incentives from the government they could be enticed to contribute their land or wealth to the cause.

This is where policy and programs have a huge role to play in collaborative housing. Far from letting our governments off the hook, community-led projects need institutional support in order to get off the ground and scale. Specifically, government programs and policies could be used to redirect some of the incredible wealth many people have built through our publicly subsidized housing market into non-profit, community-led projects engineered to preserve affordability forever.

This isn't as hard to do as some might assume. I can imagine a future where a majority, or at least an equal measure, of the money we put into housing goes into non-profit community-led initiatives instead of market development. I can imagine coaxing more landlords into selling investment properties to cohousers, co-ops and community land trusts by offering a break on their capital gains tax or some other financial incentive—especially if they sell at below market rates. I can envision a robust revival of co-op housing, with permanent funding that includes provisions for tenant-led conversions and programs to support the transition. I can envision "matching" grant programs that encourage private individuals to reinvest their housing wealth in the creation of non-profit developments that create options to age in their communities while providing affordable housing for new residents to move in. I can imagine a kind of mddl, the citizen-developer training program, geared specifically toward that goal. We could take a cue from Vienna, and use zoning to suppress speculation by requiring a majority of housing in certain areas to be non-market and community-led. And that's just off the top of my head. There are many ways to feed the good wolf.

Steps like these may not be enough to completely resolve our housing crisis, but they are essential to moving us in the direction of a permanent solution. We simply cannot get there without them. Certainly, more sweeping changes—like national rent control, landlord licensing, bans on public investments (like pension plans) in REITs, and a reassessment of how we capture, or don't, the value of land through taxation—are all worthy of consideration. But before we can build the political will and public support for such drastic legislative shifts, we need to show people why it would be worth it.

Since the advent of our housing system, governments have been loath to take steps that would lower or even stabilize the cost of housing, citing the impact to people's personal savings and nest eggs. But as long as we remain overly invested, financially and otherwise, in a profit-driven housing market where our governments ensure housing prices only ever trend up, we will continue to see the financial, ecological and social tolls mount. Some of the benefits of bringing housing costs down, not through a devastating market collapse but by building robust alternatives to the market, might seem distant and ephemeral. Results like increased productivity and innovation, reduced inequality, more economic and environmental sustainability and less political polarization may take years to filter into our lives in a recognizable way. But others will be much more immediate. Housing is where we live. It's right next door. It's across the street. It's on every corner. It is the bedrock of our lives, our neighbourhoods, our cities and our nation. When we start doing housing better, building together with health, happiness and home as a singular goal, we'll start to notice benefits almost immediately: less loneliness and social isolation; less visible poverty; more trust among our neighbours; a deeper sense of purpose in contributing to our communities; more fun, livable and enjoyable cities; more options and greater support for moving through all the stages of life with dignity and autonomy; more money left in our pockets at the end of the month to spend on literally anything else our tender hearts desire or require.

Perhaps the best case to be made for a radical reorientation of our housing system is the restoration of something that seems in short supply in these tumultuous times: hope. Almost everyone you've met in the pages of this book is an unrelenting optimist driven by a belief that building better homes—better lives—for ourselves and for our loved ones is not only possible but plausible. This belief isn't fed by blind optimism or guileless faith. It is fed by facts. When people work together toward this goal, it happens. The challenge ahead of us doesn't lie in finding solutions to our housing crisis; it is in finding the will to apply the solutions that already exist on a scale and at a pace that will fundamentally solve the problem. This is the next step, the one we owe it to ourselves and to those who will come after us to take. "We want this to benefit our grandkids," said Ryan Houston. "What if they get to come back here someday? Wow."

CONCLUSION

# WHERE THE HEART IS

It is simply not possible to spend years of your life intensely examining our cultural relationship to housing and to home without eventually turning the microscope on yourself.

When I moved to Calgary, my checklist for a good home pretty much read like a real estate listing. I wanted space, two bedrooms at least and to be in a walkable neighbourhood with bike lanes and coffee shops and close to downtown. I wanted to be near parks and green space, and I wanted the option to maybe one day own a place of my own. "If all goes well, we plan to save some money and buy a house in the next couple of years—an actual house, with a yard and everything," I wrote in that viral essay all those years ago.

I am beyond fortunate to have achieved those goals, and from the other side I see things very differently. My checklist for home is now much less tangible. It's a weighting of the elements—familiarity, haven, heaven (belonging), space, place, need and time (stability). It's trying to prioritize what will help me *feel* most at home in my life right now and for the foreseeable future. My research has informed my criteria, for sure, but so has the incredible force that is just plain old life.

When Dave and I decided to settle in Calgary for good, a major factor was that it was closer to our families. Dave's parents were in the city and mine were a manageable three-hour drive away in Edmonton. We anticipated that we'd need them if we became parents ourselves. What we didn't anticipate was becoming parents in a pandemic, cut off from family and friends. Nor did we anticipate losing my mom to a brain aneurysm when our son was just five months old. Or Dave's mom to cancer just three years after that, almost to the day. We have struggled immensely, not just through grief, but also through the profound disorientation of handling so many seismic shifts in our lives all at once. We often say that it feels as if we went to sleep one night as ourselves and woke up in the morning complete strangers firmly sandwiched between the demands of raising a young child and the challenge of caring for aging parents. We'd come to Calgary hoping to have family support; suddenly, we were the support.

The whole thing has made us totally recalibrate our relationship to housing and home and to *houses* in particular. We both saw first-hand just how fast the big, single-family houses and generational monocultures of the suburbs turned into liabilities for our loved ones. Near the end of her life, Dave's mom couldn't get up the stairs or to the bathroom on her own. Even though she had plenty of family and friends nearby, they were all older and had their own health challenges. Nobody had the right combination of dexterity, strength and eyesight required to do things like help her to the toilet, read the labels on the tiny vials of drugs or keep a steady hand with a syringe. Dave basically had to move in. When my mom was in the hospital, and while we were still hopeful she might make some form of meaningful recovery, her husband and I looked around their house full of stairs and voiced the same fear: What if she needed a wheelchair? If she lived she'd almost surely have a degree of disability. Would she ever be able to come home?

After our mothers passed away, Dave and I both experienced the same eerie phenomenon. When the person who makes a house a home is gone, it's like a spell is lifted. Our family homes stopped being places of comfort and warmth and reverted to the sum of their parts. For us, at least, these dwellings that had held so much emotional significance became just collections of floorboards, carpets, furniture and other stuff someone had to figure out what to do with. They also became sources of nagging concern.

We stressed over how our loved ones would manage—both physically and emotionally—in those now soulless and unwieldy-seeming structures. In both of our cases, trying to find long-term housing options that will keep our remaining family members safe and healthy, but also happy and fulfilled, has been a difficult, lengthy and often frustrating process.

Through all of this, our own house has done exactly what houses are supposed to do. It has kept us safe and warm and sheltered. We have been so incredibly grateful to have it, and also amazed at our luck in buying it when we did. Annoyingly, it still doesn't feel like our home. I have spent a lot of time trying to figure out why that is and I've landed on several contributing factors.

With so much big life stuff going on, many of our ambitions to personalize our space were left on the back burner for so long they've completely evaporated. I'd hoped our house would be a canvas for self-expression. More often than not, it feels like a half-completed project that adds to the stress and chaos of our lives rather than providing a refuge from it. It has also taken on a kind of symbolic status as the place we lived during an exceptionally shitty phase of our lives, one we are keen to leave behind.

The development pressure on our block has resolved somewhat. After a few more attempts to upzone by the faction of landlords, the city came back and said they can build what everyone else in the city can build under the new blanket rezoning—missing middle up to three storeys. I've come around to the idea of townhouses eventually going up next door. It seems like a reasonable and fair outcome, and our street doesn't feel as much like prey. But getting to this point inflicted some damage that's been harder to repair. That very first day at city hall planted a seed in our minds: Maybe this wouldn't, or shouldn't, be our forever home after all?

The not-so-subtle suggestion not to get too attached might actually turn out to be a blessing. For all the cultural and economic weight a single-family house carries, we are realizing life inside of one just might not be for us. When we got the keys to our 1980s split-level it felt momentous, like we'd managed to beat the odds and pull off an impossible dream. But now I wonder if that was actually *our* dream or one we just absorbed from our culture. When I think back on it, I can't remember ever explicitly wanting to own a single-family house until I realized I might never be able to. So, when the opportunity arose to acquire such a lauded symbol of middle-class success, we jumped at it without giving it much thought. Of course this is what we want. It's what everyone wants, isn't it? As it turns out, not so much.

We've actually found living in our house to be pretty isolating in a sneaky sort of way. Having space and storage is nice, but we find it gets filled with crap we don't need—especially the overflow from our downsizing and/or deceased parents. We spend so much time cleaning and sorting and organizing and purging that we find it difficult to ever get *out* of the house. And there are other barriers we continually bump up against in our quest for social connection. I thought I was doing the right thing by replacing our busted-up waist-height fence with a new, solid six-foot version, but it obliterated the tentative relationships we were forming with the people on the other side. Our front-drive attached garage is convenient for getting through a Calgary winter, but it also means we don't see our neighbours across the street for months at a time. It's a real pity, because they're great.

Since we moved in, a cluster of new families arrived on our block clearly intending to stay for the long haul. We are all raising kids around the same age and there is massive potential to cement some close neighbourly bonds. All it would take, I'm sure, is some nudging to get us into village territory. I've often thought of starting something like a babysitting exchange, an arrangement where families agree to trade off childcare, but so far, I haven't made the effort, mostly because I haven't had the energy or the time. But there's something else holding me back. It's become clear that Calgary just isn't our place.

Once upon a time, a friend who is probably the most cynical person I know told me with stone-faced sincerity that she felt Vancouver was my "spiritual home." I laughed it off at the time, but now I know she was right. I've come to realize that place ranks pretty highly in my personal hierarchy of the elements of home. It always has, but I didn't realize this was something to consider when I moved away, ironically because my attachment to Vancouver—my affinity for the landscape, the climate, the people and the culture—was so strong. I fell in love with Vancouver so easily, so quickly and so completely that I assumed it would and could happen again. I thought I could make any place "my place" with enough effort, intention and time. Now, after almost a decade of putting considerable effort and intention into becoming a successful transplant, I can definitively say: It's just not working. This is not Calgary's fault. This city has a lot going for it—I chose Calgary because it had everything I thought I needed in a home. But it doesn't have my heart.

In many ways, our time in Calgary has felt fated, like we were meant to be here during this particular phase of life. We were close to our families when they needed us most. In other ways, it's been excruciating. I don't just miss my old life in Vancouver; I can't shake the feeling that my life is still there, carrying on without me. Despite the cost of housing, which is even worse now, a lot of my friends, peers and colleagues have managed to hang on—albeit by making a lot of sacrifices. This is the cohort I belong to. Every time a classmate from university puts on a new show or takes over leadership of an arts organization, I feel like I should be there to support their work. Every time a former colleague from my newsroom days releases a book, I wish we could still be moving through our careers together. It absolutely kills me that some of my dearest, oldest friends have kids that I don't know and that they don't know mine.

In a weird twist of fate, the merciless housing market that ejected me from my home might just be the thing that allows me to go back. Thanks to the conditions that created Calgary's housing crisis, the assessed value of our house has gone up considerably since we bought it—about 40 percent in five years, if you can believe it. It is absolutely insane. Selling it won't buy us something comparable in Vancouver, not even close, but it can solve the problem I left the city to escape. It can buy us stability, either in the form of a long-term, purpose-built rental, or some kind of haven that we can own. So, we have decided to move back.

This has not been an easy decision. Relocating as an adult was hard enough, but doing it again as the parent of a small child has added a whole other world of considerations. Moving is a very big deal, even more so for a little person—you are literally taking them away from the only home they've ever known. Ultimately, it's for our son that we most feel we need to make this move. We are just better people, better parents, in a place that we love, close to the people who, despite all these years apart, are still the foundation of our support network. And like any parent, I look around this world we live in sometimes (read: all the time) with a great deal of anxiety and fear. There are so many threats to account for in raising a child right now and so many things—climate change, the manosphere, the reality-distorting effects of AI, to name but a few—that are outside of my control. The best way I can figure to give my kid the best shot at becoming a happy, healthy adult in this environment is to provide him with a good home. I used to think that meant a backyard for him to run around in and a basement to store all his toys. Now I know it's so much more complex than that. A good home is one that extends far beyond our housing and even our own family. I want to give him stability, and a sense of place he can root into as he grows, a community he belongs to full of people who are undeniably real, and true, and who are physically right there when he needs them. I want him to feel needed, to have a sense of purpose through his contributions to the world around him. Time. Place. Belonging. Need. These are the elements that we're prioritizing for this next phase of our lives.

We've decided this version of home is worth pursuing, and worth investing in, in every sense of the word.

Right after we got back from a recent trip to Vancouver, a friend tipped me off to a cohousing group looking for land in East Van. The timing was serendipitous. After researching this book and touring every cohousing development in the city (there are only three), I was convinced: This is the kind of home I want for myself and my family. A home that's more about community, less about stuff, and where the return on investment is calculated in terms of our quality of life and a positive influence on the people and the place around us. It is also important to me that the housing wealth we've accumulated by participating in a dysfunctional housing system doesn't just get cycled back into sustaining the status quo. Right now, there are not a lot of ways to do this, but cohousing is one option. It's an ideological off-ramp from the market, and with some work and some advocacy, there's potential for it to become a financial off-ramp as well. We're hoping we can convince the city to work with us to make cohousing a more affordable option for more people. The prospect of going back to Vancouver and engaging in this work actually makes me excited. It's given me a sense of purpose I've been lacking in Calgary, and a sense of optimism I never had when I lived in Vancouver before.

To be clear, Calgary needs people willing to work toward change just as much as Vancouver does. Hamilton, Halifax, New York, Toronto, Harare, Berlin, even Vienna—they all need champions as well, people willing to work for a more equitable, enjoyable, sustainable housing future. But need is a two-way street. Systemic change is a long game, and it's much easier to sustain this work when you're doing it for and from a place that you love. Like anything else in life, you're more effective when your heart is in it.

I recognize how lucky I am to even have the choice to go back and to take a chance on a different way of building a home. One of the most crippling consequences of our housing crisis is that too many of us don't have the opportunity to live where and how we feel our strongest, most supported and most capable. But I think it is something to aim for. After meeting so many incredible people around the world while working on this book, I've learned that when it comes to our homes, arguably the most important thing in our lives, we need to aim higher. We don't get anywhere by cutting corners, lowering expectations and accepting a scarcity mindset. Everything gets better when more of us have what we need to thrive.

That doesn't mean we won't ever have to compromise. As human beings, a safe, stable, nurturing home is our birthright, but it's not always going to look exactly like we imagined, or like our culture tells us it should. Personally, I've found prioritizing purpose, place and belonging has helped me embrace the unfamiliar. Part of the reason I think we defaulted toward a single-family house is because I couldn't picture myself in the most ubiquitous alternative. Frankly, I found the idea of living in a condo building extremely off-putting, owing to the sense of sterility, tension and social alienation outlined in the research we talked about a few chapters back. I certainly never envisioned myself developing one with a bunch of near-strangers. Plunging into cohousing, however, that's exactly what we signed up for.

After meeting with our cohousing group virtually for the first few months, we made a few trips to Vancouver as a family to get to know everyone better and participate in the planning process in person. So far, it's been a really positive experience. I'd even go so far as to say it's bolstered my faith in humanity. Everyone in our group is a rare mix of capable, caring, realistic, optimistic and generous. There is something about going into a setting with people who've signalled they are ready and willing to be an active participant in a community that sets the bar really high for accountability and respect. Even though many of us don't know each other that well, the intention to build a home together creates a sense of solidarity, which is essential when taking on a task as daunting as trying to buy and develop a piece of land in one of the most expensive cities on the continent. We are all terrified on some level, but doing it together takes some of the sting out of it. We've all put in a relatively small sum of money—a few thousand dollars per household—to hire some experienced consultants, including Ronaye Matthew, and explore the feasibility of a possible site. Just like I heard from federation members in Harare,

I've found that putting money into the mix is a powerful way to expedite trust. We have skin in the game. We have invested in each other and in the process we've embarked upon. I've also discovered that cohousing has the potential to ease some of the fear around development in the communities we're looking at. It's certainly not consistent across the board, but there are a lot of landowners who feel better about potentially putting up with the change and disruption of development on their street when they know it's for a community-led project. Some have even expressed interest in being a part of it.

Of course, I'm still nervous. Mostly about giving up space. We are going to be downsizing at a point in our lives where many families are expanding their housing footprint, and our space needs haven't changed all that much. We still need at least two bedrooms, a place to host overnight guests, space to hold family dinners and a place to work. Our kid still needs a safe place to run around outside. I still need a haven. But I'm open to experimenting with the shape of those things. They might look different than I imagined—heck, they might turn out even better than I could have imagined. Knowing at least some of the people who will be our neighbours makes it much easier, even appealing, to reconsider just how much personal space is "enough." I actually think I'd prefer a shared garden over a private backyard, and I've found that, especially since having a kid, I need community way more than a basement. These days, my idea of luxury at home has less to do with aesthetics and square footage and more with having someone I can call over to watch the baby monitor so Dave and I can go for a walk after dinner. We're in the market for some things money can't buy, like a couple of surrogate grandmas.

I realize cohousing or other collaborative housing forms aren't for everyone, and that is not the goal. There will always be people who want to play the market game, who choose to view housing as a financial asset or who simply value the lifestyle and status conferred by living in a typical market home. They should continue to have that choice. Choice and freedom, after all, are what our culture is supposed to be all about. But those who either can't access the market, or long for something it doesn't offer, deserve a choice too. The choice to opt out. To not participate in propping up a system that has never satisfied its intended purpose and has done a fair amount of damage along the way.

I am choosing to opt out in the way that is available to me. It is my hope that in doing so, I will inspire more people to join me. If you are so inclined, I invite you to look around and consider what off-ramps may be available to you, and where there are none, is there something you can do to help create one? This can happen in small or big ways. It can be joining or starting a tenants' union or voting for more equitable housing policies; it can be taking part in a placemaking initiative in your community or making a point of saying hi to your neighbours. It can be totally recalibrating and rethinking the value of your home and how best to invest the money your land or housing may generate. The more of us who do this, the more we can expand the options available to everyone. We can make it a little bit easier and a little less risky to choose something different. We can choose a better version of home.

# A NOTE ON SOURCES

You may have noticed that throughout this book some sources are referred to by first name only, while others are referred to by their complete name on first reference, and subsequently by last name only, in typical journalistic style. This reflects a distinction in my mind between "civilians"—people whose personal stories and differing perspectives on home added character and diversity of perspective to this book—and experts or activists—those whose work in some way puts them in the public eye in relation to housing and home. Given the sensitive and personal nature of home, I felt a pull to "protect" the full identity of civilians like Breton, John or Dorna, who in sharing with me their personal perspectives allowed me into an intimate space I felt I needed to respect with a degree of anonymity. At other times, the distinction between civilians, activists and experts blurred, such as the case of Emily Power, who was at once a resident speaking of her home and also a public figure.

You may have noticed as well that this book does not give a lot of time or mention to conventional developers, professional building associations or other people or institutions heavily involved in market housing. This is intentional. This book was conceived of in part out of my frustration with always hearing the same "side" of the housing story. The perspective of building associations, developers and financiers in the housing industry is not unimportant, but it is not hard to find. Additionally, it tends to dominate the public discourse on our housing crisis. My express intention with this book was to give voice to those we rarely hear from and shed light on parts of the housing ecosystem that, in my opinion, rarely get the exposure they deserve. In short, I wanted to start a different conversation around housing and home, and doing so required I sidestep the more conventional sources.

To account for shifts in political ideologies and governance, I opted not to interview government sources directly but pulled from resources that are widely available on the public record, such as reports and statistics. All data regarding the housing market and policies is as up-to-date as I could find at the time of publication.

# NOTES

## INTRODUCTION: HOUSE AND HOME

1 **When I moved to Vancouver at 19** In 2002, three weeks shy of my 20th birthday.

1 **When I left the city 15 years later** In 2017, just after my 35th birthday.

## 1: HEARTBREAK CITY

10 **It took me a while to figure out Vancouver** I am talking about the Metro Vancouver area here, as I lived and worked throughout much of the region. My first apartment out west was in the city of New Westminster. I went to school in Burnaby and later moved into Vancouver proper.

11 **shining example of gentrification** I am well aware I was part of this shift.

11 **As I progressed through my career as a journalist** Starting with the *North Shore News* covering the three North Shore communities of the District of North Vancouver, the City of North Vancouver and the municipality of West Vancouver. I later worked for *WE*, formerly *The Westender*, which ceased publication in 2017.

12 **Those who didn't like it were free to leave** I'm responding to comments made publicly by folks such as Bob Rennie, a Vancouver-based developer, and Shelley Fralic, a former *Vancouver Sun* columnist. At the time there was a sort of war of words, and of generations, happening in the local media, with differing views on exactly what was happening in Vancouver's housing market. A good summary, albeit through my own lens as a columnist, can be found here: Jessica Barrett, "Is It Time to Leave Vancouver," *Vancouver Sun*, June 1, 2015, https://www.vancouverisawesome.com/courier-archive/opinion/is-it-time-to-leave-vancouver-3012296.

14 **For a year-long reporting fellowship** I spent six months in Ottawa and six months in Calgary as the recipient of the Michelle Lang Fellowship with Postmedia News.

15 **writing a well-read column that had won a prestigious award** I was awarded the 2016 City Mike Award for Commentator of the Year through the Jack Webster Awards for columns I wrote for the *Vancouver Courier*, which ceased publication in April 2020 ("Courier Columnist Jessica Barrett Awarded Commentator of the Year at Websters," vancouverisawesome.com, October 21, 2016, https://www.vancouverisawesome.com/courier-archive/news/courier-columnist-jessica-barrett-awarded-commentator-of-the-year-at-websters-3040916).

16 **Empty Homes Tax** implemented in 2017, the year I left. The tax applies to properties that are unoccupied for more than six months out of the year. In 2024 that tax was 3 percent of the property's assessed value.

## 2: THE EMPEROR HAS NO HOME

20 **In the years since I left Vancouver** Though I left Vancouver in 2017, there are two recent inflection points where home prices increased rapidly: from about 2015 to 2017, when year-over-year increases in home prices were among the highest in the

world, and again during the pandemic, from 2020 to 2022, where benchmark home prices rose by about 50 percent ("Canadian House Price Rise Outstrips All but 3 Other Global Markets," *CBC News*, October 1, 2015, https://www.cbc.ca/news/business/canadian-house-price-rise-outstrips-all-but-3-other-global-markets-1.3252406; and Jean François Perrault, René Lalonde and Patrick Perrier, "Canada's Poor Productivity a Key Driver of Higher Home Prices," Scotiabank, March 19, 2025, https://www.scotiabank.com/ca/en/about/economics/economics-publications/post.other-publications.housing.housing-note.housing-note--march-19-2025-.html).

20 **fixtures on the lists** Jake Romphf, "Victoria Ranked as Canada's Third Most Expensive City: Study," *Victoria News*, July 13, 2023, https://www.vicnews.com/local-news/victoria-ranked-as-canadas-third-most-expensive-city-study-662101; and Shari Kulha, "Canada Has Four of the 10 Most Affordable and Four of the Least Affordable Cities in North America," *National Post*, October 26, 2021, https://nationalpost.com/news/canada/canada-has-four-of-the-10-most-affordable-and-four-of-the-least-affordable-cities-in-north-america.

20 **out of reach for many locals** Steve MacNaull, "Average Family Needs $114,000 More in Annual Income to Afford an Average House in Kelowna," *Kelowna Now*, March 22, 2025, https://www.kelownanow.com/watercooler/news/news/Real_Estate/Average_family_needs_114_000_more_in_annual_income_to_afford_average_house_in_Kelowna/; "Young People Living in Halifax Say They Are Being Priced Out of the City They Love," *CityNews*, May 25, 2022, https://halifax.citynews.ca/2022/05/25/young-people-living-in-halifax-say-they-are-being-priced-out-of-the-city-they-love-5403482/; and Paul James, "Housing Needs Report Shows Kamloops Renters to Face Further Market Stress," Radio NL, December 11, 2024, https://www.radionl.com/2024/12/11/housing-needs-report-shows-renters-in-kamloops-to-face-major-challenges/.

20 **loved ones struggle** Samritha Arunasalam, "Get Therapy or Pay Rent? Millennials, Gen Z Making Hard Choices When It Comes to Mental health," *CBC News*, September 25, 2024, https://www.cbc.ca/news/canada/mental-health-cost-of-living-therapy-millenials-gen-z-1.7333105.

20 **communities fracture** Michelle Cyca, "The End of Homeownership," *Maclean's,* June 15, 2023, https://macleans.ca/society/the-end-of-homeownership/.

21 **build, build, build** In fact, upon winning a minority Liberal government in 2025, Prime Minister Mark Carney had the room chant "build, baby, build" during his acceptance speech when talking about his plan for solving the housing crisis.

21 **4.8 million new homes** For most of the time I was researching this book the CMHC had projected that Canada needed an additional 3.5 million homes by 2030 in order to restore affordability to 2004 levels ("Estimating How Much Housing We'll Need by 2030," Canada Mortgage and Housing Corporation, September 13, 2023, https://www.cmhc-schl.gc.ca/blog/2023/estimating-how-much-housing-we-need-by-2030). Just before this book went to press, the CMHC released new projections for affordability, declaring that the country needs 4.8 million new homes by 2035 in order to restore affordability to 2019 levels ("Canada's Housing Supply Shortages: Moving to a New Framework," June 19, 2025, https://www.cmhc-schl.gc.ca/professionals/housing-markets-data-and-research/housing-research/research-reports/accelerate-supply/canadas-housing-supply-shortages-a-new-framework.) According to the CMHC the shifting goalposts on affordability (homes in 2004 were obviously much more affordable than in 2019) came about due to an understanding that winding back the clock by more than two decades would be impossible at this point. Even its new, updated affordability target requires more than doubling the amount of average annual housing starts—a tall order in a country with severely limited labour and construction resources.

21 **cut immigration** "Government of Canada Reduces Immigration," Immigration, Refugees and Citizenship Canada, October 24, 2024, https://www.canada.ca/en/immigration-refugees-citizenship/news/2024/10/government-of-canada-reduces-immigration.html.

21 **multiple expert analyses** Steve Pomeroy, "Exploring Causes of Escalating Home Prices: Part 1, Supply Issues," Canadian Housing Evidence Collaborative, https://chec-ccrl.ca/causes-of-escalating-home-prices/; and Steve Pomeroy, "Exploring Causes of Escalating Home Prices: Part 2, Demand Issues," Canadian Housing Evidence Collaborative, https://chec-ccrl.ca/exploring-causes-of-escalating-home-prices-part-2-demand-issues/.

21 **British Columbia** "Building BC: Housing Completions & Population Growth 2016–2021," Union of British Columbia Municipalities, March 23, 2022, https://www.ubcm.ca/sites/default/files/2022-03/Final-UBCM%20Housing%20Position%20Paper.pdf.

21 **Ontario** "Canada's Real Estate Supply Shortage Is Being Declared a Myth in Pricey Markets," Better Dwelling, March 24, 2022, https://betterdwelling.com/canadas-real-estate-supply-shortage-is-being-declared-a-myth-in-pricey-markets/.

22 **One expert I spoke to** Paul Kershaw of Generation Squeeze.

22 **two-thirds of Canadians** 66.5 percent as of 2021, a decline from a peak of 69 percent in 2011 ("Homeownership Rate Declines from 2011 to 2021 in All Provinces and Territories, Except in the Northwest Territories," Statistics Canada, November 21, 2021, https://www150.statcan.gc.ca/n1/daily-quotidien/220921/mc-b001-eng.htm).

22 **greater percentage of lawmakers** According to independent journalist Isaac Peltz, up to 95 percent of federally elected officials own their own homes, while 40 percent are landlords and/or real estate investors or have a spouse who is. Peltz created a

searchable database of elected officials and property ownership, available here: "Is My Landlord an MP," https://ismympalandlord.ca/en. In 2024, four out of five main federal party leaders were landlords, according to The Maple (Davide Mastracci, "Four of Canada's Five Federal Party Leaders Invested in Real Estate," The Maple, June 20, 2024, https://www.readthemaple.com/80-of-canadas-federal-party-leaders-invested-in-real-estate/). This is consistent with findings from the *Vancouver Sun*'s Douglas Todd, who found in 2023 that 90 percent of B.C. MLAs were landowners and close to half were landlords, as well as findings from *Global News* (Amanda Connolly, "At Least 20% of Canadian MPs Hold Rental, Investment Real Estate Amid Housing Crunch," *Global News*, April 19, 2022, https://globalnews.ca/news/8767051/canadian-mp-real-estate-investment-amid-housing-crunch/).

23 **a dearth of housing choice** Yushu Zhu and Hanan Ali, "What's Behind Canada's Housing Crisis? Experts Break Down the Different Factors at Play," Building, October 22, 2024, https://building.ca/feature/whats-behind-canadas-housing-crisis-experts-break-down-the-different-factors-at-play/#:~:text=This%20financialization%20of%20rental%20housing,vulnerability%20becomes%20effectively%20%E2%80%9Cdeadlocked.%E2%80%9D.

23 **starter homes have essentially disappeared from the market** Emily Badger, "Whatever Happened to the Starter Home?" *New York Times*, September 25, 2022, https://www.nytimes.com/2022/09/25/upshot/starter-home-prices.html.

24 **A 2024 CBC analysis** Naeil Shiab, "Where Can You Afford to Rent?" CBC News, June 11, 2024, https://newsinteractives.cbc.ca/features/2024/rentals-affordability-crisis/.

25 **Equifax found** Canadian Press, "Equifax Says Mortgage-Holders in B.C., Ontario, Increasingly Missed Payments During Q4," CBC News, March 5, 2024, https://www.cbc.ca/news/business/mortgage-holders-bc-ontario-missing-payments

-q4-equifax-1.7134085; and "Non-mortgage Delinquencies Reach Levels Not Seen Since 2009," Equifax, May 27, 2025, https://www.equifax.ca/about-equifax/newsroom/-/intlpress/non-mortgage-delinquencies-reach-levels-not-seen-since-2009/.

25 **according to Scotiabank** "Your Quick Guide to Setting Up an Emergency Fund," The Advice+ Team, Scotiabank, February 24, 2025, https://www.scotiabank.com/ca/en/personal/advice-plus/features/posts.emergency-fund.html.

25 **Only about one-third of home purchases in Canada are made by first-time buyers** Steve Pomeroy, "Want to Solve the Housing Crisis? Address Super-Charged Demand," *The Conversation,* November 25, 2021, https://theconversation.com/want-to-solve-the-housing-crisis-address-super-charged-demand-169809.

25 **between 20 and 30 percent of all housing stock is owned by investors** Akshay Kulkarni, "1 in 5 Properties Across Much of Canada Are Owned by Investors. That Makes It Harder for 1st-time Buyers," *CBC* News, February 9, 2023, https://www.cbc.ca/news/canada/british-columbia/housing-investors-canada-bc-1.6743083.

25 **condos in Toronto** Laura Hanrahan, "57% of Recently Built Toronto Condos Are Owned by Investors," Storeys, October 24, 2023, https://storeys.com/half-toronto-condos-investor-owned/.

25 **condos in Vancouver** "Investors in the Condominium Apartment Market, 2022," Statistics Canada, October 3, 2024, https://www150.statcan.gc.ca/n1/daily-quotidien/241003/dq241003a-eng.htm.

25 **seen a meteoric rise in investor ownership** "Ontario's Big Cities Saw Investors Buy up to 85% of Condos, Fueled by Gov Incentives," Better Dwelling, October 3, 2024, https://betterdwelling.com/ontarios-big-cities-saw-investors-buy-up-to-85-of-condos-fueled-by-gov-incentives/; "Half of

BC's New Condos Apartments Are Investor Owned," Better Dwelling, February 9, 2023, https://betterdwelling.com/half-of-bcs-new-condos-apartments-are-investor-owned/; and Jeremy Withers, "Addressing the Rise of Investor Ownership of Housing, Part 1: Assessing the Scale and Impacts across Canada," *Perspectives*, April 2, 2024, https://perspectivesjournal.ca/housing-investor-ownership-part-1/.

25 **Statistics Canada** Joanie Fontaine and Joshua Gordon, "Residential Real Estate Investors and Investment Properties in 2020," Statistics Canada, February 3, 2023, https://www150.statcan.gc.ca/n1/pub/46-28-0001/2023001/article/00001-eng.htm.

25 **mom-and-pop investors** Uday Rana, "Are 'Mom-and-Pop' Investors Pricing Out First-Time Homebuyers?" Global News, April 1, 2024, https://globalnews.ca/news/10394986/are-mom-and-pop-investors-pricing-out-first-time-homebuyers/.

27 **writes Jerusalem Demsas** Jerusalem Demsas, "The Homeownership Society Was a Mistake," *The Atlantic*, December 20, 2022, https://www.theatlantic.com/newsletters/archive/2022/12/homeownership-real-estate-investment-renting/672511/.

27 **the value of condos** "Why Are So Many Big-City Condos Sitting Empty?" CBC News, June 2024, https://www.cbc.ca/player/play/video/9.6428660; and Nisha Patel, "The Condo Market Is Slowing Down. Where Are All the Buyers?" CBC News, May 15, 2025, https://www.cbc.ca/news/business/condo-market-slowdown-1.7535704.

27 **the small footprints of condo units** Abby Hughes, "What Can Toronto's Real Estate Industry Do to Solve the City's Big Problem of Small Condos?" CBC News, May 20, 2025, https://www.cbc.ca/news/business/making-small-condos-bigger-1.7538637.

28 **roughly 13 percent of our gross domestic product** "Gross Domestic Product (GDP) at Basic Prices, by Industry, Annual Average (x 1,000,000)," Statistics Canada, April 30, 2025, https://www150.statcan.gc.ca/t1/tbl1/en/tv.action?pid=3610043403.

28 **writes . . . Daniel Kay Hertz**, "Housing Can't Both Be a Good Investment and Be Affordable," *City Commentary*, October 30, 2018, https://cityobservatory.org/housing-cant-be-affordable_and_be-a-good-investment/. (Note: The page contains an edit stating: "This City Observatory commentary was authored by Daniel Kay Hertz. The version published on October 26 contained an incorrect reference to the author. We regret the error"; however, the author of the post still reads as "Joe Cortright.")

29 **South America** Nicole Garcia Merida, "Digital Nomads Are the New Gentrifiers," VICE, May 22, 2023, https://www.vice.com/en/article/digital-nomads-work-from-home-gentrification/.

29 **southern Europe** Sam Jones, "Portugal's Bid to Attract Foreign Money Backfires as Rental Market Goes 'Crazy,'" *The Guardian*, July 29, 2023, https://www.theguardian.com/world/2023/jul/29/portugals-bid-to-attract-foreign-money-backfires-as-rental-market-goes-crazy.

29 **billions each year** Ben Segel-Brown and Zachary Vrhovsek, "Federal Spending on Housing Affordability in 2024," Office of the Parliamentary Budget Officer, December 12, 2024, https://www.pbo-dpb.ca/en/publications/RP-2425-023-Sfederal-spending-housing-affordability-in-2024depenses-federales-axees-abordabilite-logement-2024.

29 **tax-sheltered savings accounts** "First Home Savings Account (FHSA)," Canada Revenue Agency, March 20, 2025, https://www.canada.ca/en/revenue-agency/services/tax/individuals/topics/first-home-savings-account.html.

29 **publicly funded mortgage insurance** "What Is CMHC Mortgage Loan Insurance?" Canada Mortgage and Housing

Corporation, June 3, 2018, https://www.cmhc-schl.gc.ca/consumers/home-buying/mortgage-loan-insurance-for-consumers/what-is-mortgage-loan-insurance.

29 **shelter subsidies** Generally these are administered through provincial governments to assist low-income people who meet an income threshold cut-off to pay rent, often to private landlords.

29 **almost no mechanisms to recapture** J. David Hulchanski, "What Factors Shape Canadian Housing Policy? The Intergovernmental Role in Canada's Housing System," Homeless Hub, 2006, https://homelesshub.ca/resource/what-factors-shape-canadian-housing-policy-intergovernmental-role-canadas-housing-system/.

29 **political suicide** Hulchanski, "What Factors Shape Canadian Housing Policy?"

30 **a report from Alberta Central** "Canada's Housing Obsession Is Cannibalizing Productivity," Alberta Central, https://albertacentral.com/intelligence-centre/economic-news/canadas-housing-obsession-is-cannibalizing-productivity/.

30 **multiple studies** "High Housing Costs Making It Harder to Move for Jobs Many Are Seeking," Canada Mortgage and Housing Corporation, January 30, 2025, https://www.cmhc-schl.gc.ca/blog/2025/high-housing-costs-making-harder-move-jobs-many-seeking; and "Housing Marketing Insight—Canada," Canada Mortgage and Housing Corporation, March 2021, https://assets.cmhc-schl.gc.ca/sites/cmhc/professional/housing-markets-data-and-research/market-reports/housing-market-insight/2021/housing-market-insight-canada-68469-m03-en.pdf?rev=1d386c10-a697-4b0b-a508-f4270265f296.

30 **any nation in the G7** Nadine Yousif, "Canada's Household Debt Is Now Highest in the G7," BBC News, May 24, 2023, https://www.bbc.com/news/world-us-canada-65688460.

31 **a *New York Times* investigation** Francesca Mari, "A $60 Billion Housing Grab by Wall Street," *New York Times,* March 4, 2020, https://www.nytimes.com/2020/03/04/magazine/wall-street-landlords.html.

32 **wrote in 2017** "Report of the Special Rapporteur on Adequate Housing as a Component of the Right to an Adequate Standard of Living, and on the Right to Non-Discrimination in This Context," United Nations Human Rights Council, January 18, 2017, https://docs.un.org/en/A/HRC/34/51.

33 **I decided to write a letter too** Jessica Barrett, "I Left Vancouver Because Vancouver Left Me," *The Tyee,* October 30, 2017, https://thetyee.ca/Opinion/2017/10/30/I-Left-Vancouver/.

34 **the face of Canada's broken housing system** Jacqueline Hansen, "Ultra-low Rental Vacancy Rates Highlight 'Desperate' Struggle to Find Affordable Housing," CBC News, November 29, 2017, https://www.cbc.ca/news/business/no-vacancy-rental-struggles-1.4423963.

34 **satirized** Jacey Gibb, "Confusion Erupts as Young Woman Moves Without Writing 'Why I'm Leaving Vancouver' Open Letter," *Other Press,* November 2017, https://theotherpress.ca/confusion-erupts-as-young-woman-moves-without-writing-why-im-leaving-vancouver-open-letter/.

37 **seven people died** Benjamin Shingler, "Old Montreal Building Flagged for Violations prior to Fire That Killed 7 People," CBC News, April 28, 2023, https://www.cbc.ca/news/canada/montreal/old-montreal-fire-benamor-documents-1.6825465.

37 **Former tenants told the press** Benjamin Shingler and Sarah Leavitt, "Prior to Going Up in Flames, Old Montreal Building Was Considered 'Fire Trap' by Worried Renters," CBC News, March 25, 2023, https://www.cbc.ca/news/canada/montreal/montreal-old-port-fire-1.6788756; and Canadian Press, "Questions Raised about Safety of Old Montreal Building Destroyed by Fatal Fire," CTV News, March 25, 2023,

https://www.ctvnews.ca/montreal/article/questions-raised-about-safety-of-old-montreal-building-destroyed-by-fatal-fire/.

37 **the murder of a young couple** Bobby Hristova, "The Moments Before, During and After a Hamilton Landlord Killed His 2 Tenants: SIU Report," CBC News, September 26, 2023, https://www.cbc.ca/news/canada/hamilton/landlord-tenant-shooting-victims-siu-report-1.6978441.

37 **a shooting spree** "Vaughan Condo Shooting: What We Know about Alleged Gunman Francesco Villi," CBC News, December 19, 2023, https://www.cbc.ca/news/canada/toronto/francesco-villi-vaughan-shooting-what-we-know-1.6691201.

37 **years-long battle** Associated Press, "Canadian Man Accused of Killing 5 Had Feud with Condo Board," NPR, December 20, 2022, https://www.npr.org/2022/12/19/1144076419/5-dead-and-suspect-killed-in-toronto-area-condo-shooting.

37 **Alan O'Connor has pointed out** Alan O'Connor, "Condo: The New Structure of Housing," in *Sociology of Home, Belonging, Community, and Place in the Canadian Context*, ed. Gillian Anderson, Joseph G. Moore and Laura Suski (Canadian Scholars' Press, 2016).

38 **Paradise, California** Kirk Siegler, "A California Town Wiped Off the Map by Wildfire Is Still Recovering 5 Years On," NPR, November 8, 2023, https://www.npr.org/2023/11/08/1209471739/a-california-town-wiped-off-the-map-by-wildfire-is-still-recovering-five-years-o.

38 **Lahaina, Hawaii** John P. Rafferty, "Maui Wildfires of 2023," Britannica, April 1, 2025, https://www.britannica.com/event/Maui-wildfires-of-2023.

38 **Lytton, B.C.** Courtney Dickson, "Lytton Was a 'Magical' Place. Then It Burned to the Ground," CBC News, June 30, 2024, https://www.cbc.ca/news/canada/british-columbia/lytton-before-the-fire-1.7246077.

39 **uninsurable** Aimee Picchi, "Homes in Parts of the U.S. are 'Essentially Uninsurable' Due to Rising Climate Change Risks," CBS News, September 20, 2023, https://www.cbsnews.com/news/insurance-policy-california-florida-uninsurable-climate-change-first-street/; Gaye Taylor, comp., "'A Riskier Place to Live': Canada Could Be Uninsurable in a Decade, Says Expert," Energy Mix, January 15, 2025, https://www.theenergymix.com/a-riskier-place-to-live-canada-could-be-uninsurable-in-a-decade-says-expert/.

39 **go hand in hand** For an excellent analysis of the relationship between housing and climate change, I encourage everyone to check out the *Not Built For This* podcast: https://99percentinvisible.org/nbft/.

**3: THE ELEMENTS OF HOME**

41 **Gaston Bachelard** Gaston Bachelard, *The Poetics of Space* (Penguin Classics, 1958).

42 **an estimated 40 million people** David Farley, "Beyond Borders: A Deep Dive Into the Nomadic Way of Life," *New York Times*, October 14, 2022, https://www.nytimes.com/2022/10/14/travel/anthony-sattin-nomads-interview.html.

42 **many Indigenous cultures** Lisa-Jo K. van den Scott, "Mundane Technology in Non-Western Contexts: Wall-as-Tool," in *Sociology of Home, Belonging, Community, and Place in the Canadian Context*, ed. Gillian Anderson, Joseph G. Moore and Laura Suski (Canadian Scholars' Press, 2016), p. 38.

45 **who analyzed** Jan Willem Duyvendak, *The Politics of Home: Belonging and Nostalgia in Western Europe and in the United States* (Palgrave Macmillan, 2011).

46 **"home feelings"** Duyvendak, *The Politics of Home*, p. 26.

46 **familiarity, haven and heaven** Duyvendak, *The Politics of Home*, p. 38.

46 **"solastalgia"** Glenn Albrecht, Gina-Maree Sartore, Linda Connor, Nick Higginbotham, Sonia Freeman, Brian Kelly, Helen Stain, Anne Tonna and Georgia Pollard, "Solastalgia: The Distress Caused by Environmental Change," *Australas Psychiatry* 15 (2007): S95–98, https://pubmed.ncbi.nlm.nih.gov/18027145/.

46 **"un-homing"** Leslie Kern, *Gentrification Is Inevitable and Other Lies* (Between the Lines, 2022), p. 169.

47 **mysterious tunnel** Nicholas Köhler, "The Incredible True Story Behind the Toronto Mystery Tunnel," *Maclean's*, March 20, 2015, https://macleans.ca/society/elton-mcdonald-and-the-incredible-true-story-behind-the-toronto-mystery-tunnel/.

49 **as Duyvendak pointed out** Duyvendak, *The Politics of Home*, p. 30.

49 **"McMansions"** "'McMansion' is a slang term that describes a large, often ostentatious, mass-produced house. The name carries a rather critical connotation because McMansions lack architectural uniqueness, class, or style" (Julie Kagan, "What Is a McMansion?" Investopedia, February 11, 2025, https://www.investopedia.com/terms/m/mcmansion.asp).

49 **Subterranean "iceberg" basements** Candace Jackson, "Space-Hungry Bay Area Homeowners Are Hiding Entire 'Iceberg Homes' Underground," CT Insider, April 17, 2018, https://www.sfgate.com/realestate/article/Space-Hungry-Bay-Area-Palo-Alto-Iceberg-houses-12838744.php

50 **In 1975** Preet Banerjee, "Our Love Affair with Home Ownership Might Be Doomed," *Globe and Mail*, January 18, 2012, https://www.theglobeandmail.com/real-estate/mortgages-and-rates/our-love-affair-with-home-ownership-might-be-doomed/article4179012/.

50 **By 2010** Banerjee, "Our Love Affair with Home Ownership Might Be Doomed."

50 **condos have been shrinking** Ian Austen, "Ever-Shrinking Condos Are the Choice of Investors in Toronto and Vancouver," *New York Times*, October 5, 2024, https://www.nytimes.com/2024/10/05/world/canada/ever-shrinking-condos-are-the-choice-of-investors-in-toronto-and-vancouver.html; and "The Condo Market in Toronto and Vancouver: A Home, an Investment and Increasingly a Rental Property," Statistics Canada, March 20, 2023, https://www.statcan.gc.ca/01/en/plus/3237-condo-market-toronto-and-vancouver-home-investment-and-increasingly-rental-property.

50 **"suburban multi-family"** Ximena Gonzalez, "Suburban Calgary Seeing an Apartment Construction Boom," *Globe and Mail*, November 25, 2022, https://www.theglobeandmail.com/real-estate/article-suburban-calgary-seeing-an-apartment-construction-boom/.

51 **The emergence of "micro suites"** "Vancouver 'Micro-Lofts' Billed as Smallest in Canada," CBC News, December 19, 2011, https://www.cbc.ca/news/canada/british-columbia/vancouver-micro-lofts-billed-as-smallest-in-canada-1.997448.

51 **caused a stir** Postmedia News, "'They're Very Small': Could You Live in UBC's New 140 sq. ft. 'Nano Suite'?" *National Post*, February 24, 2016, https://nationalpost.com/life/homes/theyre-very-small-could-you-live-in-ubcs-new-140-sq-ft-nano-suite.

51 **Charles Munger caused in 2021** Maria Cramer, "After a Billionaire Designed a Dorm, an Architect Resigned in Protest," *New York Times*, October 30, 2021, https://www.nytimes.com/2021/10/30/us/charlie-munger-ucsb-dorms.html.

51 **the proposal was abandoned** Daniel Jonas Roche, "Death to Dormzilla? University of California Abandons Plans to Build 'Windowless Dorm' Munger Hall," *Architect's Newspaper*, August 9, 2023, https://www.archpaper.com/2023/08/university-california-abandons-windowless-dorm-munger-hall/.

52 **as-told-to piece** Jackie Thomas, as told to Alex Cyr, "I Moved to Alberta and Hated Everything About It. After Three Months, I Came Back to Toronto," *Toronto Life*, December 13, 2022, https://torontolife.com/city/i-moved-to-alberta-and-hated-everything-about-it-after-three-months-i-came-back-to-toronto/.

54 **"place attachment"** B.B. Brown, I. Altman and C.M. Werner, "Place Attachment," *International Encyclopedia of Housing and Home* (May 2012): 183–88, https://doi.org/10.1016/B978-0-08-047163-1.00543-9.

54 **"topophilia"** Hakon Heimer, "Topophilia and Quality of Life: Defining the Ultimate Restorative Environment," *Environmental Health Perspectives* 113, no. 2 (February, 2005): A117, https://pmc.ncbi.nlm.nih.gov/articles/PMC1277882/.

55 **trading one housing crisis for another** Behdad Mahichi, "Salt Spring Island's Housing Crisis Pushing Out Longtime Residents," *Vancouver Sun*, August 7, 2018, https://vancouversun.com/news/local-news/salt-spring-islands-housing-crisis-pushing-out-longtime-residents.

58 **people who feel a sense of purpose in their jobs** Naina Dhingra, Andrew Samo, Bill Schaninger and Matt Schrimper, "Help Your Employees Find Purpose—Or Watch Them Leave," McKinsey & Company, April 5, 2021, https://www.mckinsey.com/capabilities/people-and-organizational-performance/our-insights/help-your-employees-find-purpose-or-watch-them-leave.

58 **author Melody Warnick** Melody Warnick, *This Is Where You Belong: Finding Home Wherever You Are* (Penguin, 2016).

61 **what it was to become "21 Luxury Townhomes"** More than six years after I moved out, they still hadn't been built, and the land where the original four houses had stood remained a vacant lot.

## 4: TRICKLE-DOWN HOME ECONOMICS

65 **the for-profit health-care industry** Neha Patel and Shubham Singhal, "What to Expect in US Healthcare in 2024 and Beyond," McKinsey & Company, January 4, 2024, https://www.mckinsey.com/industries/healthcare/our-insights/what-to-expect-in-us-healthcare-in-2024-and-beyond.

66 **"mother of all other forms of monopoly"** Richard M. Langworth, "Liberty and Taxation: Churchill, George and The People's Rights, Part 2," Churchill Project: Hillsdale College, March 21, 2019, https://winstonchurchill.hillsdale.edu/henry-george-churchills-rejection/.

67 **called to answer** Mark Horton, "Returning Looted Artefacts Will Finally Restore Heritage to the Brilliant Cultures That Made Them," *The Conversation*, November 3, 2018, https://theconversation.com/returning-looted-artefacts-will-finally-restore-heritage-to-the-brilliant-cultures-that-made-them-107479.

67 **process of repatriating** "Collecting Histories," British Museum, 2025, https://www.britishmuseum.org/about-us/british-museum-story/contested-objects-collection.

67 **displacing peasants on British soil** "A Short History of Enclosure in Britain," *The Land*, 2009, https://www.theland-magazine.org.uk/articles/short-history-enclosure-britain.

67 **housing crisis Britain faces today** HDigital_Admin, "The UK Housing crisis: Causes, Impact, and Solutions," Housing Digital, March 6, 2025, https://housingdigital.co.uk/the-uk-housing-crisis-causes-impact-and-solutions/.

68 **William the Conqueror** "Norman Conquest," Britannica, https://www.britannica.com/event/Norman-Conquest.

68 **writer and activist Guy Shrubsole** Guy Shrubsole, *Who Owns England? How We Lost Our Land and How to Take It Back* (William Collins, 2019), p. 88.

69 **Sherwood Forest, of Robin Hood fame** "History of Sherwood Forest, Robin Hood and Major Oak," Nottingham City Council, https://www.nottinghamshire.gov.uk/culture-leisure/country-parks/history-of-sherwood-forest-robin-hood-and-major-oak.

69 **"Make sure they have an ancestor who was a very close friend of William the Conqueror"** Shrubsole, *Who Owns England?*, p. 75.

69 **peasant revolts over the years** "Peasants' Revolt," Britannica, https://www.britannica.com/event/Peasants-Revolt.

69 **enclosure acts** "The Enclosure Act," *History of Western Civilization* 2, Lumen Learning, https://courses.lumenlearning.com/suny-hccc-worldhistory2/chapter/the-enclosure-act/.

70 **Museum of the Home** For more, see: https://www.museumofthehome.org.uk/.

73 **habitants** Tom Wien and Suzanne Gousse, updated by Clayton Ma, "Habitant," *Canadian Encyclopedia*, February 7, 2006, https://www.thecanadianencyclopedia.ca/en/article/habitant.

73 **seigneurs** Jacques Mathieu, updated by Maude-emmanuelle Lambert, "Seigneurial System," *Canadian Encyclopedia*, August 25, 2013, https://www.thecanadianencyclopedia.ca/en/article/seigneurial-system.

73 **wide open west** Susan Jackel, updated by Julia Skikavich, "Pioneer Life," *Canadian Encyclopedia*, February 7, 2006, https://www.thecanadianencyclopedia.ca/en/article/pioneer-life.

73 **settlers building palatial dream homes** Peter Ward, *A History of Domestic Space: Privacy and the Canadian Home* (UBC Press, 1999), p. 8–18.

74 **the Halifax disaster** Information about this event has been taken from many sources, among them: H. Peter Oberlander and Arthur L. Fallick, ed. by George Anderson, *Housing a Nation: The Evolution of Canadian Housing Policy*, Canada Mortgage and Housing Corporation, June 1992, https:

//publications.gc.ca/collections/collection_2018/schl-cmhc /nh15/NH15-818-1992-eng.pdf; Isabel Buckmaster, "'A New and Thoroughly Modern City' Emerged in Halifax Following Devastating 1917 Explosion," *The Signal*, January 31, 2022, https://signalhfx.ca/a-new-and-thoroughly-modern-city -emerged-in-halifax-following-devastating-1917-explosion/; and "A city Destroyed: Experience the Halifax Explosion, 100 Years Later," CBC News, https://newsinteractives.cbc.ca /halifaxexplosion/.

76 **"clearly articulated, overriding goal"** H. Peter Oberlander and Arthur L. Fallick, ed. by George Anderson, *Housing a Nation: The Evolution of Canadian Housing Policy*, p. 4.

77 **had to swear off alcohol** Isabel Buckmaster, "'A New and Thoroughly Modern City' Emerged in Halifax Following Devastating 1917 Explosion," *The Signal*, January 31, 2022 https://signalhfx.ca/a-new-and-thoroughly-modern-city -emerged-in-halifax-following-devastating-1917-explosion/.

77 **Some scholars have posited** Richard Harris, *Creeping Conformity: How Canada Became Suburban, 1900–1960* (University of Toronto Press, 2004), p. 20.

78 **penalized by the state** Doukhobors, members of a Russian Christian sect that began settling on the Canadian prairies in the late 1800s, as well as Mennonites and Hutterites, two other groups that flocked to the prairies of early Canada, all established communities in accordance with their beliefs of shared property, pacifism and a rejection of materialism. These practices were perceived to be incongruent with the ideal of small family farms spread far apart on independently owned plots of land and many forms of communal settlement were eventually outlawed.

78 **how many unrelated adults can share a home** Michael Waters, "Where Living with Friends Is Still Technically Illegal," *The Atlantic*, May 22, 2023, https://www.theatlantic.com /family/archive/2023/05/zoning-laws-nuclear-modern

-family-definition/674117/; and Carlito Pablo, "City of Vancouver Bylaw That Defines a Family Creates Concern Over Collective Housing," *Georgia Straight*, June 7, 2017, https://www.straight.com/news/921211/city-vancouver-bylaw-defines-family-creates-concern-over-collective-housing#.

78 **the vast majority of residential land** "Is Single-Family Zoning Here to Stay?" *Civic Pulse*, June 27, 2024, https://www.civicpulse.org/post/is-single-family-zoning-here-to-stay.

78 **where lifelong renting is normalized** Ian Bickis, "What European Housing Models Could Do for Canada's Affordability Problems," Global News, November 3, 2024, https://globalnews.ca/news/10848824/european-housing-models-canada-affordability/.

78 **non-profit housing** Primarily in the form of co-operative housing, municipal housing or housing built on public land.

78 **Austria, the Netherlands, France, Denmark or Sweden** With social housing rates of 24 percent, 30 percent, 16 percent, 20 percent and 19 percent, respectively, compared to Canada's 3 percent ("The Richest European Countries Have More Social Housing," Tomorrow Building, https://www.tomorrow-building.com/richest-european-countries-more-social-housing/#:~:text=With%2030%25%2C%20the%20Netherlands%20has,the%20construction%20of%20housing%20projects).

80 **we built a *housing market* instead** In fact, it's notable that one of the definitive histories of Canadian housing policy is titled *Keeping to the Marketplace: The Evolution of Canadian Housing Policy* (John C. Bacher, McGill-Queen's University Press, 1993).

80 **when you see how our leaders clung to this ideology** H. Peter Oberlander and Arthur L. Fallick, ed. by George Anderson, *Housing a Nation: The Evolution of Canadian Housing Policy*.

80 **National Housing Act** Canada, National Housing Act, R.S.C., 1985, c. n-11, https://laws.justice.gc.ca/PDF/N-11.pdf.

80 **“contribute to the well-being of the housing sector in the national economy”** Canada, National Housing Act.

81 **encouraging new households to rely even more heavily on debt** Required down payments would continue to decline in the following decades, even getting to zero for a brief period in the 2000s. As of 2025, the minimum down payment was 5 percent of the value of the cheapest homes.

81 **lagged substantially in its per capita production of affordable, rental and non-market housing** Greg Suttor, *Still Renovating: A History of Canadian Social Housing Policy* (McGill-Queen’s University Press, 2016), p. 13–14.

81 **But like trickle-down economics** “Tax Cuts for the Wealthy Only Benefit the Rich: Debunking Trickle-Down Economics,” London School of Economics, January 24, 2023, https://www.lse.ac.uk/research/research-for-the-world/economics/tax-cuts-for-the-wealthy-only-benefit-the-rich-debunking-trickle-down-economics.

81 **It wasn’t until the 1960s** Suttor, *Still Renovating*, p. 45.

81 **prevented low-income “ghettos” from forming** Suttor, *Still* Renovating, p. 70.

82 **recognition as a trailblazer** In 1976, Vancouver even hosted a United Nations conference on the future of human settlements, the honour owing to our successful and innovative approach to social housing.

82 **between 12,000 and 20,000 units** including non-profit, co-operative and public housing. Suttor, *Still Renovating*, p. 177–182.

83 **87 percent of social and affordable housing<end boldface** https://www.pbo-dpb.ca/en/additional-analyses-analyses-complementaires/BLOG-2425-008--evolution-canada-social-housing-stock--evolution-parc-logements-sociaux-canada#ref_antn_5_0.

83 **peaking at 21.75 percent in 1981** "Canada Mortgage Rates History (1975 to 2025)," WOWA, https://wowa.ca/canada-mortgage-rates-history.

83 **aggressively lobbying for more market-friendly policies** Suttor, *Still Renovating*, p. 132.

83 **"Neoliberalism"** Liz Manning, "Neoliberalism: What It Is, with Examples and Pros and Cons," Investopedia, last updated July 2, 2024, https://www.investopedia.com/terms/n/neoliberalism.asp.

83 **Thatcher's "Right to Buy" program** Andy Beckett, "The Right to Buy: The Housing Crisis That Thatcher Built," *The Guardian*, August 26, 2015, https://www.theguardian.com/society/2015/aug/26/right-to-buy-margaret-thatcher-david-cameron-housing-crisis.

84 **Reagan, meanwhile** Peter Dreier, "Reagan's Legacy: Homelessness in America," Shelter Force, May 1, 2004, https://shelterforce.org/2004/05/01/reagans-legacy-homelessness-in-america/.

84 **when a deep recession finally hit** "Canada's Housing Market Crash History," *The Peak*, December 2022, https://www.read-thepeak.com/blog/housing-market-crash-canada.

84 **spurring a huge jump in ownership** from 66 percent to 69 percent by 2011, which may not sound like a lot but experts assured me was enough to substantially change our national psyche around homeownership.

85 **According to a wealth of research** National Academies of Sciences, Engineering, and Medicine, et al., *Permanent Supportive Housing: Evaluating the Evidence for Improving Health Outcomes Among People Experiencing Chronic Homelessness* (National Academies Press [US], July 11, 2018) https://pubmed.ncbi.nlm.nih.gov/30148580/; and Nathalie Rech, "Homelessness in Canada," Canadian Encyclopedia, July 9, 2019, https://www.thecanadianencyclopedia.ca/en/article/homelessness-in-canada.

**86** **saw the nature of homelessness fundamentally change** Emma Woolley, "Why Wasn't Homelessness a Social Problem Until the 1980s?" Homeless Hub, January 2, 2015, https://homelesshub.ca/blog/2015/why-wasnt-homelessness-social-problem-until-1980s/.

**87** **David Hulchanski has pointed out in his work** J. David Hulchanski, "What Factors Shape Canadian Housing Policy? The Intergovernmental Role in Canada's Housing System," Homeless Hub, 2006, https://homelesshub.ca/resource/what-factors-shape-canadian-housing-policy-intergovernmental-role-canadas-housing-system/.

**88** **cost our economy $5.5 billion in 2024 alone** Ben Segel-Brown and Zachary Vrhovsek, "Federal Spending on Housing Affordability in 2024," Office of the Parliamentary Budget Officer, December 12, 2024, https://www.pbo-dpb.ca/en/publications/RP-2425-023-Sfederal-spending-housing-affordability-in-2024depenses-federales-axees-abordabilite-logement-2024.

**88** **The National Housing Strategy** "Canada's National Housing Strategy," Housing, Infrastructure and Communities Canada, last updated June 9, 2025, https://housing-infrastructure.canada.ca/housing-logement/ptch-csd/index-eng.html.

**88** **little impact on affordability** Jacquie Gahagan and Ren Thomas, "Canada's National Housing Strategy: Is It Really Addressing Homelessness and Affordability?" *The Conversation*, November 16, 2022, https://theconversation.com/canadas-national-housing-strategy-is-it-really-addressing-homelessness-and-affordability-193261.

**88** **point-in-time homeless counts** "Everyone Counts 2020–2022—Results from the Third Nationally Coordinated Point-in-Time Counts of Homelessness in Canada," Housing, Infrastructure and Communities Canada, last updated January 26, 2025, https://housing-infrastructure.canada.ca/homelessness-sans-abri/reports-rapports/pit-counts-dp-2020-2022-results-resultats-eng.html#figure1.

88 **2.6 million Canadian households will be in core housing need by 2027** Segel-Brown and Vrhovsek, "Federal Spending on Housing Affordability in 2024."

89 **our rental housing consists of investment properties** "Rental supply Increases but Demand Surges," Canada Mortgage and Housing Corporation, January 26, 2023, https://www.cbc.ca/news/canada/british-columbia/housing-investors-canada-bc-1.6743083.

**5: MOBILE HOMES**

92 **have one or more spare bedrooms** "Under One Roof," Statistics Canada, August 26, 2022, https://www.statcan.gc.ca/o1/en/plus/1663-under-one-roof.

93 **biggest transfers of wealth** "The $1 Trillion Wave: How Intergenerational Wealth Transfer Is Reshaping Canadian Real Estate," Canadian Real Estate Association, March 3, 2025, https://www.kelownarealestate.com/blog-posts/the-1-trillion-wave-how-intergenerational-wealth-transfer-is-reshaping-canadian-real-estate.

93 **relocation stress syndrome, or sometimes transfer trauma** Companions for Seniors, January 11, 2021, https://companions-forseniors.com/2021/01/relocation-stress-syndrome-costs-of-uprooting-elderly/; and Charles A. Walker, Linda Cox Curry and Mildred O Hogstel, "Relocation Stress Syndrome in Older Adults Transitioning from Home to a Long-Term Care Facility: Myth or Reality?" *Journal of Psychosocial Nursing and Mental Health Services* 54, no. 1 (January 2007): 38–45, doi: 10.3928/02793695-20070101-09.

94 **more than half of Canadian seniors** "Using Your Home Equity for Retirement Income," Toronto Realty Boutique, https://torontorealtyboutique.com/using-your-home-equity-for-retirement-income/.

94 **Survey after survey** "Aging in Place—Deep Dive," *Aging in Canada*, podcast, https://www.nicenet.ca/articles/aging-in-place; and Melanie R. Fenton et al., "Growing Older at Home: Canadians' Meaning of Aging in Place," *Journal of Aging and Environment* (April 17, 2004), doi: 10.1080/26892618.2024.2329869.

95 **According to data from Generation Squeeze** "Straddling the Gap 2022," Generation Squeeze, https://www.gensqueeze.ca/straddling_the_gap_2022_housing_affordability#:~:text=It%20takes%207%20years%20of,started%20out%20as%20young%20people.

96 **One 2024 study** Jordann Kaye, "2024 Canada Housing Market Report: Homebuyers Get Thrifty to Move up the Property Ladder," ZOLO, April 3, 2024, https://www.zolo.ca/blog/2024-canada-housing-market-report.

96 **live with at least one parent** "Plateau in the Share of Young Adults Living with Their Parents from 2016 to 2021," Statistics Canada, https://www150.statcan.gc.ca/n1/daily-quotidien/220713/g-a005-eng.htm.

96 **residential mobility has declined** Jens von Bergmann, "Residential Mobility in Canada," Mountain Doodles, May 27, 2022, https://doodles.mountainmath.ca/posts/2022-05-27-residential-mobility-in-canada/.

97 **writes American historian Yoni Appelbaum** Yoni Appelbaum, "How Progressives Froze the American Dream," *The Atlantic*, February 10, 2025, https://www.theatlantic.com/magazine/archive/2025/03/american-geographic-social-mobility/681439/.

97 **housing affordability now trumps any other consideration** "Remote Work and Housing Location Preferences," Fannie Mae, 2023, https://www.fanniemae.com/media/48891/display.

97 **nearly 40 percent of prospective homebuyers say . . . and another 25 percent say they'd consider moving to a new province** Mackenzie Scibetta, "Homeownership on Hold: 67% of Millennials Delayed Buying a Home (Survey)," Zoocasa, October 10, 2023, https://www.zoocasa.com/blog/zoocasa-fall-survey-2023/.

97 **43 percent were 35 or older in 2023** "Down Payment Dilemma: Canadian First-Time Homebuyers' Fear of Falling Short Is Escalating," Royal LePage, https://www.royallepage.ca/en/realestate/news/down-payment-dilemma-canadian-first-time-homebuyers-fear-of-falling-short-is-escalating/.

97 **delaying having children** Natalie Stechyson, "Many Canadians in Their 20s and 30s Are Delaying Having Kids—and Some Say High Rent Is a Factor," CBC News, July 4, 2024, https://www.cbc.ca/news/canada/rent-canada-delaying-kids-1.7252926.

98 **harder to save for a down payment or save at all** Carrie Freestone, "Proof Point: Canadian Renters Face Higher Hurdles to Accumulating Wealth Than Homeowners," RBC Featured Insights, March 14, 2024, https://thoughtleadership.rbc.com/proof-point-canadian-renters-face-higher-hurdles-to-accumulating-wealth-than-homeowners/.

101 **adults who moved a lot as children** "Moving Repeatedly in Childhood Associated with Poorer Quality of Life Years Later," American Psychological Association, 2010, https://www.apa.org/news/press/releases/2010/06/moving-well-being.

102 **who identify as introverts** "A Portrait of Social Isolation and Loneliness in Canada Today," Angus Reid Institute, June 17, 2019, https://angusreid.org/social-isolation-loneliness-canada/#:~:text=More%20than%20seven%2Din%2Dten,both%2C%20or%20%E2%80%9Cambiverted.%E2%80%9D.

102 **are less likely to see themselves as part of a collective whole** Shigehiro Oishi and Ulrich Schimmack, "Residential Mobility, Well-Being, and Mortality," *Journal of Personality and Social Psychology* 98, no. 6 (2010): 980–4, doi: 10.1037/a0019389; and

Shigehiro Oishi, Janetta Lun and Gary D. Sherman, "Residential Mobility, Self-Concept, and Positive Affect in Social Interactions," *Journal of Personality and Social Psychology* 93, no. 1 (2007): 131–41, doi: 10.1037/0022-3514.93.1.131.

103 **That's why the United Nations** "The Human Right to Adequate Housing," United Nations Human Rights, https://www.ohchr.org/en/special-procedures/sr-housing/human-right-adequate-housing.

103 **"the freedom to choose one's city or community has become a privilege of class"** Yoni Appelbaum, "How Progressives Froze the American Dream," *The Atlantic*, February 10, 2025 https://www.theatlantic.com /magazine/archive/2025/03/american-geographic-social -mobility/681439/.

106 **author of a book about how we form friendships** Beverley Fehr, *Friendship Processes* (SAGE Publications, 1995).

107 **Research has even shown high-quality friendships** Beverley Fehr and Susan Sprecher, "Friendships and Acquaintanceships," in *The Cambridge Handbook of Personal Relationships*, 3rd edition (Cambridge University Press, 2026).

109 **as bad for us as smoking 15 cigarettes a day** Padraig Morgan, "Loneliness Is as Bad for You as Smoking, Research Shows. But the Stigma Stops People Getting Help," CBC Radio, November 21, 2023, https://www.cbc.ca/radio/thecurrent/who-loneliness-health-stigma-1.7035081.

109 **we have fewer friends today than 20 years ago** Youyou Zhou, "Want More Time with friends? It's the Ordinary Things That Matter," *Washington Post*, December 23, 2024, https://www.washingtonpost.com/opinions/interactive/2024/friends-loneliness-solitude-friendships/.

109 **one word over and over again: lonely** Roman Mars (host), *99% Invisible*, podcast, episode PB01, "The Power Broker #1: Robert Caro," January 18, 2024, https://99percentinvisible.org/episode/power-broker-01-robert-caro/.

109 **This corresponds with what surveys show us today.** "A Portrait of Social Isolation and Loneliness in Canada Today," Angus Reid Institute, June 17, 2019, https://angusreid.org/social-isolation-loneliness-canada/.

109 **"anyone, anywhere can become lonely or socially isolated"** "WHO Commission on Social Connection," https://www.who.int/groups/commission-on-social-connection.

110 **more likely to be renters** "A tale of Two Renters: Housing Affordability Among Recent and Existing Renters in Canada," Statistics Canada, October 4, 2023, https://www12.statcan.gc.ca/census-recensement/2021/as-sa/98-200-X/2021016/98-200-x2021016-eng.cfm; Egale, "Housing Challenges, Barriers, and Realities Among 2SLGBTQI People in Canada," November 2024, https://egale.ca/wp-content/uploads/2024/11/Housing-Among-2SLGBTQI-People-in-Canada_Literature-Review_V-01.pdf; "Housing Outcomes for Rural and Urban (Off-Reserve) Indigenous Peoples: A Brief Literature Review," Congress of Aboriginal Peoples, March 15, 2023, https://abo-peoples.org/wp-content/uploads/2024/05/Mini-Lit-review-housing-Outcomes-for-Rural-and-Urban-Off-Reserve-March-15-2023.pdf; and "New Data Highlights Troubling Housing Inequalities for People with Disabilities," Canadian Human Rights Commission, December 3, 2024, https://www.chrc-ccdp.gc.ca/resources/newsroom/joint-news-release-new-data-highlights-troubling-housing-inequalities-people.

111 **book *Chasing the Scream*** Johann Hari, *Chasing the Scream: The First and Last Days of the War on Drugs* (Bloomsbury, 2016).

111 **It's connection** Johann Hari, "Johann Hari: 'The Opposite of Addiction Isn't Sobriety—It's Connection,'" *The Guardian*, April 12, 2016, https://www.theguardian.com/books/2016/apr/12/johann-hari-chasing-the-scream-war-on-drugs.

**6: NEIGHBOURHOOD WELCOME**

117 **That day at city hall** Looking back over video of the public hearing, I actually appear rather calm in front of council, as do many of the other speakers that day. It was an altogether civil affair. However, there were many conversations that happened outside council chambers, including a rather heated exchange with one of the landlords on my block that left me shaken.

**7: VIENNA: A MODEL OF HOME**

122 **has topped lists** "Vienna Secures Its Position as the World's Most Liveable City for Third Consecutive Year," Economic Intelligence Unit, June 27, 2024, https://www.eiu.com/n/vienna-secures-its-position-as-the-worlds-most-liveable-city-for-third-consecutive-year/.

122 **has managed to sidestep the global affordability crisis** Binyamin Appelbaum, "The Big City Where Housing Is Still Affordable," *New York Times*, September 11, 2023, https://www.nytimes.com/2023/09/11/opinion/editorials/tokyo-housing.html.

122 **about C$930 a month (as of 2024)** "Average Monthly Rent for Apartments in the Greater Tokyo Area from 2015 to 2024, by Layout," Statista, https://www.statista.com/statistics/1202559/japan-rent-for-apartments-in-greater-tokyo-by-layout/#:~:text=In%20March%202024%2C%20the%20average%20monthly%20rent,and%20kitchen%20area%20and%20two%20separate%20rooms.

122 **to clock in at 250 square feet** Tim Hornyak, "In Japan, Designers Fit Big Ideas Into Tiny Homes," *New York Times*, December 6, 2024, https://www.nytimes.com/2024/12/06/realestate/tiny-homes-japan.html.

122 **buy their first homes directly from the government** Marc Lee, "Housing Lessons from Singapore," Canadian Centre for Policy Alternatives, August 10, 2023, https://www.policyalternatives.ca/news-research/singapore-housing/.

122 **favour heterosexual, nuclear families** "How Housing Policies Discriminate Against and Penalise LGBTQ+ Couples in Singapore // LGBTQ+ Rights in Singapore," Heckin' Unicorn. October 14, 2023, https://heckinunicorn.com/blogs/heckin-unicorn-blog/how-housing-policies-discriminate-against-and-penalise-lgbtq-couples-in-singapore-lgbtq-rights-in-singapore?currency=CAD.

123 **a "renters' utopia"** Francesca Mari, "Imagine a Renters' Utopia. It Might Look Like Vienna," *New York Times Magazine*, May 26, 2023, https://www.nytimes.com/2023/05/23/magazine/vienna-social-housing.html.

123 **Vienna's free and fair elections** The exception being the mid-1930s to the end of the Second World War, when Austria fell under authoritarian rule and was eventually annexed as part of Nazi Germany.

124 **an overview of its housing system** "Social Housing in Vienna," City of Vienna, https://socialhousing.wien/.

124 **of limited-profit or non-profit entities** These housing providers operate as associations or co-operatives and account for roughly half the social housing in Vienna and 40 percent of its total housing construction. As the name suggests, non-profit builders operate on a break-even capacity, with housing charges calculated to cover the cost of building and maintenance. Limited-profit builders can make an amount of profit limited by national legislation. Those profits must be reinvested in creating more social housing, either through the purchase of land, renovation and rehabilitation of existing housing, or new construction; in return they are exempt from corporate taxes. Both limited and non-profit housing is regulated by the Non-Profit Housing Act.

124 **all the streets are named for women** Valeriya Safronova, "Can Urban Design Have a Gender? In This Vienna District, the Answer Is Yes," *New York Times*, July 17, 2024, https://www.nytimes.com/2024/07/17/realestate/vienna-aspern-seestadt-gender.html.

126 **about €467 (C$730) per month** All currency conversions as of May 2025.

139 **to support a theory** Kunze told me she was influenced to explore this theory by the work of American sociologist Matthew Desmond, whose book *Evicted: Poverty and Profit in the American City* (Penguin Random House, 2016) is a harrowing, fact-based exploration of the impact housing insecurity has at a personal and population level. Well worth the read.

142 **The rent was just €650 a month, total** One of the benefits of Vienna's limited-profit and non-profit buildings, where Max lived, is that once costs such as construction loans are paid off, housing charges go down, in some cases resulting in rent that is even cheaper than in municipal housing. Many people also pay a certain amount, often between €30,000 and €50,000, to buy into a limited- or non-profit building, with the upfront costs offsetting monthly housing charges going forward.

### 8: BERLIN: A STREET FIGHT FOR THE CITY

146 **control of the city was carved up** "The Cold War in Berlin," John F. Kennedy Presidential Library and Museum, November 7, 2024, https://www.jfklibrary.org/learn/about-jfk/jfk-in-history/the-cold-war-in-berlin.

147 **all of this was in doubt** John Hooper, "Bankrupt Berlin Turns Off Fountains," *The Guardian*, May 28, 2001, https://www.theguardian.com/world/2001/may/28/johnhooper.

147 **As the scholar Quill R. Kukla writes** Quill R. Kukla, *City Living: How Urban Dwellers and Urban Spaces Make One Another* (Oxford Academic, 2021), p. 136.

151 **The Deutsche Wohnen & Co. Expropriation** Alexander Vasudevan, "Berlin's Vote to Take Properties from Big Landlords Could Be a Watershed Moment," *The Guardian*, September 29, 2021, https://www.theguardian.com/commentisfree/2021/sep/29/berlin-vote-landlords-referendum-corporate.

154 **it had previously sold to corporate owners** Joel Dullroy, "Berlin's Failed Rental Revolution," *The Berliner*, August 8, 2022, https://www.the-berliner.com/berlin/berlins-failed-rental-revolution-crisis-expropriation-mietendeckel-enteignen/.

154 **a five-year, city-wide rent cap** Dullroy, "Berlin's Failed Rental Revolution."

154 **released its findings** Olivia Logan, "Expropriating 240.000 Berlin Flats Is Constitutional, Expert Panel Concludes," *I Am Expat*, June 28, 2023, https://www.iamexpat.de/housing/property-news/expropriating-240000-berlin-flats-constitutional-expert-panel-concludes.

156 **Turkish migrants, who began arriving in the 1970s and '80s** Klaudia Prevezanos, "Turkish Guest Workers Transformed German Society," Deutsche Welle, October 30, 2011, https://www.dw.com/en/turkish-guest-workers-transformed-german-society/a-15489210.

157 **Kotti & Co.,** "(English) The Gecekondu Protest Hut of Kotti & Co—A Space for Housing Rights in Berlin," Kotti & Co, June 2019, https://kottiundco.net/2019/06/02/english-the-gecekondu-protest-hut-of-kotti-co-a-space-for-housing-rights-in-berlin/.

158 **a documentary I watched** Angelika Levi, dir., *Rent Eats the Soul*, Weltfilm GmbH, 2015, https://german-documentaries.de/en_EN/films/rent-eats-the-soul.9632.

159 **Rent freeze on all social housing units across Berlin** This has since been lifted by the Berlin Senate.

159 **According to an article in *Broadview* magazine** Isaac Würmann, "Berlin's Radical Renter Movement Has Lessons for Canada's Big Cities," *Broadview*, February 18, 2022, https://broadview.org/berlin-tenants-movement/.

**159** **€405 million** "Story of Berlin—Milestones in the Real Estate Market," Engel & Völkers, https://www.engelvoelkers.com/en-de/berlincommercial/blog/story-of-berlin-milestones-in-the-real-estate-market/.

**161** **chanting cheerleaders** Do yourself a favour and watch this video: Deutsche Wohnen & Co. enteignen, "Right to the City Cheerleading Tutorial (Full Video)," YouTube, 8:53, https://www.youtube.com/watch?v=JA2PzcZxKes.

**162** **Right to the City** Global Platform for Right to the City, https://www.right2city.org/the-right-to-the-city/.

**163** **ready to put them to work** Martin Neise, "A Blueprint for a Left That Wins," Rose Luxemburg Stiftung, October 28, 2021, https://www.rosalux.de/en/news/id/45255/a-blueprint-for-a-left-that-wins.

**164** **Hamburg** Peter Matthews, "'We're Closer Than Ever' What Next for Berlin's Housing Referendum?" *The Berliner*, August 9, 2023, https://www.the-berliner.com/berlin/deutsche-wohnen-vonovia-enteignen-expropriation-housing-referendum-what-next/; and Philipp Stehr, "Expropriation as a Measure of Corporate Reform: Learning from the Berlin Initiative," *European Journal of Political Theory* 24, no. 1 (2023), doi: 10.1177/14748851231197799.

**164** **Lisbon** Richard Matoušek, "In Lisbon, Residents Seek a Vote on Banning Airbnb," Jacobin, August 9, 2024, https://jacobin.com/2024/08/lisbon-housing-airbnb-ban-tourism; and Movimento Referendo pela Habitação: https://referendopela-habitacao.pt/pt/.

**164** **Spain** Joseph Wilson, "Across Spain, Tens of Thousands March to Protest the Growing Housing Crisis," AP News, April 5, 2025, https://apnews.com/article/housing-cost-protest-spain-9a4bc15ae2a0d1460950848ad2596d1b.

**9: HARARE: HEADS HELD HIGH**

**167** **defined by the United Nations** "SDG Indicator Metadata," https://unstats.un.org/sdgs/metadata/files/Metadata-11-01-01.pdf, last updated December 20, 2021.

**167** **Dolly Parton** Sarah Smarsh, "Outta That Holler," *Slate*, October 13, 2020, https://slate.com/culture/2020/10/dolly-parton-biography-she-come-by-it-natural-excerpt.html.

**167** **Bob Marley** "Bob Marley summary," Britannica, https://www.britannica.com/summary/Bob-Marley.

**167** **Pelé** Kurt Streeter, "Pele's Breakthrough Gave Soccer a Black Star," *New York Times*, December 31, 2022, https://www.nytimes.com/2022/12/30/sports/soccer/pele-kylian-mbappe-lionel-messi.html.

**167** **hotbeds of entrepreneurship and innovation** Reena Jana, "A Peek into the Future: Slums as Innovation Hotbeds," *CBS News*, October 14, 2011, https://www.cbsnews.com/news/a-peek-into-the-future-slums-as-innovation-hotbeds/.

**167** **15-minute cities** "A Guide to 15-minute Cities: Why Are They So Controversial?" University College of Estate Management, December 2, 2024, https://www.ucem.ac.uk/whats-happening/articles/15-minute-city/.

**169** **with a bulldozer** Duncan Campbell, "Homeless and Hopeless: Bulldozers Carve Out a Bleak New Reality for Poor Zimbabweans," *The Guardian*, July 5, 2005, https://www.the-guardian.com/world/2005/jul/05/zimbabwe.duncancampbell.

**170** **they often destroy critical items** Ruth Talbot, Asia Fields, Nicole Santa Cruz and Maya Miller, "Swept Away," Propublica, October 29, 2024, https://projects.propublica.org/homeless-encampment-sweeps-taken-belongings/.

**171** **opted to criminalize them** Nazish Dholakia, "How the United States Punishes People for Being Poor," Vera, September 21, 2023, https://www.vera.org/news/how-the-united-states-punishes-people-for-being-poor.

171 **It is very expensive** "Cost of Ending Homelessness," Homeless Hub, https://homelesshub.ca/collection/homelessness-101/cost-of-ending-homelessness/#:~:text=Ironically%2C%20it%20costs%20more%20to%20ignore%20our,Canadian%20economy%20around%20$10%20billion%20per%20year.

173 **Zimbabwe Homeless People's Federation** "Who We Are," Dialogue on Shelter for the Homeless in Zimbabwe Trust, https://www.dialogueshelter.org/index.php/about-us.

173 **"time is money"** "Advice to a Young Tradesman [21 July 1748]," Founders Online, https://founders.archives.gov/documents/Franklin/01-03-02-0130.

174 **Jockin Arputham** Srinath Perur, "Jockin Arputham: From Slum Dweller to Nobel Peace Prize Nominee," *The Guardian*, June 12, 2014, https://www.theguardian.com/cities/2014/jun/12/jockin-arputham-mumbai-slum-dweller-nobel-peace-prize-nominee.

176 **Harare Slum Upgrading Project** "Dzivarasekwa Slum Upgrading Project, Zimbabwe," https://world-habitat.org/wp-content/uploads/2019/11/Zimbabwe_FULL-Project-Summary.pdf.

178 **"credit is a human right"** Randeep Ramesh, "'Credit Is a Basic Human Right'" *The Guardian*, January 5, 2007, https://www.theguardian.com/world/2007/jan/05/outlook.development.

178 **A 2021 investigation by Bloomberg** Gavin Finch and David Kocieniewski, "Big Money Backs Tiny Loans That Lead to Debt, Despair and Even Suicide," *Bloomberg*, May 3, 2022, https://www.bloomberg.com/graphics/2022-microfinance-banks-profit-off-developing-world/.

178 **a litany of academic studies** Thomas Dichter, "Whatever Happened to Microfinance? A Cautionary Tale," American Foreign Service Association, June 2021, https://afsa.org/whatever-happened-microfinance-cautionary-tale.

181 **a number of awards** "Dzivarasekwa Slum Upgrading," World Habitat Awards, 2019, https://world-habitat.org/world-habitat-awards/winners-and-finalists/dzivarasekwa-slum-upgrading/; James Tayler, "SDI Receives the Skoll Award for Social Entrepreneurship," SDI, 2014, https://sdinet.org/2014/04/sdi-receives-the-skoll-award-for-social-entrepreneurship/.

181 **include Hillary Clinton** "Clinton Backs Microcredit Pioneer Yunus in Bangladesh," BBC News, May 6, 2012, https://www.bbc.com/news/world-asia-17973267.

181 **Nobel Peace Prize in 2006** "Muhammad Yunus Facts," Nobel Prize, 2006, https://www.nobelprize.org/prizes/peace/2006/yunus/facts/.

181 **Arputham was also nominated in 2014** Perur, "Jockin Arputham."

185 **the Gates Foundation . . . as major funders** "480 DZ Families Benefit from Gates Foundation," *The Herald*, April 24, 2015, https://www.heraldonline.co.zw/480-dz-families-benefit-from-gates-foundation/.

187 **more than a billion people worldwide live in slums** "Goal 11: Make cities Inclusive, Safe, Resilient and Sustainable," United Nations Sustainable Development Goals, https://www.un.org/sustainabledevelopment/cities/.

191 ***"Never doubt that a small group of thoughtful, committed citizens can change the world; indeed, it's the only thing that ever has."*** No one can really pinpoint the source of this quotation. It is widely attributed to Margaret Mead, an anthropologist who rose to fame in the late 1920s after releasing her book *Coming of Age in Samoa*, though it doesn't appear in any of her writing. It is thought that it may have been something she uttered in a speech or interview throughout her career. Some people take issue with it, arguing it is patently not true—only large movements seem to have changed the world.

I love this quote regardless. I first encountered it as a mural painted on the side of one of my favourite restaurants in Vancouver on Main Street, the dearly departed radical vegetarian eatery The Foundation, and it has always stuck with me. First, as an embodiment of the kind of scrappy DIY artist circles I was a part of in Vancouver in my early days. What I loved about the city was that my corner of it really did seem propelled by small groups of people doing cool off-the-cuff stuff that later became theatre companies or venues or festivals. The quotation later came back into my consciousness while working on this book. White it's true that achieving a critical mass is important to successful systemic change, it is also true that these movements start with small groups and sometimes even individual acts. A neighbourhood savings group, a knock on a door to commiserate with a neighbour about a rent increase, a group of people occupying a hut on the sidewalk. It's through these small actions and small connections that movements gain their momentum and lead to change.

**10: HOME FEELINGS**

193 **flocked to Calgary** Mackenzie Rhode, "Calgary Remains Fastest-Growing City in Canada, According to U-Haul Data," *Calgary Herald*, January 13, 2025, https://calgaryherald.com/news/local-news/alberta-top-province-for-growth-in-2024-calgary-top-city#:~:text=Alberta%27s%20population%20projections%20report%20cites%20job%20opportunity,and%20rapidly%20growing%20tech%20and%20finance%20sectors; and Sheri Block, "Alberta Called. I Shouldn't Have Answered." *Maclean's*, April 9, 2025, https://macleans.ca/society/alberta-called-i-shouldnt-have-answered/.

193 **in core housing need** Michael Franklin, "'A Housing Crisis': 1 in 5 Calgary Households Couldn't Afford Costs, City Says," CTV News, September 6, 2023, https://www.ctvnews.ca/calgary/article/a-housing-crisis-1-in-5-calgary-households-couldnt-afford-costs-city-says/.

193 **In a province with no rent control** In Alberta, there is no limit on how much landlords can increase rent, though they can only implement an increase once a year.

197 **Calgary City Council held a marathon public hearing** "Calgary Councillors Hear Summary of Marathon Rezoning Hearings," CBC News, May 20, 2024, https://www.cbc.ca/news/canada/calgary/calgary-city-council-rezoning-hearings-summary-1.7199831.

197 **the "missing middle"** "Missing Middle Housing," https://missingmiddlehousing.com/.

198 **Minneapolis** Gabrielle Bruney, "Minneapolis, Tackling Housing Crisis and Inequity, Votes to End Single-Family Zoning," *The New York Times*, December 13, 2018, https://www.nytimes.com/2018/12/13/us/minneapolis-single-family-zoning.html.

198 **Toronto** "Expanding Housing Options in Neighbourhoods," City of Toronto, https://www.toronto.ca/city-government/planning-development/planning-studies-initiatives/expanding-housing-options/.

198 **Vancouver** "Vancouver Reforms Single Family Neighbourhoods," City of Vancouver, September, 15, 2023, https://vancouver.ca/news-calendar/vancouver-reforms-sf-neighbourhoods.aspx.

198 **Halifax** Haley Ryan, "Halifax Zoning Changes Could Allow for Some 200,000 New Housing Units," CBC News, April 18, 2024, https://www.cbc.ca/news/canada/nova-scotia/halifax-zoning-changes-could-allow-for-200-000-new-housing-units-1.7177029.

198 **Edmonton** Laura Krause, "What Does Edmonton's New Zoning Bylaw Mean for You?" City News, October 24, 2023, https://edmonton.citynews.ca/2023/10/24/edmonton-new-zoning-bylaw/.

198 **Oregon** Laurel Wamsley, "Oregon Legislature Votes to Essentially Ban Single-Family Zoning," NPR, July 1, 2019, https://www.npr.org/2019/07/01/737798440/oregon-legislature-votes-to-essentially-ban-single-family-zoning.

**198 California** Kenneth Schrupp, "California Quietly Ended Single Family Zoning, Allowing Four Homes per Lot," *Center Square*, December 31, 2024, https://www.thecentersquare.com/california/article_ec839ece-c7af-11ef-a03d-93f8e3efc572.html.

**198 in a 9–6 vote** Kylee Pedersen, "Calgary City Council Passes Amended Rezoning Bylaw after Longest Meeting Ever Held," CBC News, May 14, 2024, https://www.cbc.ca/news/canada/calgary/calgary-city-council-rezoning-land-use-bylaw-amended-1.7204465.

**199 one councillor told the local news** Pedersen, "Calgary City Council Passes Amended Rezoning Bylaw."

**199 attack on their property rights** An interesting pattern I've noticed in this and other hearings is that homeowners opposed to increased density often cite their fear it will decrease their property value, when it's more likely to do the opposite. Living in a neighbourhood that's been rezoned to allow for more density generally increases property values because land becomes worth more to developers, who can build more units of housing and make a bigger profit. That's why Calgary's mayor told me if we signed onto the rezoning on our block, our house would be worth a lot more. I've developed a theory that the reason people constantly cite concern for "property values" in development hearings is because they lack language to describe the fear and discomfort they feel about change and potentially being "un-homed," even if they're not at risk of being displaced. Lacking this language, they tend to put their discomfort in terms most likely to get action in our culture, which is using the language of money. City councils don't tend to respond to people's emotional loss over property development, but they do tend to consider financial loss more seriously. I often wonder how much quicker and more productive these processes would be if we could just talk about, and acknowledge, feelings more plainly.

200 **launched a court challenge** Alejandro Melgar, "Calgary Court Challenge on Blanket Rezoning Going to Appeals Court," City News, January 26, 2025, https://calgary.citynews.ca/2025/01/26/calgary-zoning-bylaw-challenge-appeals-court/.

200 **restrictive covenants on their properties** Scott Strasser, "Homeowners Against Blanket Zoning Turn to Restrictive Covenants to Block Redevelopment," *Calgary Herald*, September 24, 2024, https://calgaryherald.com/news/calgary-homeowners-against-rezoning-use-restrictive-covenants.

200 **In California, a court challenge** Liam Dillon, "Law That Ended Single-Family Zoning Is Struck Down for Five Southern California Cities," *Los Angeles Times*, April 29, 2024, https://www.latimes.com/homeless-housing/story/2024-04-29/law-that-ended-single-family-zoning-is-struck-down-for-five-southern-california-cities.

200 **have also turned to restrictive covenants** Chad Pawson, "Burnaby Neighbourhood Hopes Covenants Will Defend Against Density," CBC News, August 23, 2024, https://www.cbc.ca/news/canada/british-columbia/brentwood-park-covenants-single-family-homes-densification-provincial-legislation-1.7303509.

201 **INTERACT** For more on INTERACT, see https://teaminteract.ca/.

201 **In one study** J. Karmann, M. Najjar, C.A. Ottoni, M. Shareck, S. Lord, M. Winters, D. Fuller and Y. Kestens, "'They Didn't Have to Build That Much': A Qualitative Study on the Emotional Response to Urban Change in the Montreal Context," *Emotion, Space and Society* 46 (2023): 1–8, doi/10.1016/j.emospa.2022.100937.

203 **staff received racist threats of violence** Kylee Pedersen, "Walking Tour on Rezoning Proposal Cancelled Due to Safety Concerns," CBC News, March 17, 2024, https://www.cbc.ca/news/canada/calgary/rezoning-bylaw-walking-tour-capitol-hill-cancelled-safety-concerns-1.7146391.

**205** **gradually "thicken up" existing neighbourhoods** Charles L. Marohn Jr. and Daniel Herriges, *Escaping the Housing Trap: The Strong Towns Response to the Housing Crisis* (Wiley, 2024), p. 156–159.

**206** **Her dissertation** Teresa Goldstein, "Bringing Back the Love: The Emotional Connection of Growth and Change through Multi-Community Local Area Planning in Calgary, AB" (Ph.D. diss, University of Calgary, 2023), doi: 10.11575/PRISM/41582.

**11: GOOD NEIGHBOURS**

**213** **Streetcar tracks got ripped out** Joseph Stromberg, "The Real Story Behind the Demise of America's Once-Mighty Streetcars," *Vox*, May 7, 2015, https://www.vox.com/2015/5/7/8562007/streetcar-history-demise.

**213** **Sidewalks got much narrower** Avi Selk, "The Death of the Sidewalk," *Washington Post*, June 30, 2019, https://www.washingtonpost.com/lifestyle/style/the-death-of-the-sidewalk/2019/06/28/b89c9bb2-9900-11e9-8d0a-5edd7e2025b1_story.html.

**213** **Robert D. Putnam** *Bowling Alone: The Collapse and Revival of American Community* (Simon & Schuster, 2000).

**213** **megaplex movie theatres** Marissa Matozzo, "Movie Theaters Are Trying Everything to Bring Audiences Back—From Pickleball to Cocktail Bars," *New York Post*, March 28, 2025, https://nypost.com/2025/03/28/lifestyle/movie-theaters-are-shaking-things-up-to-survive-heres-how/.

**213** **shopping malls have been stripped of their status** Matthew Christopher, "The Life and Death of the American Mall: The Indoor Suburban Shopping Center Is a Special Kind of Abandoned Place," *Atlas Obscura*, January 10, 2024, https://www.atlasobscura.com/articles/the-life-and-death-of-the-suburban-american-mall.

213 **the reliable din of the dinner rush** Jessica Barrett, "How Restaurant Delivery Services Are Impacting Calgary's Dining Scene," *Avenue Calgary*, May 13, 2019, https://www.avenuecalgary.com/restaurants-food/eating-in/how-restaurant-delivery-services-are-impacting-calgarys-dining-scene/.

214 **as a chief design consideration** Derek Thompson, "The Anti-Social Century," *The Atlantic*, January 8, 2025, https://www.theatlantic.com/magazine/archive/2025/02/american-loneliness-personality-politics/681091/.

214 **Multitudes of studies** Meredith Sones, "How Social Connectedness Between Neighbours Supports Health and Well-Being," Hey Neighbour! Collective, June 3, 2022, https://www.heyneighbourcollective.ca/2022/06/how-social-connectedness-between-neighbours-supports-health-wellbeing/; "A Portrait of Social Isolation and Loneliness in Canada Today," Angus Reid Institute, June 17, 2019, https://angusreid.org/social-isolation-loneliness-canada/; and Emily A. Greenfield and Laurent Reyes, "Continuity and Change in Relationships with Neighbors: Implications for Psychological Well-being in Middle and Later Life," *Journals of Gerontology: Series B: Psychological Sciences and Social Sciences* 70, no. 4 (2014): 607–18, doi: 10.1093/geronb/gbu084.

215 **One study I looked at** Thomas O'Rourke, "The Decline of Trust and Neighborliness," Institute for Family Studies, October 3, 2023, https://ifstudies.org/blog/the-decline-of-trust-and-neighborliness.

215 **As *Atlantic* writer Derek Thompson points out** Thompson, "The Anti-Social Century," https://www.theatlantic.com/magazine/archive/2025/02/american-loneliness-personality-politics/681091/.

216 **Hey Neighbour! Collective** For more, see: https://www.heyneighbourcollective.ca/.

217 **when a 2012 survey from the non-profit Vancouver Foundation** "Connections and Engagement: A Survey of Metro Vancouver," Vancouver Foundation, June 2012, https://www.vancouverfoundation.ca/sites/default/files/documents/VanFdn-SurveyResults-Report.pdf.

217 **a growing body of research** Meg Holden and Yushu Zhu, "Can Highrises Be Neighbourly? It's Complicated" *The Tyee*, April 22, 2024, https://thetyee.ca/Analysis/2024/04/22/Can-Highrises-Be-Neighbourly/.

217 **knowledge synthesis on the topic** "Social Quality of Life in High-Density Built Environments: Knowledge Synthesis for the Emerging Asocial Society," Simon Fraser University, November 7, 2022, https://summit.sfu.ca/item/35349.

218 **Happy Cities** For more, see: https://happycities.com/. This firm was co-founded by urbanist and author Charles Montgomery, whose book, *Happy City: Transforming Our Lives Through Urban Design* (Anchor Canada, 2014) is very much worth a read.

219 **A pilot project** "Supporting Residents to Become Community Connectors in Multi-Unit Housing Practice Guide," Hey Neighbour! Collective, https://www.heyneighbourcollective.ca/wp-content/uploads/2023/01/Practice-Guide-1-v2.1.pdf.

221 **several completed multi-family buildings** "Building Social Connections: Toolbox of Design Actions to Nurture Wellbeing in Multi-Unit Housing," Hey Neighbour! Collective, July 2024, https://www.heyneighbourcollective.ca/wp-content/uploads/2025/04/Building-social-connections-toolkit-v2-1.pdf.

223 **"placemaking"** "What Is Placemaking?" Project for Public Spaces, 2007, https://www.pps.org/article/what-is-placemaking.

225 **called ParkPark** For more, see: https://www.calgarymlc.ca/projects/park-park. I was interested to see the project had been decommissioned a few months after the walking tour I took with Schwartz. The space has since been returned to its "natural" state as a plain old surface parking lot.

227 **mddl** For more, see: https://www.mddl.co/.

227 **Canada Mortgage and Housing Corporation's Housing Supply Challenge** "Round 5's game-changer winners from the Housing Supply Challenge," Canada Mortgage and Housing Corporation's Housing Supply Challenge, July 23, 2024, https://www.cmhc-schl.gc.ca/professionals/project-funding-and-mortgage-financing/funding-programs/all-funding-programs/housing-supply-challenge/round-5-housing-supply-challenge/round-5-game-changer-winners.

232 **the two wolves** "The Two Wolves: A Cherokee Story," San Diego State University, n.d., https://theacademy.sdsu.edu/wp-content/uploads/2015/06/two-wolves-cherokee-story.pdf.

### 12: BUILDING FOR THE VILLAGE

233 **Little Mountain Cohousing** For more, see: https://www.littlemountaincohousing.ca/.

233 **about three times a week** Common meals are a core tenet of cohousing, but every development does it differently.

233 **Taking a page right out of . . . socially connected design guidelines** In reality, it was the other way around. Little Mountain and many other cohousing developments served as case studies for socially connected design, informing the guidelines Happy Cities eventually came up with (see "Building Social Connections," Happy Cities and Hey Neighbour! Collective, July 2024, https://www.heyneighbourcollective.ca/wp-content/uploads/2025/04/Building-social-connections-toolkit-v2-1.pdf).

234 **net you a fine from building management** When Dave lived in his rented high-rise condo in Vancouver we ended up nicknaming the building "luxury prison" for the ways in which it felt like we lived in a surveillance state where one was always assumed guilty until proven innocent. Dave was once charged a "move-in" fee for having a couch delivered via the elevator

(how else is one supposed to get a piece of furniture up to the 21st floor?) and another time was charged for violating the building's non-smoking policy, despite never having smoked a cigarette in his life. It seemed a neighbour smelled cigarette smoke emanating from a balcony and decided it was coming from Dave's unit with absolutely no proof. The fine arrived with zero avenue for appeal; it took him months to track down someone from the condo board to correct the record.

237 **community-focused way of building housing** Ronaye Matthew and Margaret Crtichlow, *Community Led Housing: A Cohousing Development Approach* (Page Two, 2024).

237 **only what it cost to build** This doesn't mean things come cheap. Building costs are still substantial, including the cost of land, construction, financing and fees for professionals such as architects and consultants. But without the added margin of profit, costs can be kept lower.

238 **many experts** "Scaling-Up the Non-Market Housing Sector in Canada," National Housing Council, March 2025, https://cms.nhc-cnl.ca/media/Scaling%20Non%20Market%20Housing%20Report%20-%20V10%202.pdf; and Yushu Zhu, Hanan Ali, Meg Holden and Natasha Mhuriro, "Busting Four Damaging Myths about Community Housing," *The Tyee*, May 14, 2024, https://thetyee.ca/Analysis/2024/05/14/Four-Damaging-Myths-Community-Housing/.

238 **World Habitat** For more, see: https://world-habitat.org/our-programmes/community-led-housing/.

238 **URBACT** For more, see: https://urbact.eu/.

239 **core qualities in common** E.J. Griffith, M. Jepma and F. Savini, "Beyond Collective Property: A Typology of Collaborative Housing in Europe," *International Journal of Housing Policy* 24, no. 1 (2022): 121–41, https://doi.org/10.1080/19491247.2022.2123272.

239 **similar-sounding moniker of co-living** Will Coldwell, "'Co-living': The End of Urban Loneliness—Or Cynical Corporate Dormitories?" *The Guardian*, September 3, 2019, https://www.theguardian.com/cities/2019/sep/03/co-living-the-end-of-urban-loneliness-or-cynical-corporate-dormitories.

241 **existed in some form since the 1960s** Danny Milman, "The History of Cohousing," Canadian Cohousing Network, https://old.cohousing.ca/about-cohousing/history-of-cohousing/.

241 **most prominently in Europe** Cohousing is a big part of Barcelona's anti-gentrification strategy, where they are often built on municipal land and operated as non-profit co-ops. In Vienna, cohousing design techniques are also often used in the creation of non-profit and limited-profit buildings (see "Cohousing," https://www.habitatge.barcelona/en/access-to-housing/cohousing; and https://world-habitat.org/wp-content/uploads/2024/12/2024AI1.pdf).

241 **There are fewer than 25 completed** As of 2025, according to the Canadian Cohousing Network, https://cohousing.ca/.

242 **environmental standard** Many are what's called "passive houses" with an extremely low carbon footprint.

242 **developer levies** Uytae Lee does a very good explanation of developer levies and other taxes on new construction in this video: About Here, "How Cities Taxed Their Way into the Housing Crisis," YouTube, 17:11, https://www.youtube.com/watch?v=ZEUR9bj89lo). His entire series "About Here" is worth watching for armchair urbanists.

242 **decreased substantially or dropped entirely** The foremost example of this in my mind is what happened during the lead-up to the 2010 Olympics in Vancouver ("Vancouver Cuts Olympic Village Social Housing," CBC News, April 23, 2010, https://www.cbc.ca/news/canada/british-columbia/vancouver-cuts-olympic-village-social-housing-1.882070).

242 **Driftwood Village** For more, see: https://www.driftwood villagecohousing.com/.

242 **25 percent below market price** Carlito Pablo, "Cohousing Opens the Door to Affordability in City of North Vancouver," *Georgia Straight*, June 27, 2018, https://www.straight.com /news/1095141/cohousing-opens-door-affordability-city -north-vancouver.

243 **more than a quarter million people** "Facts and Figures," Co-operative Housing Federation of Canada, n.d., https: //chfcanada.coop/about-co-op-housing/facts-and-figures/.

243 **waitlists that can be years long** Ximena Gonzalez, "People Love Living in Co-ops—So Why Did Canada Kill the Program?" *Ricochet*, November 7, 2023, https://ricochet.media/justice /housing/people-love-living-in-co-ops-so-why-did-canada -kill-the-program/#:~:text=Decade%2Dlong%20waiting% 20lists%20for%20co%2Dops%20The%20limited,for%20 most%20Canadians%2C%20despite%20being%20so% 20in%2Ddemand.

244 **vulnerable to eventual redevelopment** "This Vancouver Housing Co-op is Facing a $1M Tax If It Wants to Renew Its Lease for More Than 30 Years," CBC News, May 15, 2025, https://www.cbc.ca/news/canada/british-columbia/vancouver -housing-co-op-property-transfer-tax-1.7536390.

244 **reinvestment in housing co-ops** Paul Weinberg, "Housing Crisis Pushes Once-Thriving Co-Op Movement Back into the Spotlight," *The Breach*, March 31, 2023, https://breachmedia.ca /solutions-canada-housing-crisis-co-ops/.

244 **unveiled a $1.5 billion fund** "Canadians Want More Co-Op Housing: New Report from Abacus Data," Co-operative Housing Federation of Canada, March 6, 2025, https://chf canada.coop/canadians-want-more-co-op-housing-new -report-from-abacus-data/; and "Federal Government Launches New $1.5 Billion Program to Build a New Generation

of Co-Op Housing," Government of Canada, June 6, 2024, https://www.canada.ca/en/housing-infrastructure-communities/news/2024/06/federal-government-launches-new-15-billion-program-to-build-a-new-generation-of-coop-housing.html.

244 **during our golden era** Greg Suttor, *Still Renovating: A History of Canadian Social Housing Policy* (McGill-Queen's University Press, 2016).

244 **market-oriented solutions** "Progress on the National Housing Strategy," Government of Canada, June, 2024, https://housing-infrastructure.canada.ca/housing-logement/ptch-csd/reports-rapports/prog-nhs-june-2024-juin-snl-eng.html; and "2024 federal budget analysis," BC Non-Profit Housing Association, https://bcnpha.ca/resource/2024-federal-budget-analysis/.

244 **it costs about $500,000 to build a new unit of affordable housing** Numbers vary across the country. This is the cost estimate used by organizations such as the Co-operative Housing Federation of Canada and the Parkdale Neighbourhood Land Trust.

244 **According to a 2022 analysis** Steve Pomeroy, "Updating Analysis on Erosion of Lower Rent Stock from 2021 Census," Canadian Housing Evidence Collaborative, October, 2022, https://chec-ccrl.ca/wp-content/uploads/2022/10/Updated-Analysis-on-Housing-Erosion-from-2021-Census-Steve-Pomeroy.pdf.

245 **now a few fledgling funds** See: Rental Protection Fund (https://rentalprotectionfund.ca/) and Canadian Housing Acquisition Fund (https://www.acquisitionfund.ca/).

245 **cost of housing artificially high** Yushu Zhu and Hanan Ali, "Canada's Housing Crisis Is a Feature, Not a Bug," *The Tyee*, November 1, 2024, https://thetyee.ca/Analysis/2024/11/01/Canada-Housing-Crisis-Feature-Not-Bug/; and "Want to Solve the Housing Crisis? Address Super-Charged Demand," *The Conversation*, November 25, 2021, https://theconversation.

com/want-to-solve-the-housing-crisis-address-super-charged-demand-169809.

245 **the growth of renters is outpacing buyers** Pamela Heaven, "Posthaste: Renter Nation? Number of Tenants in Canada Hits Unprecedented Heights," *Financial Post*, June 11, 2024, https://financialpost.com/news/canada-renters-hit-record-heights.

246 **the Caroline Co-op was born** For more, see: https://caroline-cooperative.com/about-us/; and Justin Chandler, "Hamilton Co-op Residents Celebrate Their 1st Holidays in a Building They Worked over a Year to Own," CBC News, December 23, 2024, https://www.cbc.ca/news/canada/hamilton/caroline-co-op-1.7412629.

248 **cities like Montreal** CBC News, "Montreal Uses Right To Refusal to Buy Another Rooming House in Fight Against Housing Crisis" July 10, 2023, https://www.cbc.ca/news/canada/montreal/montreal-rooming-house-buy-1.6902559.

248 **while Washington, D.C.** Yesin Sayin and Emilia Calma, "TOPA's Promise and Pitfalls: Balancing Tenant Rights, Affordability, and Housing Investment in Washington, D.C.," D.C. Policy Center, March 13, 2025, https://www.dcpolicycenter.org/publications/topas-promise-and-pitfalls-in-dc/.

248 **San Francisco** Eli Underwood, "A Guide to Rights of First Refusal," California Lawyers Association, n.d., https://calawyers.org/real-property-law/a-guide-to-rights-of-first-refusal/.

250 **Community land trusts** For more, see: https://www.communityland.ca/.

250 **the ultimate container** One of the things that excites me most about CLTs is that they play so nicely with other forms of collaborative housing. It's entirely possible to have a cohousing co-operative on land managed by a CLT.

251 **Toronto's Parkdale Neighbourhood Land Trust** For more, see: https://pnlt.ca/.

251 **portfolio of 86 properties** Eighty-two of these are low-density "scatterhomes"—single-family homes or small buildings—that were once owned by a municipal housing authority that was struggling with maintenance, upkeep and adequately filling the homes with tenants. This is the type of housing that is often sold to private owners and upgraded to market housing when municipalities or other government housing agencies find them unwieldy and difficult to manage. In acquiring these properties, the PNLT was able to fix them up and keep them as social housing stock, saving 155 units of affordable housing (https://pnlt.ca/land/scatterhomes).

251 **Downtown Eastside Community Land Trust** For more, see: https://dtescommunitylandtrust.ca/.

252 **the number of affordable SROs is dwindling** "The Fight to Save Vancouver's SROs," downtowneastside.org, October 19, 2024, https://downtowneastside.org/the-fight-to-save-vancouvers-sros/; and Dan Fumano, "'We Are Opening the Floodgates': Vancouver Councillors Raise Alarms about Loss of SRO Units," *Vancouver Sun*, April 17, 2025, https://vancouversun.com/opinion/columnists/vancouver-councillors-raise-alarms-loss-sro-units.

252 **while some have been gutted by fires** Elizabeth McSheffrey and Angela Jung, "Operator of Vancouver SRO Gutted in Deadly Fire Went Years Without Key Review, Inquest Hears," Global News, February 1, 2024, https://globalnews.ca/news/10266195/winters-hotel-bc-coroners-inquest-day-nine/; and Jen St. Denis, "SRO Fires Are Causing an Endless Cycle of Displacement," *The Tyee*, September 30, 2022, https://thetyee.ca/News/2022/09/30/SRO-Fires-Causing-Endless-Cycle-Displacement/.

252 **buying SROs a few years back** Jen St. Denis, "After Two Disastrous Decades, Vancouver Gets Serious about Protecting SROs," *The Tyee*, November 13, 2020, https://thetyee.ca/News/2020/11/13/Two-Decades-Now-Vancouver-Serious-Protecting-SROs/.

252 **amidst a series of public scandals** Jen St. Denis, "Youth and Tenants with Mental Illness Lived in a Filthy, Violent Government SRO," *The Tyee*, March 18, 2024, https://thetyee.ca/News/2024/03/18/Tenants-Lived-Filthy-Violent-Government-SRO/.

252 **an unfit and undignified form of housing** Mike Lloyd and Hana Mae Nassar, "Vancouver SROs 'Not Fit Housing,' Are Being Addressed: Premier Eby," CityNews, January 10, 2023, https://vancouver.citynews.ca/2023/01/10/vancouver-sro-housing-dtes-eby/.

252 **government would no longer support** Amy Judd and Christa Dao, "'Replace with Dignified Housing': Vancouver's SROs Need to Be Phased Out, Says B.C.'s Premier," Global News, January 10, 2023, https://globalnews.ca/news/9401254/sro-vancouver-future-phased-out-plan/.

253 **agreed to purchase and renovate** Ian Holliday, "Province Acquires Shuttered Vancouver SRO, Says Building Will Reopen in 'Spring 2025'," CTV News, October 17, 2023, https://www.ctvnews.ca/vancouver/article/province-acquires-shuttered-vancouver-sro-says-building-will-reopen-in-spring-2025/.

253 **The first community land trust** For more, see: https://www.newcommunitiesinc.com/.

253 **a way to claim land and build wealth** Audrea Lim, "We Shall Not Be Moved: Collective Ownership Gives Power Back to Poor Farmers," *Harper's*, July, 2020, https://harpers.org/archive/2020/07/we-shall-not-be-moved-collective-ownership-black-farmers/.

254 **the Hogan's Alley CLT** For more, see: https://www.hogansalleysociety.org/.

254 **was demolished to make way for a never-completed freeway** Sherlyn Assam, "A Black Neighbourhood Destroyed Half a Century Ago Is on the Brink of a Comeback," *The Walrus*, May 18, 2023, https://thewalrus.ca/black-neighbourhood-come-back/.

254 **CLTs have been established in Kensington Market as well as the city's Chinatown** For more, see: https://kmclt.ca/ and https://chinatownlandtrust.ca/.

254 **CLTs have been established to serve the interests of Indigenous groups** For more, see: https://www.communityland.ca/solidarity/.

254 **T'it'q'et community** For more, see: https://www.bcafn.ca/first-nations-bc/lower-mainland-southwest/titqet.

254 **St'át'imc Nation** For more, see: https://statimc.ca/about/about-us/.

255 **a real estate market that rivals Vancouver's and Toronto's** Cathy Ellis, "Valley Real Estate Prices on Par with Vancouver, Toronto," *Rocky Mountain Outlook*, June 27, 2019, https://www.rmoutlook.com/local-news/valley-real-estate-prices-on-par-with-vancouver-toronto-1574413#:~:text=A%20long%2Dawaited%20housing%20needs%20assessment%20shows%20that,million%20in%20Banff%2C%20which%20compares%20to%20$1.&text=While%20real%20estate%20data%20for%20Canmore%20and,Toronto%20but%20less%20than%20$804%2C000%20in%20Vancouver.

255 **For most of its existence** "History of Canmore," Canmore Kananaskis, n.d., https://www.explorecanmore.ca/plan-your-trip/about-canmore/canmore-history/.

255 **no place left for Canmore's permanent population of 16,000 to affordably live** Jim Pyecroft, "Opinion: 'Lack of Vision' at Heart of Canmore Housing Crisis," *Calgary Herald*, December 19, 2024, https://calgaryherald.com/opinion/columnists/poor-leadership-not-owners-of-second-homes-driving-canmore-housing-crisis.

255 **Canmoreland CLT** For more, see: https://canmoreland.ca/.

257 **2024 wildfire that wiped out a third of Jasper** "Jasper Recovery Efforts Continue as Insurers Finish Clearing Debris

Left by 2024 Wildfire," CBC News, May 2, 2025, https://www.cbc.ca/news/canada/edmonton/jasper-recovery-efforts-insurer-led-program-clear-debris-1.7525233.

257 **when a wildfire swept through** Ashifa Kassman, "'Absolutely Apocalyptic': Fort McMurray Evacuees Describe Terror of Alberta Wildfires," *The Guardian*, May 5, 2016, https://www.theguardian.com/world/2016/may/05/alberta-fort-mcmurray-wildfires-canada.

258 **selling investment properties** The federal Liberal party platform released in 2025 did include a promise to "facilitate the conversion of existing structures into affordable housing units by reducing the tax liability for private owners of multi-purpose rental when they sell their building to a non-profit operator, land trust, or non-profit acquisition fund—so long as the proceeds are reinvested in building new purpose-built rental housing" ("Mark Carney's Liberals Unveil Canada's Most Ambitious Housing Plan Since the Second World War, n.d., https://liberal.ca/wp-content/uploads/sites/292/2025/03/Mark-Carneys-Liberals-unveil-Canadas-most-ambitious-housing-plan-since-the-Second-World-War.pdf).

258 **"matching" grant programs** There is precedent for this in programs like the Canada Greener Homes Grant, which gave rebates to private homeowners who invested in energy-saving retrofits such as heat pumps, solar panels or better insulation (for more, see: https://natural-resources.canada.ca/energy-efficiency/home-energy-efficiency/canada-greener-homes-initiative/canada-greener-homes-grant).

258 **use zoning to suppress speculation** In most provinces this would require the approval of provincial governments.

258 **non-market and community-led** This doesn't mean these communities should all be low-income. There is considerable evidence mixed-income communities are the most socially cohesive and economically resilient. Vienna's threshold of

60 percent social housing, which includes non-market options for middle-income households, seems like a good standard to follow.

259 **national rent control** Arguments against rent control mainly centre on two beliefs: 1) that it can disincentivize the construction of market rental housing by limiting how much income landlords can make from rent, and 2) that it discourages mobility of tenants who may be inclined to downsize or upsize but are staying put in an affordable, rent-controlled, apartment. To the first point, studies have been largely inconclusive as to whether rent control actually supresses construction of market rentals. In fact, CMHC analyses of rental construction did not find evidence of lower rental starts in jurisdictions with rent control compared to those without ("Rent Controls, Rental Prices and Rental Supply," Research Insights [CMHC], November 2020, https://assets.cmhc-schl.gc.ca/sites/cmhc/data-research/publications-reports/research-insight/2020/research-insight-impact-rent-control-housing-affordability-69677-en.pdf?rev=66c07ffc-7a0c-4044-bdd2-549484582312). To point number two, the problem of decreased mobility can be solved by tying rent control to units rather than to tenancies, meaning that when people move the rent on a unit will remain predictable rather than being hiked to the going market rate, freeing people to move as needed. Additionally, concerns about the impact of rent control on the production of market housing are exacerbated by the fact that we are so overly reliant on market housing. The more non-profit, non-market options we have, the less of an issue this becomes.

259 **landlord licensing** Am I the only person who thinks it's weird that you need a licence in this country to officiate a wedding, serve alcohol or drive a car but not to manage something as critical as someone's home? We require businesses to be licensed in order to operate. Becoming a landlord is getting into the business of housing. I think it's prudent for landlords

to *at least* go through a form of online training proving they have read and understand provincial tenancy laws, maintenance requirements, et cetera, before being able to get into *the business* of providing housing.

259 **bans on public investments (like pension plans) in REITs** Recent years have seen a rise in people and institutions divesting from companies with questionable environmental or social impacts. While the most obvious example of this is fossil fuel companies, which have increasingly been forced to answer to shareholders for dubious environmental practices, real estate has largely been given a pass in the realm of sustainable or ethical investing. I think it's time we place more scrutiny on REITs and other large-scale residential real estate companies, either by divesting from those with a demonstrated track record of evicting tenants and pushing housing prices up, or by putting pressure on those companies to behave more ethically as shareholders.

259 **a reassessment of how we capture, or don't, the value of land through taxation** The most obvious option here would be to make the sale of primary residences subject to capital gains tax, as we do on the sale of businesses and other assets. Given the amount of public money that goes into increasing property values (by ensuring people can qualify for mortgages through government programs, through housing subsidies that supplement market rents, and with public infrastructure like roads, sewers, transit, greenspace and public services that make our neighbourhoods safe, desirable places to live), it makes sense that we should be reclaiming a portion of that on resale. But there are other options that are perhaps an easier sell to the general public given our ingrained culture of entitlement to housing wealth. One idea gaining traction is a land value tax advocated for by organizations such as Common Wealth Canada (https://www.commonwealth.ca/), which would tax land at its "highest and best use" rather than its current use.

That means an empty lot owned by an individual or developer in the inner-city that could become housing or another badly needed amenity would be taxed at the rate of what it *should* be—housing, a community centre, transit station, whatever—rather than what it currently is—vacant land—thus deterring people from sitting on undeveloped land for years waiting for market peaks in order to sell or develop.

# ACKNOWLEDGEMENTS

Endless thanks are due to my family, without whom this book never would have been written. David McKeone, my partner, held down the fort at home and supported me in every way imaginable through the much-longer-than-anticipated process of research and writing. In hindsight, birthing a human baby and a book baby in quick succession was perhaps not the best plan, timing-wise, but I think both turned out pretty well. Neither would have happened if not for you. Ellis, my son, was as patient as a small child can reasonably be expected to be while I was away on long trips or long hours at my computer. Thank you for the snuggles, comic relief and inspiration to keep on going. Karen McKeone provided the backup childcare and emotional support necessary to even consider taking on a project of this magnitude at a very sensitive and demanding phase of my life, especially given the travel required. Karen, you were the best grandma we could have asked for and we miss you every day—thank you from the bottom of my heart. Thank you also to my mom, Deborah Barrett, who made me promise that I would one day write a book—I only wish you could have been here to see me do it. Mike McKeone kept the mood light with his jokes and his generous contributions of Air Miles that helped cover travel costs. My surviving parents, Bob and Pam Barrett, provided support, feedback and great conversation along the way. I am beyond grateful for all of you in my life, as well as for my siblings and niblings.

My agent, Rob Firing at Transatlantic Agency, believed in me and this project from the outset. Thank you, Rob, for your confidence in me and for expertly shepherding me through the process of finding a publisher as well as connecting me with the perfect editor in Laura Dosky of Penguin Random House Canada. Laura, you've been a champion of this work from day one, and your insight and direction has been critical in refining and shaping my ideas and my words. Vaani Sai's additional input and hype-girl energy gave me the boost I needed to get across the finish line.

Fellow authors who walked this path before me were instrumental in encouraging me to embark on this journey and connecting me with the resources to make it possible. Marcello Di Cintio basically forced me to come sit in his office as writer-in-residence at the Calgary Public Library, a meeting during which I voiced the idea for this book out loud to a peer for the first time. Your receptivity and interest was instrumental in getting the ball rolling, as was your constant advice on navigating the complex world of arts grants. Harrison Mooney, thank you for your faith in my potential, for your friendship and for your feedback on my early work, as well as for helping me get a foot into the publishing world. Christina Myers took the time to answer a panicked Facebook message from a near stranger and talked me down from the ledge that is writing a book.

Several dear friends acted as early readers, asking great questions and engaging in thoughtful dialogue about how to shape my narrative and where to focus my efforts. Kalie Bredo, you were the most consistent and thorough reader of this book—your time, insight and encouragement was invaluable. Janel Snider, Patrick Martin, Helen Pike, Melanie Kuxdorf, Scott Greenfield, Amber

Hopgood, Kelly Pickford, Noa Nattrass Moses, Sylvia Nicholles, Tim Bedford and the rest of the camp crew also provided feedback and sounding boards throughout my process. Morgan Vanek's stunning intellect was and continues to be a delight to engage with. It's been so great to have you as a fellow ambitious woman, writer and mother in my corner. Thank you also for helping me access research material through the University of Calgary, a favour also aided by Jessica Shaw.

Kathryn Gretsinger continues to be a mentor: Thank you for the wonderful conversation around housing and for connecting me with Mashal Butt, my fact-checker. Mashal, your organization and thoroughness was truly a lifesaver.

My deepest gratitude goes out to everyone who shared with me their own reflections on home and experiences within the housing market both here in Canada and abroad. Your vulnerability, honesty, creativity and willingness to reflect was critical to helping me formulate ideas and recommendations for better homes for us as a society, and has also changed how I think about my own home. Many of your words and insights did not make it into this book in direct references, but they nonetheless informed a huge part of this project. Thank you in particular to Kalle Kunkel for seamlessly connecting me with Berlin's housing activists, and to Matthias Coers and Giorgios Thodos, whose interviews, translation and background information were integral in my understanding of Berlin's tenants' movements. Veronika Iwanowski in Vienna was not only a source but a resource, ensuring I had the right interviews with the right people. Beth Chitekwe-Biti helped me connect with the Dialogue on Shelter for the Homeless in Zimbabwe Trust as well as the People's Process on Housing and Poverty in Zambia. Tarisai Natalie Manyowa was a constant resource and companion to my research in Zimbabwe who provided invaluable context, explanation and translation. Melanie Chirwa in Zambia was an open-hearted and dedicated guide to housing issues and progress in Zambia, which, though not included in this book, was pivotal to my understanding of finding home in slum communities. All the members of the Zimbabwe Homeless People's Federation and Zambia Homeless and Poor People's Federation who so openly shared with me, I am forever grateful for your generosity.

This book has been assisted by the Province of Alberta through Alberta Foundation for the Arts, its arts funding agency.

We acknowledge the support of the Canada Council for the Arts.

# INDEX